IN SEARCH OF A
NEW LEFT

CANADIAN POLITICS
AFTER THE
NEOCONSERVATIVE
ASSAULT

JAMES LAXER

VIKING

VIKING
Published by the Penguin Group
Penguin Books Canada Ltd, 10 Alcorn Avenue, Toronto, Ontario, Canada M4V 3B2
Penguin Books Ltd, 27 Wrights Lane, London W8 5TZ, England
Viking Penguin, a division of Penguin Books USA Inc., 375 Hudson Street, New York,
New York 10014, U.S.A.
Penguin Books Australia Ltd, Ringwood, Victoria, Australia
Penguin Books (NZ) Ltd, 182–190 Wairau Road, Auckland 10, New Zealand

Penguin Books Ltd, Registered Offices: Harmondsworth, Middlesex, England

First published 1996
1 3 5 7 9 10 8 6 4 2

Copyright © James Laxer, 1996

Printed and bound in Canada on acid free paper ∞

Canadian Cataloguing in Publication Data

Laxer, James, 1941–
In search of a new left: Canadian politics after the neoconservative assault

ISBN 0-670-85901-X

1. Socialism - Canada. 2. Canada - Politics and government - 1993-   .* I. Title.

HX109.L38 1996   320.5'31'0971   C95-930197-6

To my mother and father

ACKNOWLEDGMENTS

IN writing this book, I have had the benefit of the advice and assistance of a number of people. Peter Bleyer, Josie Harlow and Vernon Bassue read drafts of the manuscript and made valuable suggestions. Maude Barlow was an invaluable source on the development of social movements in Canada. Gerald Caplan was diligent in commenting on every aspect of the book and gave indispensable advice on the last chapter. John Smart was helpful on the history of the NDP, the Waffle in particular. Panagiotis Damaskopoulos made useful comments on the evolution of the global economy. Linda McQuaig pushed me to hone the analysis advanced in this book and suggested ways to strengthen the flow of the argument.

At Atkinson College, Louise Jacobs helped make it possible for me to work on the book, while I was doing many other things. Kathryn Dean was a meticulous editor, whose efforts have been invaluable. Jackie Kaiser, my editor at Penguin, has been an inspiration. I am much indebted to her for her major contribution to every aspect of the book.

I thank my two youngest, Jonathan and Emily, for their good cheer. I am deeply grateful to my wife, Sandy Price, for her support, both personal and intellectual, while the book was being written.

Contents

CHAPTER 1

THE BEST OF TIMES, THE WORST OF TIMES

WE live in an age in which even our anxieties have been privatized.

In our time, most people are overworked and are on edge about whether they will keep their jobs, while many others are overwrought because they are unemployed or underemployed and can't find a way back into the world of full-time work. Passage from the world of the overworked to the netherworld of the underemployed preys on the minds of an enormous number of people.

An acquaintance of mine, a skilled machinist, works overtime almost every week. He almost never gets a full weekend off. In his early forties, he'd rather do without the overtime, but fears that if he makes that choice, he'll be out of a job. He says some of the younger guys in the shop like all the overtime they can get, but many others don't.

Meanwhile, every time decent industrial jobs are advertised, thousands apply for them from among the vast army of unemployed and underemployed. Does it make sense for industrial workers to be putting in more hours per week on average than at any time in fifty years, while others can't get a decent job at all?

Then there are the private sector middle managers I know, men and women about my age, who mostly agree with the way the system picks winners and losers. That is until they lose their own jobs. And middle managers are a highly vulnerable lot.

When a company restructures, or when one company acquires another, a full-scale bloodletting can be expected to follow among middle managers between the ages of forty-five and fifty-five. And many of those who lose their jobs will never work again. These believers in the system that destroyed them are condemned to a slow loss of self-esteem, a waning of respect from family and friends. Often they become chronically ill or alcoholic. A highly rational use of people at the height of their powers, isn't it?

In the universities, there are the young scholars who are scraping by in part-time teaching positions. They are full of energy, intelligence and creativity. But for them, as for many other highly qualified people, the door to a full-time position is all but closed. Many of them will experience years of waiting, and not a few will be shut out altogether.

And then there are the stressed professionals of our age—lawyers, accountants and the rest—who are prisoners of our new and supposedly liberating technology. That technology means they can and do work while they are in their cars, in airplanes and hotel rooms, and at home. For them, the job never goes away.

Technology exacts a still more cruel toll from those who do the lion's share of white-collar work. Many administrative assistants and receptionists have been herded together in computer pools, driven to do the low-end repetitive work that is one outcome of the new technology. For them, new technology means a loss of the relative autonomy they previously enjoyed. These galley slaves of the computer age experience none of the adventure spoken of by the apostles of the internet. Their fate is to be ground down by the new machines, or even worse, to be laid off because the new machines make them unnecessary.

And of course, there are the crazed two-income families of the nineties. When I was a kid growing up in downtown Toronto, the one-income family was the norm. The men worked in industrial plants and the women stayed home. On weekends, few people worked. Those families owned their own houses and were buying cars and TVs. There were no fast food restaurants, and everyone ate at home.

I'm not advocating a return to the sexist division of labour of the 1950s. But I reject the assumption that, over the decades, progress is being made toward the goal of a more humane, intelligent and prosperous society. Ruefully, I think back to my days as a student in the 1960s, when it was commonplace to believe that we were moving toward a society where managing our leisure time would be a major social problem. It didn't turn out that way.

Is the new capitalism fertile ground for the extension of human freedom? Hardly.

—————

For Canadian social democrats, the first half of the 1990s was the best of times and the worst of times. The New Democratic Party held office in three provinces—Ontario, British Columbia and Saskatchewan. Over 50 percent of Canadians were governed by NDP provincial governments. And while the party had won office once before in British Columbia, and many times previously in its historic Saskatchewan bastion, it had never before come to power in Ontario.

In September 1990, the stunning victory of the Ontario NDP under its leader, Bob Rae, the Rhodes Scholar, appeared to unlock the door to major party status for the NDP right across Canada. Ontario, after all, was the commercial and industrial heartland of the country, home to nearly ten million people. All previous social democratic governments in Canada had been in the West, but with Bob Rae's victory, the party had won office in a province from which business could not easily flee, or go "on strike" (by delaying capital investments) to put pressure on the social democrats to keep them in line. Here was the golden opportunity to implement changes that generations of social democrats had hoped for. On that surprising day in early September when the Ontario New Democrats scaled heights never before achieved by their party, it seemed that anything was possible. Surely a victory by the party at the federal level was only a matter of time.

Yet within a few years, it became apparent that the NDP provincial victories in the 1990s were merely Pyrrhic. So compromised were the New Democratic provincial governments by the policies they adopted and by the times in which they governed that social democrats descended to a level of despair unparalleled in their history. And they sank further when the federal NDP under the leadership of Audrey McLaughlin was decimated in the federal election of October 1993—partly because of the negative public view taken of NDP provincial governments. They plunged from forty-three to nine seats in the House of Commons—and a mere 7 percent of the popular vote. Since they had fallen below the twelve-seat mark, they no longer had official party status in the House of Commons, were given no guaranteed share of questions in Question Period and had no research staff. The NDP became a nonfactor in national politics. Social democrats suddenly had less visibility at the national level than at any time since the mid-Depression election of 1935, when the NDP's predecessor, the Co-operative Commonwealth Federation (CCF) had first won seats in Parliament.

Instead of changing the country in ways their constituency had hoped for, NDP provincial governments jettisoned most of what they had long espoused, adopting instead the new and alien politics of restraint, cutbacks and adaptation to globalization. The lesson learned from this turn of events was a devastating one: social democrats do not deliver on their promises. They talk a good game, but in the end, their policies differ little from those of other parties. Still worse, their policies could be portrayed as expensive and even unaffordable—and of no more advantage to ordinary people than those of the other political parties. At a time when increasing proportions of government budgets were being eaten by interest payments, government services declined and the taxes of the nonaffluent remained high. All these developments made the NDP extremely vulnerable to attacks from political opponents.

If Ontario's Rae government represented the pinnacle of the NDP's electoral success, it also became the symbol of the New Democrats' inability to carry out provincial programs in the 1990s. In the past, social democrats had been pathsetters in establishing new social programs: hospitalization, medicare and public auto insurance were all first established by social democratic provincial governments. So great expectations were vested in the Rae government, and its failure to meet them had national significance.

In December 1994, long after his government had gone on the defensive, Bob Rae said in an interview, "The choice isn't between capitalism and socialism. The question is what kind of capitalism do we want to have." Rae went on to say that he favoured the "democratic solidaristic model" of capitalism, featuring a partnership between business and government.[1] His comments were perfectly logical given the record of his government, but they represented a distinct departure from what Canadian social democrats had advocated in the past. After more than four years of presiding over a government that had steadfastly avoided "socialist" reforms, Bob Rae was simply acknowledging reality. His government lacked any vision that challenged capitalism.

The defining episode in the life of the Rae government was the imposition in 1993 of the so-called social contract regime on public sector employees. The social contract, with its Orwellian nomenclature, implying consent where there was none, forced the reopening of the contracts of public employees. The critical provision of the social contract concerned the "Rae day" salary rollbacks—unpaid holidays that gave the government a means of cutting the cost of public services. The most notorious feature of the process, as far as public sector unionists were concerned, was that those who went along with it were rewarded with lighter rollbacks, while those who resisted were penalized. As Thomas Walkom noted in *Rae Days*, his account of the Ontario NDP government: "Unions that agreed to enter the social contract voluntarily would be rewarded with access to an unemployment-insurance top-up fund. Those that did not agree would be denied access to this fund, and would be punished with a larger wage roll-back."[2]

The social contract violated the most basic of political principles—that it is unwise to humiliate your allies and delight your enemies. What left a foul taste in the mouths of trade unionists was the conviction that the Rae government had turned on its own. And even though Bob Rae always believed he would be forgiven for the social contract, because trade unionists ultimately had nowhere else to go politically, enthusiastic support from the whole of the trade union movement was to elude Rae right down to the very last days of his government. In the campaign that led to the humiliating and overwhelming defeat of the Rae government on June 8, 1995, trade unionists offered only tepid support. Many, such as Buzz Hargrove, president of the Canadian Auto Workers Union (CAW), chose to remain on the sidelines.

Bob Rae was so confident of the value of his social contract policy that when he called the election in the spring of 1995, the NDP election team made the strategic decision to highlight Rae Days during the campaign in free-time political broadcasts and TV advertising. The advertising made the point that the Rae government had figured out how to cut back government spending without laying off thousands of public sector workers—a policy the provincial Conservatives and Liberals were both planning to institute, taking their cue from the federal Liberal government, which had already put such policies in place. The implicit message was just as eloquent: the Rae government knew how to deal with public sector workers and their unions and could be trusted to keep them in line.

In another unprecedented departure from social democratic tradition, the party campaigned without a full platform. Jettisoning this trademark of Canadian social democracy, the NDP campaigned instead on the issue of leadership—the usual bailiwick of Conservatives and Liberals. The party also argued that the experience it had gained in office made it the most fit of the three parties to govern—thus unwisely calling attention to embarrassments that had occurred in the early days of the government, largely because of the inexperience of some of its members.

A mere five years before, in 1990, the party had defeated the incumbent Liberals under David Peterson, when they had campaigned on a wide range of social and political pledges, including public auto insurance. The platform had been published with great fanfare under the title "Agenda for People." Ironically, in 1995, while the NDP was relying overwhelmingly on the personality of its leader, Bob Rae, and its claims of governing experience, the Conservatives and Liberals both unveiled detailed programs signalling their intention to shift the province more or less sharply to the right. The Conservatives had issued their detailed campaign promises a year before the election under the title "Common Sense Revolution," and the Liberals issued an eighty-two-page policy book during the campaign. The NDP produced a sixteen-page booklet, summarizing the record of the Rae government and presenting its general philosophy—omitting any clear social democratic vision for the future.

When asked by the media to explain this wholly uncharacteristic failure to issue a platform, Bob Rae gave a testy response that made him sound more like a deputy minister than a premier and party leader: "You don't know what the federal transfers are going to be like in 1998, do you? No, do you know? We think we know what they're going to be in '97. Do you know what they're going to be in '98? Do you know what they're going to be in '99? In 2000? We don't know what the federal government is going to do. We don't know what the demands are going to be."[3]

The Ontario NDP was oddly inarticulate in the 1995 campaign, and this was not because its leader was incapable of personal eloquence. What had happened was that traditional social democracy had lost its way. The Rae government, on the eve of its defeat, had nothing to say except that its leader was superior to his opponents, both intellectually and in terms of political experience. And while this was undoubtedly true, it was the stunning absence of social democracy in any recognizable form that told the real story. While the Liberals and Conservatives fought over right-wing political turf, exchanging blows over which party would be more punitive to welfare recipients, the NDP said virtually nothing about the plight of the poor, the unemployed and the disadvantaged in society. On the eve of its defeat, the Ontario NDP abandoned its historic role.

It seemed that what the NDP was offering to the public was Bob Rae, not the Bob Rae of old, but the Bob Rae who had imposed the social contract on the labour movement, the Bob Rae who had spent so much time in power trying to woo the business community. Holding office in Ontario, where the party had never governed before, changed the national fortunes of social democracy. So, too, inevitably, did the defeat of the Ontario NDP have implications for social democracy right across Canada. After the rise and fall of the Rae government, it was inevitable that Canadian social democracy would have to be completely rethought.

But if Bob Rae played a prominent role in bringing on the crisis of Canadian social democracy, he was far from being personally responsible for it. No individual could be responsible for an historical change of such depth—partly because the crisis that afflicts Canadian social democracy is by no means limited to this country alone. It is part and parcel of an alteration that has affected social democracy in Europe as well as in Canada—as illustrated by the following brief survey of developments on that continent.

• In Britain, the Labour Party, which for decades had served as a model for Canadian social democrats, has been out of office since 1979. While the party is highly favoured to win the next general election against the ineffectual Conservative government of John Major, Labour has retreated far from the principles on which it was originally built. To win power after a generation in the wilderness, Labour has picked a centrist leader, Tony Blair, whose main promise to the electorate is that he will not challenge the fundamentals of the harsh new capitalism that has grown up in Britain over the past seventeen years. Instead of making clear what Labour will do, Blair's strategy is to let the Conservatives defeat themselves. While the electoral prospects for Labour are highly favourable, their position is not the fruit of a penetrating new analysis or strategy. It results from the British people's exhaustion with the tawdry outcome of nearly two decades of militant conservatism.

• The French Socialist Party, which came to power with such high hopes in 1981, is in tatters. Despite many achievements during the fourteen-year presidency of François Mitterrand, the

Socialists have lost their sense of direction and have collapsed into a coterie of feuding factions, each centred on the ambitions of a chieftain who is a survivor of the days of the party in power. The state of the party is symbolically captured in the tragic death of the last Socialist prime minister, Pierre Beregovoy, who took his own life just weeks after leading the Socialists into oblivion in the National Assembly elections of March 1993.

In the spring of 1995, the French Socialists saw their fortunes significantly revived in the presidential election campaign, when Lionel Jospin, a former minister of education, ran a close second to Gaullist Jacques Chirac. But even Jospin's extraordinary race for the presidency did not stop rivals in his own party from continuing their campaign of divisiveness. The great social upheaval of the autumn of 1995, with hundreds of thousands of workers and students protesting the Gaullist government's social program cuts, had little to do with the Socialist Party.

- In Sweden, although the Social Democrats returned to power in the fall of 1994, the prospects for their political option were less than clear. For sixty years, from the 1930s on, Swedish social democracy had been the most advanced in the world. Swedish social democrats had constructed the world's most generous system of social programs and the most egalitarian distribution of income. All this had been achieved through a structure of decision making in which labour and business, in partnership with government, set national standards. While the Social Democrats were able to reassert themselves as the country's preferred party of government after three years of ineffectual right-wing rule, Sweden had been caught up in the transformation of capitalism that was sweeping the world. Faced with a rise in unemployment, and threatened by the deregulation of capital in Sweden and the increasing tendency of Swedish business to invest abroad, the Swedish labour movement had lost ground in its ability to stand up to business in the system of nationwide bargaining.

In the autumn of 1994, Swedes voted to join the European Union (EU), a decision that was sure to add a progressive voice to Europe but that was also bound to undermine the distinctiveness of Sweden's own economic and social arrangements. Even though they were back in power, Sweden's Social Democrats had lost the sense that they were genuinely leading their country to a new, and as yet uncharted, socialism.

- Out of office since 1982, Germany's Social Democrats (SPD) saw the federal election of 1994 slip away, as Helmut Kohl's Christian Democrats were returned to office with a razor-thin victory. On the continent, the German Social Democratic Party was the flagship of social democracy, the party to which Karl Marx had once belonged. The SPD, which later turned its back on revolutionary socialism and adopted a gradualist program, finally declared itself non-Marxist in the late 1950s.

  German social democracy had been centrist at least from the days of Helmut Schmidt's chancellorship in the seventies and early eighties. Today, the party defends the welfare state and promotes environmentalism, under the constant pressure of the Greens. But it has been decades since German social democracy had anything to say about a genuine shift in power away from business to the people at large.

- In Spain, the Socialist Party of Prime Minister Felipe Gonzalez played a critical role in building a post-Franco democracy—an immense achievement. During its long tenure in office, however, the Gonzalez government has moved ever further away from policies that could be characterized as socialist. In the winter of 1996, sullied by financial scandals involving members of the government, the Socialists were narrowly defeated in general elections by their right-wing opponents in the Popular Party.

- In Italy, the left did succeed in winning power in elections held in April 1996. Italian voters chose the left-wing Olive Tree alliance, led by Romano Prodi, in preference to the right-wing

Freedom alliance, led by Silvio Berlusconi, the tycoon and former prime minister. What gave the election historic significance is that it brought the left to power in a country whose political system has been designed to prevent that from happening for half a century. The largest branch of the Olive Tree is the Democratic Party of the Left, a party established by former communists. The alliance comes to power with the backing of the Communist Refoundation Party.

Within the new governing coalition, there is a range of views, from those in the centre, who want to tackle Italy's debt problem, to those on the left, who want to fight unemployment (at 12.6 percent in March 1996) and strengthen social programs. While the left has been shut out of power at the national level until now, many of its leaders have had a great deal of experience running regional governments in Italy's industrial north. It was thought ironic in a country where corruption involving business and government was endemic, that some of the cleanest and most efficient regional regimes were run by communists who often got on famously with profit-making industrialists.

Despite the important electoral success in Italy, as this brief survey suggests, social democracy, in Canada and across Europe, has been confronting a crisis of definition and political effectiveness.

In the postwar decades, social democrats were seen as pointing the way to the future; today they have lost their compass. Where social democrats once pioneered the development of social programs to improve the lot of the majority of people living under capitalism, a new, market-centred capitalism is everywhere in the ascendancy. While there are immensely important differences between capitalism in one place and in another, the overall trend away from the great social compromise of the postwar decades cannot be doubted.

Gerald Caplan, long-time NDP strategist, says that he is "astonished by the magnitude of the defeat of social democracy in every walk of life." He believes, and has dedicated much of his life to his conviction, that the "only signs of genuine civility in our society are things social democrats pushed for." "The way the free market has won and we have lost," he says, "is so Orwellian that I can't begin to cope with it. We are steadily going backwards into a world that we thought would never exist again, with its poverty, breadlines and its ever higher 'acceptable' levels of unemployment."[4]

Joe Levitt, a retired historian at the University of Ottawa and a long-time left-wing activist, draws pessimistic conclusions from the experience of recent history. He goes so far as to say that he "has lost confidence in the common man" as a consequence of what has happened, and that he no longer dares believe that ordinary people are likely to rise above the problems of their everyday existence to struggle for greater social justice.[5]

Pessimism about the future and suspicion of the young—these sentiments have pervaded the left in recent years. And they are the most significant telltale signs of the defensive posture the left has now adopted—for optimism about the future has always been its stock-in-trade in the past.

CHAPTER 2

DEMOCRACY IN PERIL

IN our age the predominant assumption is that the form of liberal, globalizing capitalism that now prevails is the only possible economic and social system for the advanced, industrialized world. This system—received opinion now asserts—will endure into the indefinite future. There is no point, therefore, in having ideological debates. Such debates are a part of the past, not the future. And they will not be appropriate to the future.

A central premise of this book is that this outlook is the product of a fleeting contemporary reality and that any analysis based on this view will not endure. Today's consensus in the capitalist world is born out of resignation much more than deep conviction. What, then, has given such vogue to the idea that liberal capitalism is the only conceivable system for the industrialized world?

Two enormous transformations have contributed mightily to the conviction that the present form of capitalism has disposed of any potential challengers: the collapse of Soviet communism and the economic, social and political changes that together go under the label "globalization."

The collapse of communism, beginning in Eastern Europe in 1989 and climaxing with the demise of the Soviet Union in December 1991, lent vast support to the notion that liberal capitalism had conclusively demonstrated its superiority as a social system. After all, had not the Bolsheviks themselves proclaimed that their October 1917 revolution was only the first step in what would be a worldwide socialist transformation? Had the Marxist-

Leninists not declared that capitalism was a doomed system, bound to collapse and to be replaced by socialism? Since these prophecies had not come true, did that not suggest that the entire world should move towards liberal capitalism? Particularly in North America, the era that followed the Second World War was understood in Cold War terms—as a twilight struggle between liberal capitalism and Soviet communism. The collapse of one of those systems was taken as proof of the superiority of the other.

Ironies abound concerning the impact of the Soviet Union on Western radicalism. Although socialists in the Western world had long ago written off the Soviet Union as an abortive experiment that had nothing to do with their own aspirations, there is no denying the fact that the collapse of the Soviet system struck a blow at their political fortunes. For Western socialists, both Marxist and non-Marxist, the demise of Lenin's state has forced a fundamental rethinking of the history of the twentieth century and the place in that history of the Bolshevik Revolution of 1917—an event that had once been celebrated by Marxists as even more liberating than the French Revolution. From the vantage point of the 1990s, it is evident that the Bolshevik Revolution opened the way, not to a new democracy broader in scope than that of liberalism, but instead to the tyranny of Stalinism.

Socialists cannot escape the debate about the causes of Stalinism and what they mean for any radical project that seeks to remake society. Was Stalinism the inevitable consequence of Lenin's concept of a highly centralized political party, which put ultimate power in the hands of a single leader? Or was it the chance product of a paranoiac who got control of a great revolutionary movement? As a mass murderer, Stalin may actually have surpassed Hitler in the sheer number of victims. In *Hitler and Stalin: Parallel Lives*, historian Alan Bullock puts the number of those who died as a result of the Stalinist repression at up to twice as many as the number killed by the Nazis.[1]

However interpreted, Stalinism destroyed the humane and liberating impulses of the Russian Revolution of 1917, replacing them with a totalitarianism not unlike that of Nazi Germany.

Although Nazism was conceived as a mirror to Marxism (its purpose being to negate the idea of a revolution of the working class with a revolution in which the Aryan race would rule the earth), the Hitler and Stalin regimes had much in common. The totalitarian state deploying terror against its own population, the notion of remaking humanity under the tutelage of an omniscient leader—these were features of both. The "black" and "red" terrors of Nazism and communism were virulent outbreaks of the twentieth-century "disease" wherein nonadherence to a total ideology was a capital offence.

For much of the twentieth century, Marxism was seen as a potentially viable alternative to Western liberalism. But in the end, Stalinism vitiated the potential of Marxism to replace Western liberalism. The eventual collapse of the Soviet Union posed a less direct threat for social democrats in the West than it did for Marxists. But if the demise of Soviet communism has not struck a direct blow to Western social democracy, it has contributed to social democracy's loss of direction in both Canada and Europe. The idea that there is no fundamental alternative to Western capitalism, an idea that was powerfully reinforced by the demise of the Soviet Union, has undermined the claim of social democrats to represent a distinct and significant option.

The second major factor contributing to the decline of social democracy was the transition to globalization, beginning in the 1970s. To make sense of the importance of that transition for our own era, we first have to consider the highly unusual historical circumstances three decades earlier, which gave rise to the golden age of social democracy in the postwar decades.

What opened the door to postwar social democracy was the construction of the political and military alliance that defeated the fascists and the Nazis in the Second World War. The wartime coalition included antifascist conservatives like Winston Churchill, liberals, social democrats, and after the invasion of the Soviet Union in June 1941, communist parties as well. In social terms, the antifascist coalition necessitated something that had been unthinkable previously in capitalism—an alliance between business and labour in opposition to the common foe. And to make that coalition work, the role of the state in the economy and in society had to be substantially altered. Constructing the antifascist coalition changed the political and economic thinking of the wartime allies and thus transformed their societies in the decades following the war.

Although the international coalition that eventually defeated Nazism and fascism is usually remembered in military terms, it was much more than military. Not only was fascism pushed to the political margin, but even traditional conservatism found itself in disgrace for many years after the war. The dominant political force to emerge in Western Europe after the conflict was Christian democracy, which would eventually become the basis for new parties of the right and a modified conservatism. But the postwar Christian democrats subscribed to a reform philosophy that included a much more central place for social programs and organized labour than that of traditional conservatism. Socialists and social democrats also emerged as a powerful political force in the new Western Europe. In addition, particularly in France and Italy, the communists who had been crucial to the resistance against the fascists were a force to be reckoned with for decades to come.

Not only was the traditional political right in disgrace after the war, much of business was too. In Germany and Italy, business had been massively involved in the crimes of the fascist regimes. After the war, its record became a major argument in favour of public ownership of large parts of the economy in Italy, and for a role for worker management of industry in West Germany.

In France, the record of collaboration of top elements of business was a reason for the large-scale nationalization of industry, including that of key firms, such as the automaker Renault. In France, postwar economic strategy was developed by the so-called "Plan," an agency of government run by Jean Monnet, who later became the master builder of the European Community. The Plan brought government, business and initially labour together to set targets for the economy.

In the English-speaking world, the laissez-faire economic ideas that had allowed the Depression of the thirties to drag on for so long were jettisoned. The new doctrines, which asserted that governments could greatly influence the direction of the economy and could intervene to assure full employment, retained their vigour for a quarter of a century after the war.

The working class enjoyed much more power in postwar Europe than it had before the war. The consequence was an emphasis on full employment and on the development of the welfare state. For Western Europeans, the postwar decades opened the door to mass affluence on an unprecedented scale. The blend of capitalism and social democracy ensured, for the first time in history, that the majority of the population was not poor.

In Britain, just after the end of the war, the Labour Party swept to power. And while it failed to deliver the socialist transformation promised in the party platform, it did establish a wide range of social programs, the most important being the National Health Service.

In the United States, the war entrenched the reforms of the New Deal era, including the social security system, which even the Reagan administration in the 1980s was unable to dislodge. Moreover, the debate about what role blacks could play in the armed forces placed the general plight of blacks on the national agenda for the first time in decades. This opened the way for desegregation in the decade after 1945—a development that had been unthinkable before the conflict.

Similarly, in Canada, the war legitimated important political goals of the left. It demonstrated how quickly full employment could be restored in a society that had long been plagued by unemployment if the government acted directly. It showed that government was capable of executing an effective plan for economic development, thus demonstrating that a basic social democratic idea was workable in practice. And it had the effect of eliminating the force of antisocialist and anticommunist agitation. After all, if the Allies could make common cause with the Soviet Union, how could socialism and communism be dismissed as totally alien ideas? While the election of the CCF in Saskatchewan in 1944 was largely explainable as a local phenomenon, it was clearly aided by the new mindset that developed during the war. In 1943, the CCF briefly led the Liberals and Conservatives in a national Gallup poll as the first choice of Canadian voters.

Everywhere in the industrialized world, the predominant point of view was that the state could and should pursue full employment and the further extension of social programs. That perspective prevailed until the 1970s, when another great socioeconomic shift changed things dramatically. The golden age of social democracy was drawing to a close.

Following the global inflation of the early 1970s, the viability of the social programs and progressive, full-employment policies of governments was called into doubt by alternative schools of economic thought, the most influential being monetarism, whose leading proponent was Milton Friedman. This economic philosophy was a harbinger of the new conservatism that has become the dominant political tendency in our era.

The global oil price crises of the 1970s stoked the fires of inflation, adding to the generation of what was called "stagflation"— high inflation combined with economic stagnation. As industrialized economies slowed, higher levels of unemployment became the norm, and the cost of unemployment insurance and welfare programs skyrocketed. Governments were forced to spend more on social outlays, while the much reduced rate of economic growth caused tax revenues to stop rising or even shrink. This was the onset of the fiscal crisis which, to a greater or lesser extent, has confronted all the states in the industrialized world. It was also the transition to the age of globalization.

By the end of the 1970s, the new conservatism was gathering strength, intellectually and politically, especially in Britain and the United States. These movements, whose political chieftains were Margaret Thatcher and Ronald Reagan, sought to resolve the growing problems of the economy and society by putting an end to the postwar social compromise. Their plan was audacious: take control of the state to undermine the strength of the labour movement and reverse the growth of the welfare state. And they were quite prepared to accept the cost of economic crisis, with slow growth and high unemployment, to achieve their goals. Once in power, both Thatcher and Reagan were bold in taking on the power of the unions. In his first year in office, Reagan fired all the air-traffic controllers to punish them for their illegal strike. And Thatcher fought a savage campaign against the National Union of Miners—the same union that had once been so effective in mobilizing the country against the Conservative Party.

What hurt the power of labour even more than these direct assaults, though, were the economic policies of neoconservative regimes in Britain and the United States—whose chief ingredient was the hard-line stance against inflation. Thatcher and Reagan used as justification the works of the monetarists, who believed in squeezing inflation out of the system by restricting growth in the money supply. And while there were plenty of problems with their theoretical position, policies based on their ideas did succeed in reducing inflation—as well as in pushing the British and American economies into severe recessions in the early 1980s. Recessions fostered unemployment, and unemployment hobbled the trade union movement for the simple reason that when there is surplus labour, unions lose their bargaining power.

Economic recovery, when it came after the great recession of the early 1980s, was the consequence of the contradictory elements of Reaganomics. The Reagan administration cut taxes and increased defence spending. These measures, along with a fortuitous fall in global oil prices, helped reignite the American economy. Increased American economic demand then became the focal point for export-led recoveries throughout the industrialized world.

But Reagan's recovery floated on a sea of red ink. The U.S. public sector deficit skyrocketed, as did the U.S. current account deficit. Not only was Reaganomics putting Washington in debt for the long term; it was putting Americans into debt with the rest of the world.

In social terms, the Reagan recovery was also extremely uneven. The gap in income between the rich and the poor widened appreciably, and while millions of low-wage jobs were created, full employment was not achieved. And with the onset of a new and deeper international recession at the beginning of the 1990s, the full scope of the new socioeconomic malaise became starkly apparent.

Between 1973 and 1991, the share of total income going to the bottom 60 percent of Canadian families with children was declining, while that of the top 40 percent of families with children was increasing.[2] In this stagnant economy, social programs became extremely expensive. The social democratic political coalition of the golden age of social democracy was breaking up in the new and unaccustomed circumstances of the 1990s.

Social democracy had flourished during the postwar decades, in a social setting that was much more homogeneous than it is today. This was the high point of traditional industrialism, with its mammoth workplaces and large phalanxes of workers. Secondary manufacturing was the largest single source of jobs, in a male-centred system of employment. It was not difficult for the male workforce, in an era when trade unions were stronger, to see its self-interest very much at stake when it came to proposals to strengthen social programs. They benefitted from the programs directly, and they could easily see that other people like them also benefitted.

Today's transformed economy and heterogeneous society are quite another matter. The service sector is now central. Female labour is no longer secondary. And cultural, racial and lifestyle differences in the population have made it more difficult for people to identify with each other on the basis of social class. The old cleavage of poor versus rich is now overlain with other cleavages. In these times of chronically high unemployment and underemployment, much of the working class, for instance, has become disillusioned with affirmative action programs aimed at overcoming the historic disadvantages of women, racial minorities and the disabled; they see them as being undertaken at their expense.

To those with jobs, whose incomes are not increasing and whose tax burdens have been mounting, social programs such as welfare often seem to be nothing but an additional burden. The antagonism of those with jobs toward those on welfare or even on unemployment insurance is no new thing. I can recall encountering it when canvassing for NDP candidates in the east end of Toronto as long ago as the 1960s. But now that the jobless are everywhere in working-class neighbourhoods and the government debt has mushroomed, these antagonisms have grown much more politically salient. The consequence is that the social cement that held the welfare state together is coming unstuck. While this host of societal developments can hardly be laid at the door of the neo-conservatives, it is indisputable that the attack on inflation, which was at the heart of conservative economic policies, has actually formed an assault on the organized power of the working class. As we will see in later chapters, these policies have evolved at the behest of those who now dominate global capitalism: the corporate and institutional interests that finance the world's long-term debts and provide capital for the bond market. The overriding concern of these interests is to ensure a reliable rate of return on their invested capital. For them, inflation is the deadly enemy, because it threatens investors with the repayment of their loans in devalued currency. The consequence is that the bond market has become a fetter, standing in the way of economic growth. At the first sign of a growing economy, where jobs are being created, the bond market slumps, forcing up long-term interest rates. And with high interest rates, finance ministers are placed under immense pressure to cut government spending, which, in turn, has the effect of slowing the economy, increasing joblessness and slashing social programs.

Watching the rise of the new capitalism is like watching a history film rolled backwards. As the economic and political pillars on which it rested have collapsed, the great social compromise of the postwar decades has been shattered. The coalition that defeated Nazism and fascism in the Second World War has long since disappeared. Under the cover of revolutionary technology and globalizing markets, a new conservatism has restored capitalism to its prewar values.

The term *globalization*, ubiquitous in our era, refers to the transformation—economic, social and political—that has been underway since the 1970s. Globalization is a word with a dual meaning. It refers not simply to the ways the world has been changing, but also to the ways the economically dominant want the world to change to serve their interests. As a consequence of new technology and policies of free trade and deregulation, a new kind of global economy has indeed emerged over the past two decades. Never before has business been able to produce goods and services in so many diverse locations across the face of the world and to market them virtually everywhere. And never before has capital flowed so freely around the globe as it does today. As we will see in later chapters, this latter fact is the very hallmark of globalization, stamping its character on the new capitalism of our time.

In addition to those objective changes, there is the other use of the word globalization. Globalization is not merely a description, it is a prescription as well. What can be called the globalization agenda has become the conventional wisdom of the English-speaking world's business elite. This wisdom holds that we have to reshape our economy and our social order to make ourselves competitive in a world dominated by technological revolution and the rising might of the new economies of East Asia. We are challenged repeatedly to shape up to meet these challenges. To shape up, we have to cut two kinds of costs—the cost of labour and the cost of social programs.

Cost cutting, of course, is no socially neutral phenomenon. It establishes a very clear hierarchy of winners and losers. It is based on a precise notion about what is essential and what is secondary in contemporary society. At the centre of society, according to the "globalization" perspective, is the marketplace. The most important people are entrepreneurs, those who take risks investing their own money, and those who manage large and small enterprises. Investors and managers are the indispensable actors who carry the whole of society forward, through their creative responses to the ever-shifting whims of the market.

The globalization agenda presents the worldview of the right as more than a set of aspirations. It presents it as necessity itself.

In a way quite unprecedented since at least the 1920s, the

worldview of the right has become accepted as the voice of realism. Even though conservatives actually speak for the most powerful vested interests in society, it has been the great accomplishment of the right that it has managed to make the left appear to represent what are called "special interest groups" (i.e., those who stand in the way of the imperatives of globalization).

Moreover, the current drive to the right shows no sign of stopping with the mere unravelling of the postwar welfare state. Emboldened by its victories, elements of the right now have their sights set on a much grander goal—the undoing of the legacy of the Enlightenment, the eighteenth-century social transformation that gave rise to the enfranchisement of the working classes in the French Revolution and formed the foundation of modern democracy.

It is widely assumed in the West that there is a fundamental link between democracy and capitalism, that democracy and capitalism are mutually reinforcing. In fact, when we examine the history of the West since the French Revolution, we see that the relationship between democracy and capitalism has been anything but simple. Moreover, given the political trajectory of the hegemonic right in the West today, the relationship between democracy and capitalism needs to be critically evaluated.

The central working assumption of a capitalist society is, and must always be, that selfishness and greed liberate the creative energies of human beings more effectively than any alternative set of values and motivations. It is true that the rise of capitalism was accompanied by an immense expansion of economic output and repeated rounds of technological advance. It is also a matter of historical record that the struggle to free capitalism from the remaining fetters of feudalism and the European *ancien régime* threw open the doors to the notions of democracy and human equality. But if there is no question that the rise of capitalism was crucial to the initial advance of democracy, it is certainly the case that while freedom, democracy and human rights have sometimes been allies of capitalism, they are by no means permanent or necessary parts of it.

To make the transition from the *ancien régime* to full capitalism, the then revolutionary capitalist class needed to invoke the notions of equality and citizenship to mobilize mass support for their project. In France, the capitalists of the late eighteenth century could not have overturned the entrenched order unless the mass of the population were prepared to be their footsoldiers. Capitalists had to venture far beyond their narrow class interests to alter their society so that the market could be legitimated as a central fact of life.

Having once invoked the rights of the mass of the population, however, it proved to be more difficult to dismiss those rights when they became inconvenient later on. Ever since the French Revolution, struggles have been waged within society about the rights that became a part of the Western consciousness as a result of the revolution. At times of political reaction, those rights have been suppressed and negated, but never forgotten. At other times, as a consequence of the power of the labour movement and other social and political movements, those rights have been broadened and deepened.

During the period following the Second World War, the rights of citizenship were broadened from narrowly defined political freedoms to include new concepts of economic and social citizenship. The right to a job with a living wage, the right to social assistance for those unable to work, the right to high-quality health care and the right to an education were crucial elements of this broader notion of citizenship. Since the early 1970s, however, the trend has been entirely different. A new capitalism has enabled the affluent and their political representatives to launch a highly effective assault on the welfare state and on the gains won by the working class. No less than a full-scale attack on social citizenship has been undertaken by the affluent, who have retreated to their perfumed stockades so they can live lives of comfort and privilege, unaffected by the storms their actions have provoked in society at large.

In the postwar period, it was assumed that the government had a responsibility to ensure that anyone who wanted to work could find a job. That assumption is now gone—so much so that when

I talk about the postwar idea of full employment my students often find it a bewildering notion.

In *Socialism: Past and Future*, the book he wrote just before his death in 1989, the great American socialist Michael Harrington made the case that the future of democracy depended to a considerable extent on the future vitality of socialism. Without a vast movement of reform from below, he maintained, democracy would wither, and the great gains made in the capitalist epoch would atrophy.[3] Harrington's warning about democracy is even more relevant today than it was when he issued it.

In both Europe and North America, a potent and growing far right now poses a threat to the democratic order, surpassing anything experienced in the West since the days of the Nazis and the fascists. The social tensions engendered by a new and meaner capitalism, with all its attendant threats to traditional forms of social organization, have combined to brew far-right political movements across Europe and North America. These movements threaten political violence in varying degrees, on a scale that would have been unthinkable only a few years ago.

In Europe, the movements of the far right are broadly connected in their lineage to the fascist past. The largest of them, the Front National in France, led by former paratrooper Jean-Marie Le Pen, is authoritarian, and has its source of political energy in the charisma of its leader. The Front National promulgates a harsh French nationalist creed, the goal of which is to protect the country from a supposed excess of immigration, particularly from North Africa. Le Pen promises that, with power, he would expel three million foreigners—which happens to be close to the number of unemployed in France—and thereby guarantee employment for all the French. Other European far-right movements and parties, such as the Republican Party in Germany and the Austrian Freedom Party, have similar exclusionist and racist programs.

In the United States, extremism has a quite different, homegrown face. For a year before the bombing of the U.S. federal building in Oklahoma City in April 1995, paramilitary units with an extreme right-wing political outlook had been organizing in various parts of the country. These militias formed the outer edge of the American extreme right, bringing two novel features to its frothy mixture: the formation of armed bands organized into paramilitary units and the dissemination of an ideology that claimed the right of such militias to defend the true nature of the American constitution, if necessary, through opposition to the U.S. government by means of force.

What came to light in the period following the Oklahoma City bombing was the existence of a far from miniscule paramilitary and political movement prepared to use extralegal means to confront their federal government. Not since the 1920s, with the fascist paramilitary in Italy and Hitler's brown shirts in Germany, had there been such a radical, militaristic challenge to the elected government in a major capitalist state. In its threat to use force, the militia movement in the United States exceeds anything on the far right in Europe, where no major challenge to the state's monopoly over the means of force has yet been attempted. Even parties like Le Pen's Front National have no paramilitary wing of any significance. On the other hand, the European neofascist right has developed better known leaders and has a much clearer political program—focused on the exclusion of foreigners and opposition to European union—than is the case with the American militia movement. It may be armed, but it remains less politically mature than its European counterparts.

It is clear that the rise of these associations, beginning with the formation of the Michigan Militia in April 1994, was intimately connected to developments in the mainstream right—and in particular with the ideological offensive against the Clinton White House quarterbacked by Newt Gingrich of the Republican Party in 1994. That assault, which challenged the legitimacy of the Clinton presidency in extravagant fashion, was unique in its intensity. The Republican Party was only the partisan voice of a much wider right-wing crusade against the Clinton White House which involved newspapers, radio and TV talk shows, evangelical

Christian organizations and the anti-abortion movement. Activists in this crusade portrayed President Clinton as a liberal, a draft dodger, a supporter of big and intrusive government, and because of all this, as completely unfit to uphold and defend the U.S. constitution.

The alarming rise of the extreme right in both Europe and North America is an important feature of an era in which democracy is in retreat. What is important about the far right is not its outré behaviour or its sensational characteristics, but precisely its organic connection with the mainstream right, whose contemporary stance also challenges democracy in important ways. It is the posture of mainstream conservatism that, in the short to medium term, poses a more basic threat to democracy than does the far right.

For its part, the mainstream right has been shifting away from fiscal conservatism—the great issue on which it achieved its present ideological hegemony—to a more radical agenda. Where the monetarists had few goals beyond restraining government spending, members of the new right see themselves as social revolutionaries. An agenda that implicitly promoted the legitimacy of inequality has become an explicitly anti-egalitarian agenda. Mainstream conservatism has embraced the idea that the poor, the disadvantaged and the insane will be with us always and that acceptance of this fact is preferable to attempts to push forward the frontiers of equality.

The mainstream conservative drive for inequality started with the assault on the idea of full employment, the cornerstone of the economic and social agendas of postwar governments. The idea of full employment has been replaced by the notion that permanently high joblessness is a price that has to be paid for economic advance. For the past twenty-five years, the acceptable level of unemployment has been revised steadily upward. In 1960, the Marxist notion that capitalism maintains a "reserve army of unemployed" to drive down the price of labour was customarily cited as a proof that Marxism was out of date. As we near the year 2000, however, that "reserve army" has again become reality.

To the contemporary right, full employment is a noxious idea, not just because the global capitalism of our era makes it virtually impossible to attain, but also because of the values that accompany it. Policies of full employment afforded a measure of dignity and independence to ordinary citizens. This struck at the underlying conservative idea that only a tiny proportion of the population has the drive and courage to achieve excellence.

The conservative predilection against egalitarianism has a very long pedigree, and predates the Enlightenment of the eighteenth century. It is almost instinctual for conservatives to suspect that most people are lazy, fearful and irrational, more suited to being compelled by their superiors than to being allowed to think and act for themselves. It has never been difficult for conservatives to regard egalitarianism as an unnatural suppression of the innate differences between human beings. Equality pushed too far, conservatives believe, condemns society to sameness and mediocrity, the wretched pursuit of security and safety, and thereby blocks the way to true greatness and excellence.

Today's conservative attack on full employment has been accompanied by an assault on social programs, again not merely for narrowly economic reasons. The desire to put people in their place is easily seen among contemporary conservatives, who have been feeling triumphalist in recent years. The most advanced social programs—decent levels of social assistance and unemployment insurance, childcare leave for parents, generous old age security, universal medical care—have the effect of reducing the harsh impact of the market on ordinary citizens. Conservatives aspire to demolish these nonmarket features of advanced capitalist society and to force the majority of the population once again into a completely market-centred existence.

Nothing reveals this more clearly than the onslaught against welfare recipients in both Canada and the United States. They have become ideal targets for conservatives, who have the goal of dividing the working class against itself. Those who have jobs and pay taxes can be embroiled against those who have no jobs and receive social benefits. But the welfare issue goes well beyond the question of government deficits and taxation. For conservatives, welfare is a moral issue. It is ideal ground on which to drive home the lesson that there is a deep divide in society between the decent and hard working, and the slothful who want to live on handouts.

A student of mine who was working for the Ontario Conservative Party expressed the view that welfare recipients have a good life. As he put it, they get to sit at home all day, watching television and drinking beer. His tone was derisive. He saw those on welfare as coarse beings, lacking in moral fibre, driven only by the lowest appetites. To redeem them and society, they had to be made to work.

The sentiments expressed by my student were far from original. Indeed, loathing for the poor has always been a feature of our civilization. The current assault on welfare recipients has a specific intellectual source, however. It was launched in the mid-1980s by Charles Murray, an American right-wing ideologue, in a book entitled *Losing Ground*. Murray formulated the notion that social assistance payments have the effect of trapping the poor in a cycle of dependency. Cutting off welfare, he argued, even if this were to mean destitution for some, was the only way to wean most of those on social assistance away from the enervating culture of dependency. According to Murray, the welfare system constituted a magnet, drawing people to it in preference to work. He further maintained that, particularly among young black women, welfare was attractive as a sort of substitute career, actually motivating them to conceive children out of wedlock.[4]

Murray's thesis was immensely attractive to American conservatives. At a time when their economic policies were driving up unemployment and widening the gap between rich and poor, here was a theory that shifted the blame squarely and unequivocally onto the backs of the welfare recipients themselves.

The attraction of the theory was not accompanied, however, by accuracy. The theory of welfare dependency is a counterfeit analysis of a serious social condition. The fact is that advanced capitalism has evolved from a system of relatively full employment to one of chronic underemployment. In a terrible irony, the very failure of the new capitalism to provide full employment has strengthened capitalism politically—for the moment, anyway. The reason for this is that chronic joblessness has enormously increased the cost of unemployment and welfare programs. The tax burden to pay for those increased social costs has fallen squarely on wage and salary earners. The consequence of this has been a sharpening political division between those with work and those without. Conservatives have been highly successful in selling the idea that the welfare system, rather than the economic system, is at fault—a neat trick in which reality is stood precisely on its head, so that the high welfare bill becomes a cause of our economic problems instead of a consequence.

A key part of the antiwelfare crusade has been the focus on welfare cheaters. The media loves to feature stories of those who rip off the system—collecting more than one welfare cheque or placing themselves on social assistance illegitimately. In fact, the available evidence suggests that the number of people cheating on welfare is very low. The 1994 study of the welfare system, "Managing Social Assistance in Ontario," undertaken by the Ontario government, pointed to a rate of deliberate welfare cheating of less than 2 percent of cases.[5]

Meanwhile, it is standard practice for people doing household repairs—roofing, carpentry, eavestroughs, and so on—to ask for cash, so that they can avoid paying the federal Goods and Services Tax (GST). People crossing the border from the United States to Canada regularly fail to declare some of the goods they are importing to avoid paying duty.

And then there's the thorny question of income taxes. There's nothing wrong with affluent citizens trying to pay as little tax as possible, provided they don't cheat—and most affluent people are honest. But there is a good deal of tax cheating on the part of well-to-do citizens and a lot of what tax expert Neil Brooks, professor of law at Osgoode Hall in Toronto, calls "borderline tax evasion."

Many businesspeople put spouses and children on the payroll. This lessens the amount of income the proprietor has to declare at the highest marginal tax rate. It's perfectly legal to hire family members, provided they do all the work they're paid for. But padding the number of hours worked and jacking up the rate of pay for family members is tax evasion. According to Brooks, it's not uncommon for proprietors to hire their offspring for the summer and pay them much more for the work than they'd normally pay someone else.

The right of businesspeople to deduct 50 percent of business entertaining is also widely abused. Most of the lunches at high-priced restaurants in major cities are being written off, as are most of the season tickets for major league hockey and baseball games. And the write-offs are commonplace, even when friends and family members are the beneficiaries.

The super-rich also shelter tens of millions of dollars from Revenue Canada in places like the Cayman Islands. The law requires the Canadian beneficiaries of foreign trusts to pay Canadian taxes, but the rich have found a way around that. Wealthy Canadians can direct millions of dollars to an entity in the Caymans that is like a trust, but is not exactly a trust. They send the trustees there a letter of intent about who the fund is to benefit. Strictly speaking, though, the beneficiaries have no legal, enforceable claim, and that means that they don't have to pay any Canadian tax.

In the types of cheating or borderline tax evasion I have cited, as in the case of welfare cheating, the effect is that taxpayers in general end up with a higher bill to pay. And yet, public morality is such that the perpetrators are treated in different ways than are welfare cheaters. These perpetrators meet with wide public acceptance, even though the effect of their activities increases the tax bill for everyone else. Moreover, these perpetrators are so sure of the social acceptability of what they are doing that they often brag about their activities to others, even to casual strangers.

In truth, cheaters take their toll on all public and private institutions to a certain extent. That has always been true, and it always will be. Welfare cheating has been inflamed and dramatized, however, not because it is intrinsically more important than other varieties, but because it advances a particular ideological agenda. No one ought to deny that welfare cheating is wrong, just as the other forms of cheating I have mentioned are wrong. But it is not accidental that only welfare cheating has become a salient political issue.

It is not for nothing that the only form of cheating discussed in the Common Sense Revolution, the program on which the Ontario Conservatives won office in 1995, is welfare cheating. Under the heading "Welfare Fraud and Overpayments," the Tories pledge that "fraud and overpayments must be stopped."[6]

What the Tories were doing was vilifying all welfare recipients, even though the overwhelming majority of them are honest, and once in office, the Conservatives proceeded to cut the benefits of welfare recipients by 21.6 percent. You wouldn't know from the Tory campaign against them that welfare recipients are required by law to prove they are seeking work and that the majority of those living on welfare are children, single mothers, the elderly, the disabled and the permanently unemployable.

Stereotyped and isolated, it's too late for many welfare recipients such as one who wrote to tell me her story. Her fifty-nine-year-old husband, a lifelong construction worker, has suffered deterioration of the cartilage in his hands, elbows and shoulders. The doctor says he can no longer work at anything requiring "extension and repetitive use of the arms and hands."

With his grade ten education, he's never going to get an office job, but technically he's not disabled. And he and his wife are too honest to go looking for a doctor who will say his condition is worse than it is. So they took the cut and now are subsisting on $680 a month.

Adding fuel to the antiwelfare backlash has been a perception about the make-up of those receiving benefits. Writing in the *Toronto Star* the day before the 1995 Ontario election, Dalton Camp commented on Bob Rae's political decline: "One of the problems Rae had with welfare, as a political hot button issue, was that a lot of the public suspected a lot of those on welfare were 'foreigners'—like Jamaicans, or Maritimers—which was an even hotter button. Some of those who pressed the welfare issue knew damn well the passions it aroused in the body politic."[7]

Under Mike Harris, the Ontario Conservatives won power chiefly on the following pledges: a 30 percent income tax cut; the conversion of the system of welfare to one of mandatory workfare; and the elimination of employment equity legislation, which required employers to establish hiring plans reflecting the community-at-large and thereby helping women, minorities and the disabled find jobs.

The Conservative message was perfectly geared to the social cleavages that existed in recessionary Ontario. In disproportionate numbers, white males, convinced that they were the targets of reverse discrimination, supported the Tories.

If right wingers have succeeded in standing reality on its head on welfare and employment issues, they have been similarly effective in their assault on those who work in the public sector. The campaign against the public sector has been going on since the 1970s. Civil servants in Canada who have had to live with epithets such as "snivel servant" or "swivel servant" are regularly accused of being less productive than private sector counterparts and unfairly benefitting from a level of job security that is absent in the private sector.

There are many nonsocialist democrats, such as Liberals and traditional Tories, who regard the rise of the right with anxiety and dismay and who are highly aware of the threats to democracy it entails. But socialists have a critical role to play in resisting the antidemocratic tendencies of the right. Socialism and socialist politics, as I will argue in this book, are essential to the defence and extension of democracy in our era.

At its centre, socialism is about the struggle from below for the fullest possible extension of democracy. Historically, the great extensions of democracy have come much more through movements from below than as a consequence of enlightened reform from above. Without the English Civil War, the American and French revolutions, the struggles of the Chartists in nineteenth-century Britain, the Paris Commune, the campaigns of the suffragists, the drive to organize industrial workers in Canada and the United

States in the 1930s, and the electoral victories of socialist and social democratic political parties in many countries, the broadening of political and economic democracy would never have occurred.

Socialism starts from the premise that social justice is concerned, first and foremost, with the condition of the nonaffluent. While it can be noncommittal about the utility of the market, socialism does not see the market as the proper arbiter of social relations. It is on this point, and on its identification with the interests of the working class, that socialism is radically at odds with other ideologies.

But it is not for reasons of tradition that today's socialism continues to be rooted in these distinguishing features. Capitalism has returned, with a vengeance, to the idea of the untrammelled market. The new capitalism has reduced traditional social democracy to an uncertain and largely ineffectual political vessel, even when social democratic governments have managed to stay in office. Instead of acting as a clear opponent of the new capitalism, social democracy has often tried to show how well it can manage the new capitalism, and in doing so has often divided and demoralized its own constituency.

Social democracy flourished at a time when the balance of forces within capitalism was favourable to labour. Its leaders learned that they could play a centrist role in politics and could realistically aspire to form governments. Today, however, with the new capitalism, social democratic leaders have shown themselves to be ineffectual. Social democracy has lost its way.

CHAPTER 3

THE GLOBAL CRISIS OF SOCIAL DEMOCRACY

THE French Revolution anticipated the history of the modern world. The elements that would combine to create the ideologies and political systems of the past two centuries were forged in its white hot furnaces. One of those ideologies was socialism. Perhaps it would be better to say that socialism was the *foundling* of the French Revolution. Unwanted, unanticipated—once socialism came on the scene, capitalism could never be at peace. It has been the curse of capitalism that at the moment of its great historical triumph, centuries in the making, when France threw off the remnants of feudalism and bourgeois society emerged fully formed, so too did its negation make a brief and spectral appearance.

The socialism of Gracchus Babeuf, the leader of the Conspiracy of Equals, arose for a brief moment during the most revolutionary phase of the revolution. Although primitive by the standards of later socialist thinking, the essential idea that working people had interests unlike those of capitalists was already there. A mere flash across the stage of history to be sure, but once the idea of socialism had appeared, it was not erased, nor could it be erased.

Some may object to the contention that socialism first appeared in the French Revolution. Of course, as with any such complex and historically necessary idea, there were numerous antecedents dating back as far as ancient Greece and Rome. When it comes to the socialisms of the modern world, however, the French Revolution was truly the moment of creation—and to understand the crisis of contemporary social democracy, we first need to look at the traditions of socialist thought and action that have developed since that time.

In its simplest form, socialism embraces much that is essential to liberalism, at the same time as it negates the rest. For two centuries before the French Revolution, liberal thinkers waged an assault against the *ancien régime*, drawing on new paradigms of knowledge in a host of fields: politics, religion, psychology, economics, history and philosophy. The work of Hobbes, Locke, Newton, Voltaire and Rousseau elaborated a new conception of the universe and humanity's place in it and contributed mightily to the vast transformation wrought by the French Revolution. Liberalism struck at the idea that inherited privilege was a part of the divine order of things. It tore away at the justification for a hereditary aristocracy and monarchy. It insisted that in essential respects, human beings were cut from the same cloth and were, therefore, equal. At the same time, the growth of commercial capitalism and the development of the national state established the material basis for a wholesale challenge to the *ancien régime*.

Beneath the exo-skeleton of the old order, a new capitalist society took shape. Wealthy merchants, bankers and lawyers formed nonaristocratic elites in the burgeoning cities of France. The aristocracy, with its political privileges, remained the locus of a great deal of formal power, while the new capitalist wealth created the potential, indeed the necessity, for a new system of power relations. The French Revolution pierced the shell, allowing the new society to emerge. When we look beneath the exterior trappings of the various phases of the revolution, the subsequent Napoleonic era, and even the restoration of the Bourbon monarchy, we see that the assumptions of capitalist society were enshrined in the workings of the state. Once the revolution had occurred, France could never go back to a system in which a hereditary aristocracy predominated. The capitalists had arrived, and though they might themselves aspire to titles and favour a monarchy, the marketplace, the banks, commerce and cities had taken centre stage. Alexis de Tocqueville captured the spirit of the age: "In democracies, nothing is greater or more brilliant than commerce. It attracts the attention of the public and fills the imagination of the multitude."[1]

After the French Revolution, liberalism, the ideology of capitalism, was entrenched in the citadel of the established order. For capitalists, the overthrow of the aristocracy and the enthroning of money, business and the marketplace was the end of the revolution. But not everyone felt that way. Having prevailed against the *ancien régime*, it was now the turn of capitalism and liberalism to defend themselves against revolutionary challenge. Socialism was the challenger, and it mounted its offence on behalf of those who were economically disenfranchised within the order of liberal equality.

The working class is at the centre of socialism, as it has been from the beginning. That is completely natural, since the working class was created by capitalism, and capitalism could not exist without a working class. And yet the working class can make capitalism function only through its own exploitation. It is this essential contradiction at the heart of capitalism that gives rise to socialism.

By working class, I mean all those who make their living by earning a wage or salary in nonmanagerial positions—about 80 percent of the population of industrialized countries. There is, of course, a wide range of differences in income, wealth and education within the working class as I have defined it. In North America, much of what I call the working class is normally referred to as the middle class: teachers, skilled workers, technicians and nurses, for example. Quibbling over these terms is pointless, but what does matter is to distinguish between the majority of the population, which sells its labour power to earn a living (however skilled and well rewarded they may be), and those who earn their living primarily from the profits made on invested capital. While there may be a considerable difference between the circumstances faced by a part-time labourer and a teacher, there is a much wider difference between both of them and Conrad Black.

Liberals believe that while capitalism has its problems, these difficulties are resolvable within the logic of the system itself. In fact, liberals customarily view the social inequality encountered within capitalism as evidence that the system has not been pushed to reach its logical potential. It is not that liberals deny there are marked inequalities in society. The question is how to explain them. To a liberal, economic and social problems are explained as a sign of imperfections in the market. Repair the market, make it whole, and equality will be restored—that is the liberal faith.

In contrast, the new right sees equality as the enemy of liberty. Leading spokespersons of the new right are forthright in their insistence that equality has been pushed too far and we have thus headed down the road to mediocrity. They want society reformed so that individual initiative is restored to its rightful place as the source of human advance. If the many must be trampled for the few to excel, then so be it. In this, the new right is merely recycling the harsh thinking of the Social Darwinists of the late nineteenth century, who believed that life and business involved an inexorable struggle between the fit and the unfit. Asked to justify his ruthless efforts to destroy the competitors of Standard Oil, John D. Rockefeller once said: "The American Beauty rose can be produced in the splendor and fragrance which bring cheer to its beholder only by sacrificing the early buds which grow up around it. This is not an evil tendency in business. It is merely the working out of a law of Nature and of God."[2]

Socialists do not share the liberal faith that as the market approaches perfection, human problems will thereby be resolved. As far as socialists are concerned, the exploitation of the working class is essential to capitalism. Letting the market work may improve economic efficiency in certain circumstances, but it will always involve the exploitation of the working class.

Early European socialism was an amalgam of many streams of thought. German philosophy, the example of the French Revolution and British political economy all contributed to its heady brew. Its advocates ranged from utopian visionaries, who dreamed of a world of cooperation and brotherhood, to Marxists, with their claim to having created a new and scientific understanding of human society that pointed toward the inevitable collapse of capitalism. Marxists preached the replacement of capitalism by a revolutionary workers' state and eventually by a classless society in which human exploitation would be abolished.

In the early twentieth century, socialism divided into two very broad streams: Marxism (or revolutionary socialism) and social democracy (reformist socialism). While Marxist socialism has had many internal divisions, it has been dominated by what became its orthodox branch, the Communist Party of the Soviet Union, ever since the Bolshevik Revolution of 1917. Social democracy, on the other hand, has had no such overpowering orthodox centre. It differs in its traditions and goals from country to country.

In the mid-Victorian era, Karl Marx presented his "scientific socialism," a claim that depended on the notion that the class struggle was central to the historical process. According to Marx, recorded history was, in fact, the history of societies divided into social classes in which there was a ruling class and an exploited class. Ancient societies were divided between a slave-owning minority that ruled over a majority whose slave labour produced the necessities of life. In mediaeval Europe, feudal society was divided between a land-owning nobility and serfs, who worked the land on their behalf. For its part, capitalist society was divided into two essential classes: a capitalist class, which owned the means of production and the sources of wealth (banks, factories, land) and a working class, which sold its labour to the capitalists for a wage. While there were certainly other social classes—a self-employed middle class, for example—it was the capitalist class and the working class that gave capitalism its particular character. Moreover, according to Marx, the fate of the entire society would be determined by the interaction between these two major classes.

Marx spent most of his time analysing capitalism, so while his conception of socialism might have been sketchy, he delved in painstaking detail into the workings of capitalism and its evolution as a system. Marx concluded that capitalism was propelling itself toward an ever greater concentration of capital in the hands of a smaller and smaller number of people, as big business over-whelmed and acquired small businesses. In the process, more and more people from the middle social strata were being driven out of their intermediate position in society and into the working class. As capitalism advanced, according to Marx, the working class was being forced to take employment in ever-larger factories. Moreover, the exploitation of the working class was continually increasing, reducing the vast majority of the population to a state of immiseration so that all it was capable of doing was gaining enough sustenance to allow it to do the work demanded of it.

Where would this lead in the end? According to Marx, a high-ly contradictory process was at work: the system of production was being increasingly socialized, with huge numbers of workers employed in companies that were becoming monopolies. Meanwhile, the profits from the system were being privatized to a greater and greater degree. A point would be reached, Marx argued, when a huge and organized working class would be faced with a tiny ruling class. At this stage, the working class would seize power, and the system of socialized production would be appropriately matched by a system of socialized sharing of the spoils.

The Marxist perspective on the fate of capitalism—as a system progressing inexorably toward a revolutionary break in which the working class would seize power—was not shared by all people who regarded themselves as socialists. Another entire tradition, a tradition of nonrevolutionary socialism, developed among those who believed that the transition from capitalism to socialism did not need to involve a sharp rupture, but instead could take place through legally achieved reforms, over a long period of time. Eventually, the socialists who continued to regard themselves as orthodox Marxists mostly ended up in the communist parties and movements that were prominent following the Bolshevik Revolution of 1917, while most of those who believed in a grad-ual, legal, parliamentary road to socialism ended up being called social democrats. (The nomenclature is by no means precise and can often be confusing. In France, for example, the name *socialist* continued to be applied to political movements and parties that would be called social democratic in Germany or Sweden. In Britain, the Labour Party is reasonably regarded as a social democratic party. Among adherents of the CCF-NDP in Canada, the terms *social democrat* and *democratic socialist* have been used almost, but not quite, synonymously. In general, those regarding themselves as somewhat more radical have tended to prefer the word *socialist*, regarding the term *social democratic* as more centrist.)

From the time of Marx, the German Social Democratic Party played a critical role in the development of ideas that became associated with social democracy. A century ago, Eduard Bernstein, who regarded himself as a Marxist, developed an interpretation of the dynamics of capitalist society that came to be seen as antithetical to classical Marxism. While Marx had argued that capitalism tended to divide society ever more into an immense and immiserated working class and a small and all powerful bourgeoisie, Bernstein maintained that the working class need not be immiserated. He reckoned that social democrats, making use of parliamentary democracy, could introduce reforms into the system that would give the working class gains in well-being and in the exercise of social power. This way socialism could be achieved gradually. He believed that the ultimate transition to socialism, far from being the revolutionary upheaval Marx had contemplated, could occur almost imperceptibly. In place of revolution, Bernstein's watchword was gradual advance for the working class: "I cannot believe in a final aim of socialism. But I strongly believe...in the march forward of the working classes to a real democracy."[3]

Orthodox Marxists contemptuously referred to Bernstein, and those who came after him, as "revisionists," and the term *revisionism* came to be synonymous with right-wing abandonment of revolutionary analysis and intent. Social democrats of the parliamentary school also came to be known as gradualists, because of their belief, as pioneered by Bernstein, that socialism could be achieved over a long period of time. In Europe, the division of socialists into the social democratic and communist camps was especially bitter, and had tragic historical consequences. In the Germany of the early 1930s, the failure of social democrats and communists to close ranks against Hitler helped open the way for the Nazis to take power.

In the English-speaking world, while these divisions also existed, socialist politics developed out of other traditions as well which meant the European splits had less impact there. In Britain, for instance, trade unionism and reform protestantism combined in a new political stream that led to the formation of the Labour Party. Trade unionists, who believed the cause of the working class required political action, and Protestants committed to social reform—the so-called social gospellers—were crucial to the development of Canadian social democracy.

After the Bolshevik Revolution, the struggle for socialism in the industrialized world was overwhelmingly divided into two rival and irreconcilable camps—the communist camp, which took its direction from Moscow, and the gradualist social democratic camp. Over time, the strengths and limitations of the two approaches became evident and seemed to be so enduring as to be set in stone.

Communist parties displayed resilience and strength based on internal political discipline and the commitment that came from a deep-seated and highly articulate antagonism to capitalism. From the end of the First World War to the early 1950s, in Europe, and to a lesser extent, in the English-speaking world, communist parties were able to recruit idealistic and talented young adherents. Such members characteristically devoted great energy and selflessness to the cause.

The communist parties, however, carried two historic millstones around their necks: their theory of political organization and their subservient link to Moscow. Like the Bolsheviks in the Soviet Union, the communist parties in the West subscribed to the idea of "democratic centralism." In principle, this was based on a system in which debate on fundamental questions was open within the party at specific times, but that once positions had been adopted, they were to be followed with unquestioning loyalty. Dissent from adopted positions would not be tolerated.

In practice, the communist version of democratic centralism meant that party members were subjected to a whole lot of centralism and almost no democracy. As was the case with the Communist Party of the Soviet Union, power was concentrated tightly at the centre. Indeed Joseph Stalin's elimination of his potential rivals and consolidation of his reign of terror, using the position of Secretary of the Soviet Communist Party as his formal instrument of power, was to determine the course for the communist parties of the West as well. From the beginning of the 1930s, Western communist parties took their political line from Moscow and ran their internal affairs on the model of the Soviet party—with the obvious and important exception that the party leadership could not execute and imprison rivals and dissidents, as was notoriously the case in the Soviet Union. One of the truly dark miracles of Western communism was the way highly intelligent, creative individuals could suspend their critical judgment and subordinate themselves to a top-down leadership whose political strategy could change fundamentally on Moscow's whims.

Although communist parties in the West did not have this bloody legacy, they were nevertheless used, with ruthless cynicism, as instruments of Stalin's foreign policy. They changed their basic political line according to Stalin's dictates, not in terms of the pursuit of socialism in particular countries, about which the Soviet leader cared little, but to further the short-term goals of the Soviet Union itself. As a consequence of this, in the early 1930s, communist parties adopted an extremely hostile attitude to social democratic parties, styling them as "social fascists." When Moscow became alarmed by the threat posed by Nazi Germany in mid-decade, the line was changed to favour the formation of "popular fronts" with social democrats, liberals and others who could be won over to an antifascist position. Antifascism remained at the core of the policies of Western communist parties right up to the eve of the Second World War, and this made these parties attractive to young militants and intellectuals who were gravely alarmed by the rising influence of Hitler and his allies in the other Axis powers.

Then, in August 1939, after lengthy negotiations to achieve an alliance against Hitler with Britain and France, Stalin did an abrupt turnaround and opened the door to a diplomatic initiative from Berlin. After whirlwind talks, the Nazi-Soviet Pact was signed in Moscow. With it Stalin acceded to the imminent German invasion of Poland, with the caveat that the Soviet Union would be allowed to occupy eastern Poland and to impose its strategic will on the Baltic States.

The impact of the Nazi-Soviet Pact on Western communist parties was instantaneous and devastating. After Hitler's armies invaded Poland on September 1, 1939, communist parties, which had been building an antifascist coalition for years, refused to support the declarations of war by Britain, France and Canada against Germany, choosing instead to describe the war as an "interimperialist" conflict, in which the working classes should not opt for one side over the other. Communist parties in the West remained loyal to Moscow and stood in the way as their governments prepared for war against the Nazis. In Canada, communists made common cause with French Canadian nationalists, who were organizing to oppose any move on the part of the federal government to adopt conscription. The Canadian Communist Party's opposition to the war effort was countered by the government declaring it an illegal organization, and communist militants were interned in camps alongside profascist Germans and Italians.

Western communist parties continued their opposition to the war until June 22, 1941, when the world situation was again transformed by the Nazi invasion of the Soviet Union. From the moment the Soviet Union was attacked, communist parties in the West reversed their position, and came out fully in favour of the war effort to defeat the Nazis. From then until the end of the war, the communists were among the most stalwart proponents of the war effort, even opposing trade unions and social democrats in the West who stood up for the economic demands of workers during the conflict. In France, where the communists had previously contributed to the mood of defeatism that weakened the country against the Nazi onslaught in June 1940, the Party became the heroic backbone of the Resistance. In Canada, communists clamoured to join the armed forces, often volunteered for front-line duty and condemned the French Canadian nationalists for their continued opposition to conscription.

Once the Soviet Union joined the Grand Alliance against Hitler, communist parties were able to regain some of the standing they had lost during the notorious period of the Nazi-Soviet Pact. The respite did not last much beyond the end of the war, however. In the years immediately following the war, the Grand Alliance broke apart, forming two opposing blocs in the Cold War, and communist parties throughout the West declined. In the United States, communism replaced Hitlerism as an alien menace, and writers and artists who had briefly flirted with communism or with organizations that had included communists were themselves shut out in the days of the Hollywood blacklist. Reaching its peak with the hysteria of McCarthyism, anticommunism pushed the very idea of left-wing reform off the American agenda.

In Italy and France, the communist parties had emerged with immense popular legitimacy at the end of the war. By the late 1940s, however, they were out in the cold, having lost all hope of participating in governing coalitions. (In 1981, the once-mighty French Communist Party, which had been the dominant force on the left at the end of the war, entered the cabinet of the newly elected socialist government, as distinctly junior partners to the socialists.) In West Germany, for a time, the Communist Party was banned as an extremist organization. And while the party was legal in Canada, it was hard hit by a spy scandal, when its only member of Parliament, Fred Rose, was convicted of providing classified information to the Soviet Union, sent to prison and forced to resign his Montreal seat in the House of Commons. The Canadian party, renamed the Labour Progressive Party, also suffered the spillover effects of McCarthyism in the United States, so that by the early 1950s, it was a small and alien organization within the Canadian body politic. It continued to have influence in a few industrial unions, and enjoyed some local electoral support, but otherwise it remained marginal.

The virtual destruction of the smaller communist parties in the West was precipitated by two events, both of which occurred within a few months of each other in mid-1956: the Soviet invasion of Hungary and Nikita Khrushchev's revelation of the unspeakable crimes of the Stalin era.

In the face of the Hungarian revolution of 1956, which had brought to power a government bent on democratization and on distancing the country from the Soviet Union, Moscow, after brief hesitation, sent its tanks into Budapest. Hungary's reform prime minister, Imre Nagy, faced a secret trial and was executed and buried in an unmarked grave. Thousands died and tens of thousands of others fled the country, a large number of them coming to Canada.

The invasion of Hungary made it agonizingly clear, even to dedicated Communists in the West, that the relationship of Eastern European countries to the Soviet Union was that of satellite to imperial power. For those who continued to cling to the idealistic theory that the Soviet Union was the centre of a worldwide struggle for liberation, this was a crushing blow. And the blow was accompanied by another, which was at least as devastating.

In the summer of 1956, at a closed session of the Twentieth Congress of the Soviet Communist Party, Nikita Khrushchev presented a carefully tailored, partial look at the true nature of the Stalin regime, which until that time had been closely guarded. The full text of Khrushchev's speech, with its details about the horrors of Stalin's purges of the Communist Party, and his technique of extracting fake confessions from high-ranking rivals in the party before condemning them to death, was published in newspapers throughout the West. Although stories about the Stalin purges had been published in the West since the late 1930s, they had always been dismissed by loyal communists as nothing more than smears. But now, suddenly, the leader of the Soviet Communist Party was the source of the charges, and party adherents could no longer ignore them.

Tens of thousands of people left the communist parties in the aftermath of these twin hammer blows, and Western communist parties became mere remnants—with the exception of the highly particular cases of Italy and to some extent France, where they had a strong enough political base to survive as mass organizations. For a minor communist party, like the Canadian one, there was no recovery from the events of 1956, and any discussion of the party's history necessarily notes that date as the effective end of its influence. A dozen years later, when the Soviet Union sent troops into Czechoslovakia to crush the reform regime of Alexander Dubcek, who had opened the way for the democratic and artistic outpouring of the so-called "Prague spring," there were so few independent spirits left in the communist parties of the West that there was no exodus on the scale of the departures of 1956.

The final chapter in the history of the communist parties of the West came, not surprisingly, with the demise of the Soviet Union itself and of the Soviet Communist Party. The once mighty and feared Soviet party apparatus stumbled through an ignominious attempted coup in August 1991 as it briefly held Soviet President Mikhail Gorbachev prisoner in an attempt to regain its power. The incompetent authors of the coup finally succumbed to the resistance of Boris Yeltsin and his Muscovite supporters.

In the months that followed, the Soviet Union itself ceased to exist and the party that had given it birth was closed down. (The party sprang back to life a few years later, however, its renewed political energy fuelled by the despair of many Russians, for whom capitalism meant joblessness, inflation levels that wiped out their savings, crime, official corruption and the deterioration of health care. Despite the fact that many militants of the new party had been in the old Communist Party, its rebirth was linked to conditions in post-Soviet Russia rather than to the Soviet past.)

In the end, the communist parties of the West, despite the dedication and selflessness of their members, were the purveyors of a perverted politics. They were manipulated from Moscow, until the Moscow centre itself collapsed. As for the struggle for socialism in the West, the communist parties had taken people on a vast and agonizing detour. The very memory of how the parties had been betrayed and in turn had betrayed their followers, would make the resumption of the journey all the more arduous.

If the communists followed a course that was recognizably similar everywhere, the social democrats differed enormously in strategy and analysis from country to country. The great strength of parliamentary social democracy in the West is that it arose out of the particular political culture of each society. Despite the trials through which it passed, it was never easy to marginalize social democracy by depicting it as the product of an external and therefore alien society. With its philosophical links to liberalism, social democracy could always present itself as the voice of moderate and workable reform, even if at the other end of its spectrum it stood for a much more radical rejection of the system. On the other hand, the radicalism of social democracy, including its critique of the shortcomings of capitalism, was essential to its capacity to recruit dedicated members whose goal was to achieve fundamental change.

In Europe and Canada, in the decades after the war, social democratic parties often appeared schizophrenic. To the public at election time, it was not unusual for them to speak of workable reforms in a tone of moderation, while keeping the idea of truly radical change discreetly in the background. At conventions of the party faithful, the more radical call to transform society and build socialism was regularly heard. Both sides—the moderate public face and the radical internal vision—were necessary to win votes and hold onto adherents.

As social and economic circumstances changed, social democracy changed too, sometimes presenting a more pragmatic, reformist face, sometimes a more radical one. This oscillation of perspective has been characteristic of both Canadian and European social democracy. There was nothing haphazard about the pattern of oscillation between moderation and radicalism, however. As social democratic movements have evolved into political parties, they have developed a professional, bureaucratized leadership, dominated by those who see politics as a vocation. For these leaders, the desire to succeed in a career could not help but affect the content and direction of their politics, and career ambitions varied depending on political circumstances.

In Canada, the ambition of an NDP politician might be limited to winning and holding a seat in Parliament, or to becoming leader of the federal party. In provincial politics, at least in British Columbia, Saskatchewan, Manitoba and Ontario, the goal has been to win office. For the leadership of the major social democratic parties of Western Europe, the goal has been to win power at the national level. However "power" has been defined, the quest for it has had, not surprisingly, a great effect on social democracy. For many years, I have observed NDP MPs at close range, and while they have certainly professed radical ideas at times, their desire to hold onto their parliamentary seats has also imbued them with an unmistakable conservatism. Watching a sitting MP coming back to his or her office after a day on the hustings has often reminded me of a small businessperson in action.

When I worked as research director of the federal NDP in the early 1980s, it was perfectly obvious to me just how anxious caucus members were to hold onto their seats. No doubt this was so they could achieve worthwhile reforms, but it was also because, for many of them, it was the best job they had ever had and they could not bear the thought of losing it. What was true of individual MPs was even more evident among party leaders—particularly those who stood a good chance of winning office. As political parties developed an ever more elaborate bureaucracy, often as a consequence of the growth of tax-deductible donations, the separation between party leaders and the rank-and-file membership yawned ever wider. Social democratic parties, which prided themselves on a process of internal democratic decision making at party conventions, turned more and more for advice to professional pollsters and media consultants. (Many of the polls we used at federal NDP research were photocopied and sent to us by provincial NDP governments in Manitoba and Saskatchewan. So apart from being the poor cousins who had to read the charts in black and white instead of colour, there was not much difference between us and our counterparts in the offices of the Liberals and Conservatives.)

While, in theory, NDP leaders took their policy cues from the party membership, in practice, the professionalized leadership insulated itself ever more from the party and set its own course. The four election campaigns run by NDP leader Ed Broadbent between 1979 and 1988 provide striking examples of a party leadership setting its own themes, with very little observable reference to the body of party doctrine as established at conventions. For any professionalized leadership of a social democratic party, however, the drive for power and central control is ever present. Indeed, they have won power in Western Europe, Canada, Australia and New Zealand frequently enough that it is possible to draw general conclusions about the performance of social democrats as governors.

Understanding how social democrats behave in office requires a brief discussion of the nature of the state in a capitalist society. To that end, it must be noted that the state is made up of much more than the government; to use the words *state* and *government* as synonyms is highly misleading. The state is a vast apparatus with many functional divisions. On the federal level, some of these divisions include the armed forces, the Supreme Court, the Royal Canadian Mounted Police and crown corporations and agencies, which in Canada include such important entities as the CBC, VIA Rail and Canada Post. Provincial states operate enormous health care and school systems, as well as highway ministries and vast electric power corporations. Taking both federal and provincial states together in Canada, when we include public funds paid out to individuals for such things as pensions and welfare, close to 40 percent of the Gross Domestic Product (GDP) of the country passes through the state in one way or another.[4] As socialist political scientist Leo Panitch has noted, "a...reason for delineating clearly the institutions of the state is that it leads us away from assuming, as social democrats consistently do, that election to governmental power is equivalent to the acquisition of state power."[5]

Social democratic governments are faced with an additional problem in gaining control of power, in that senior levels of federal and provincial ministries and of crown corporations and agencies are staffed by people who are similar in outlook and training to those at the top levels of private sector bureaucracies. The social background of deputy ministers and senior government bureaucrats is often similar to that of managers in the private sector. They customarily attend the same universities, where they are influenced by the same perspectives on economics and administration. Often, top managers in the public and private sectors move in the same circles, and it is not at all unusual for senior government bureaucrats to move to top private sector jobs, where they can expect to make a lot more money. As a consequence, social democratic governments have often been described as "guests in power." Getting the vast state apparatus to perform on behalf of the goals of a social democratic government can be a daunting challenge.

Despite the fact that social democrats have often been immersed in the small details of daily politics, they have also achieved great victories. Sometimes they have run on distinctly radical platforms and won. Two such cases, to be explored later, are the victory of the Labour Party in the British general election in the spring of 1945, and the French presidential and national assembly elections in 1981, which were both won by the Socialist Party.

Any government of the left, with truly radical objectives, necessarily occupies a contradictory position. While implementing the sweeping changes it has signalled, it also needs to deal with immediate concerns, not the least of which is the need to keep running the agencies of the state effectively, and it also has to take steps to prevent an economic crisis. The first thing on the minds of leaders of a newly elected social democratic government in any country is to reassure business, and particularly the domestic and international lenders of capital, that all is well, since social democratic governments are never elected with the support of capital. They are elected only in the face of greater or lesser degrees of business hostility. Conrad Black expressed this sentiment with respect to the Rae government in his 1993 memoirs, in which he wrote, "No one in his right mind would invest a cent in Ontario under this regime…" and then went on to chastise the "petulance and naivete of the Ontario voters in delivering over half the GNP of Canada to such a regime of economic thieves and vandals…."[6]

While business doesn't like to inflict wounds on itself, it is certainly not averse to choosing to locate in a jurisdiction that is favourable to capital in preference to one where a social democratic government is in power. The most ideologically right-wing elements of business would go so far as to move to another jurisdiction in order to disrupt the economy and thus thwart the plans of an unwelcome social democratic government. Aware that a crisis with business, and especially with the financial community, is a real possibility, the leader of a social democratic government is often motivated to select a finance minister from the ranks of the more conservative members of the parliamentary caucus. Thus, when the British Labour Party was in power in the 1970s, its chancellor of the exchequer was Denis Healey, a tough political operative from the right wing of the party, and not someone like Michael Foot or Tony Benn, from the left. (In the case of Ontario's NDP government, there was initial surprise when Floyd Laughren, a long-time left-wing caucus member, was appointed finance minister by the newly elected Premier Bob Rae. Within two years of his appointment, however, Laughren had transformed himself into a hard-line deficit fighter.) On first being elected NDP premier of British Columbia in 1972, Dave Barrett flew to New York to assure Wall Street that he was not the "Allende of the north." Such gestures have been the norm for newly elected social democratic governments.

Once a social democratic government has put its most moderate face forward to calm the business community, it has to turn its attention to an immense, long-term task—gaining mastery of the vast state bureaucracy, without which it is impossible to fashion and implement new policies. When the CCF government was first elected in Saskatchewan in 1944, socialists across the continent watched how the new government dealt with this challenge, regarding it as a test for how well the CCF would perform. Since health care reform was to be such a major priority for the CCF, Premier Tommy Douglas kept the portfolio of health minister for himself. In a television interview I conducted with him in 1979, Tommy Douglas told me that when he had his first meeting with the deputy minister of health, he quickly concluded that the man was not well suited to introducing the reforms the CCF wanted. Instead, he decided, the deputy minister would be ideal as the chief administrator of a major hospital. Douglas soon appointed him to run Saskatoon's largest hospital, leaving the way clear for someone else to oversee the introduction of the government's reforms.[7]

It took the CCF a considerable period of time to gain effective control of the relatively small Saskatchewan bureaucracy of the mid-forties. It was not that the senior echelons of the provincial government bureaucracy were hostile to the CCF. They simply did not share its assumptions about a radically different role for government. Not until many top bureaucrats had been replaced by appointees sympathetic to the CCF did members of the Douglas government feel that their policies would be understood and supported by those who had to implement them. Whether control is ever effectively established is partly a function of whether bureaucrats feel that the social democratic government is likely to win re-election. In Ontario's ill-fated NDP regime, which often seemed to be afraid of its own shadow, top bureaucrats whispered to one another that their goal was "to survive 'til '95," at which point they would be liberated from serving a government whose goals were remote from their own. By contrast, media watchers marvelled at how quickly the subsequent Harris regime settled into power.

What the analysts had forgotten was the fundamental difference between a conservative and a social democratic government: one has the full support of business, while the other can expect constant sniping at best, and efforts at destabilization at worst. When the Harris government was three weeks old, it announced

$1.9 billion in cuts to government programs, the largest coming at the expense of the province's poor, in a 21.6 percent reduction of welfare payments. Four months later, billions of dollars in additional cuts were made to hospitals, municipalities, schools and universities. To some analysts, this was daring stuff—a government quickly implementing the program on which it had been elected. It was not long before this take on things showed up on the business pages: Steve Saldanha of Nesbitt Burns Inc., for one, praised the Tories, saying that "neither an economic slowdown, accounting gimmicks, nor special interest groups will prevent them from taking the steps necessary to clean up the province's fiscal house." In the same vein, economist Patti Croft of Wood Gundy Inc. was quoted saying that the Tories were "digging themselves out from a deeper hole than we thought and the fact that they have already done this much adds to their credibility."[8] What had happened was no mystery: the party of business had returned to power.

Socialist scholar Leo Panitch has commented on this close relationship between business and the party of business: There is, he writes, "an ideological hegemony emanating from both the bourgeoisie and the state which is awesome, which is reflected in the sheer pervasiveness of the view that the national interest and business interests are at one, and which certainly ensures the smooth functioning of the relationship between the state and the capitalist class."[9]

Beyond the hazards social democratic governments face in gaining control of the state and preventing business from destabilizing the regime, there is the enormous challenge of defining and implementing the social democratic project. What ought to be the goals of a social democratic government?

Naturally, this depends to a considerable degree on economic and social conditions and on the kind of mandate won by the social democrats during their campaign for power. In 1959, the CCF government in Saskatchewan won a highly specific electoral mandate to introduce medicare. On the other hand, when the Ontario NDP, under the leadership of Bob Rae, was elected in

1990, the electorate was, in many ways, passing a negative judgment on the Liberal government of David Peterson. The 37 percent of the electorate who voted for the NDP in 1990 appeared to be open to the ideas of the party and to be willing to trust the NDP to run the affairs of the province. Beyond that, it would be difficult to claim that Bob Rae and the New Democrats had a clear mandate from the public.

While provincial social democrats have won mandates of varying significance over a period of half a century in four provinces, there is no disputing the fact that the two most significant electoral victories for social democrats in the industrialized world were the British Labour Party's win in 1945 and the victory of the French Socialists in 1981.

Labour's sweeping 1945 victory was unprecedented. While the party had been in office previously, it had never come to power entirely on its own, without having to form a coalition with other political parties. This victory, all the more surprising, was won at the end of the war at the expense of Winston Churchill, the most celebrated British prime minister of the century.

During the election campaign, Labour had issued a platform calling for broad-based nationalization of British industry. Once installed in office, Clement Attlee, the new Labour prime minister, seemed to be in a position to chart an entirely new course for the country. The potential appeared to exist for a democratic socialist transformation of British society, with a vast transfer of power from the business class, and the still potent aristocracy, to the ordinary people of Britain.

What followed, however, fell far short of both the hopes of Labour militants and the fears of the Tories and their business supporters. Eschewing the fundamental transfer of power its program had called for, the new government took important steps to create a welfare state and to nationalize a number of industries, the most important being coal and steel.

During the war, the British government, which had included Conservative and Labour ministers, had undertaken a comprehensive review of British social conditions under the direction of

Lord Beveridge. The *Beveridge Report* identified what it saw as the severe ills of British society, graphically depicting them as the five "giants": "want," "sickness," "squalor," "ignorance" and "idleness." The report proposed a system of universal social security, the most important component of which was the creation of a national health service. It also recommended the pursuit of economic policies aimed at preventing a return to the mass unemployment of the 1930s.

To a considerable extent, the *Beveridge Report* shaped the agenda for Attlee's Labour government. And in comparison with the industrial strategies being mounted on the European continent by postwar governments, the Labour government's policies were rather pale. In place of socialism, Labour delivered the welfare state, buttressed by state ownership of industries that tended to be concentrated in the declining north of the country, a region that was a critical electoral base for the party. Instead of transforming Britain's class system, the Labour Party set out to ameliorate its worst excesses.

The second great case when socialists came to power in Western Europe (without having to form a coalition with a moderate centrist party) led to results similar in kind to those of the Attlee government in Britain. The French Socialist Party won a stunning victory in 1981 in both the presidential and the subsequent national assembly elections. For the first time in the history of the French Fifth Republic, whose constitutional structure had been established by Charles de Gaulle, the left came to power. Indeed, the only comparable victory of the left in the history of France had come in the mid-1930s, when Léon Blum's Popular Front took office. François Mitterrand's triumph in 1981 was even more unambiguous, however, and appeared to open the way for a major shift of power within French society.

During the 1981 election campaign, Mitterrand had presented voters with the so-called 110 propositions, a program whose stated goal was to make France the citadel for the "liberation of man and the construction of socialism." The Socialists campaigned for political liberalization, decentralization and workers' rights—what they proclaimed as a "new style of citizenship."

The elements of the Socialist platform included the following:

- widespread nationalization of industry, to place the main levers of economic development in the public sector,
- the pursuit of an interventionist industrial strategy, so that government could plan the future direction of key industries,
- the investment of large sums of money into traditional industries on the theory that they could be made productive and therefore competitive, and become a bountiful source of new jobs,
- reflation of the economy through government spending on social programs and public works in order to revive economic growth sufficiently to sharply reduce unemployment, and
- democratization of industry, so that worker representatives would have a say in the running of companies for which they worked.[10]

Taken as a whole, the Mitterrand program offered France the entire panoply of measures that had been on the socialist agenda for decades. In this sense, the Mitterrand presidency can be considered an historic testing ground. But while the Mitterrand regime was not to be without successes of vital significance to the future of Europe, straightforward progress toward socialism was not to be one of those. The Socialists plunged ahead with major elements of their ambitious program, but soon ran into increasingly stubborn difficulties.

For one thing, the effort to stimulate the economy could not have been attempted at a worse time. The severe global recession of the early 1980s was just beginning in the United States, and although it was never as severe in continental Europe, it undermined the efforts to reduce unemployment in France. Additional spending by the new French government, which in part took the form of higher incomes for public sector employees, did create a short-lived growth spurt in France. But additional demand for goods in France had the predictable effect of sharply increasing the country's imports at the same time as its exports were suffering because of the overall slowdown in the global economy. Rising imports and stagnating exports pushed France toward a balance of payments crisis, so that in 1981, by the end of Mitterrand's first year in office, France had a trade deficit of 105 billion francs, up dramatically from 20 billion francs the previous year. This put severe downward pressure on the value of the French currency, forcing several devaluations of the franc against the German deutschmark. In addition, between 1980 and 1983, the public sector deficit quadrupled and inflation jumped to 14 percent.[11]

These woes pointed to the immense difficulties that are encountered when a single country tries to buck the trend of the global economy—even when that country is as large as France. The fate of the French reflation program demonstrated how unworkable the classical Keynesian tools, so favoured by social democrats in the postwar decades, had become.

Mitterrand's problems extended to the nationalization program as well. The Socialists started out with the idea that if you invested enough money in traditional industries, you could make them work. There was no such thing as an inherently uncompetitive industrial sector, Industry Minister Pierre Chevenement insisted. Billions of francs were invested by the government to take over banks and industrial companies and to rebuild the capital base of companies already in the public sector. In 1981–82, the government spent forty-seven billion francs to acquire twelve industrial firms, thirty-six banks and two finance companies.[12]

The idea of state involvement in the economy had deep roots in France, going all the way back to the Napoleonic era. At the end of the Second World War, for example, the state took over a number of key industries, in some cases because the previous owners had collaborated with the Nazis during the German occupation—as in the case of the automotive manufacturer Renault. But the nationalizations undertaken by the French Socialists added appreciably to the already large number of publicly owned industries in France.

In marked contrast to the major English-speaking countries,

the idea that state-owned industries could help boost productivity and keep the country competitive was strong in France. "Indicative planning" was practised by the postwar French government, the idea being to achieve a national consensus involving business and the state (and labour in the beginning) on the goals of the economy. Successive plans were intended to move the economy forward through various stages of economic development.

When the Socialists came to power in 1981, their goal was to add significantly to the already large publicly owned sector. They also wanted to democratize the running of public industry, which was already notorious for behaving just like the private sector in its top-down approach to labour. In the new round of nationalizations, a great deal of capital was invested in mature industries, such as steel, with the idea that new jobs could be created in the traditional sectors, whose workers were a key electoral base for the Socialist Party. Particularly here, nationalization involved large outlays of capital in sectors with doubtful prospects.

As early as the spring of 1982 and definitely by 1983, the Socialists reversed the major elements of their economic program, adopting what was then featured as a new economic realism. What became known as the "U-Turn" involved the dropping of the idea of economic stimulus and the thought of still further nationalization. The emphasis shifted dramatically toward the quest for productivity and the success of individual firms, and the locus of economic development shifted away from France on its own to France as an integral part of the new Europe.

By 1984, François Mitterrand had clearly moved away from socialism and adopted a neocapitalist European strategy. The strategy centred on the idea that for Europe to compete successfully with the United States and Japan, European economic and political union were essential. And for such a union to be consummated, France would have to return to the extremely close alliance it had established with West Germany to establish and develop the European Community (EC). Mitterrand, who had been a proponent of European union as a young man in the postwar years, now became its chief architect in the 1980s and early

1990s. He was the political force behind the EC's single-market program and later a key sponsor of the Maastricht Treaty on European union.

It could be argued, as Mitterrand did indeed argue, that European union would act as a bulwark against the more primitive capitalism of the English-speaking countries and East Asia, and therefore as a protection for the more advanced welfare state and the socialist potential of Europe. Whatever one might think of the merits of that argument, it was undeniable, however, that Mitterrand and the French Socialist Party had abandoned any recognizable attempt to achieve socialism in France.

In France in the 1980s, as in Britain in the postwar years, a major political opening toward socialism had led somewhere other than socialism. Numerous other social democratic governments have followed the same path—in West Germany, Scandinavia, Spain, Australia, New Zealand and Canada. Social democrats could make the case, as they often have, that their regimes had the effect of humanizing capitalism to a considerable degree. They have even claimed that, under their governance, capitalism was less crisis prone and more capable of pursuing the goals of higher productivity and sustained economic growth. But from our vantage point at the end of the twentieth century, looking back over many decades of experiments with social democratic governments, it is reasonable for us to ask whether social democracy cannot go beyond the welfare state and some solid successes in industrial strategy. Is social democracy unable to initiate a basic transfer of power from the capitalist class to the rest of society?

Even the most advanced case of social democracy, the one developed in Sweden since the 1930s, appears in our own era to be incapable of going beyond the creation of an extensive welfare state to a true transfer of societal power.

At the centre of the Swedish model was a system of national bargaining in which labour met capital on a comparatively equal footing. Labour, in close collaboration with the country's social democrats, pursued what was called a "solidaristic" wage policy. The policy was aimed at increasing the wages of those at the bottom at a higher rate than those at the top. This meant, of course, restraining the ability of the highest paid and most skilled workers to strike the best possible deal for themselves. The solidaristic wage strategy was helpful both to big business and to the least well paid workers. Its upshot was that big business was not squeezed by workers in their collective bargaining and was perennially able to earn profits to be reinvested in the development of new labour-saving techniques. This boost to productivity was accomplished at the same time as the wages of those at the bottom were kept very high in comparison to those in other developed countries. In fact, the lowest-paid workers in Sweden were paid about 75 percent as much as those with top wages, an exceedingly narrow division between top and bottom in comparison to other countries. What this meant was not that top wages were low in comparison to other countries, but that wages at the bottom end were high.

In the early 1980s, the Swedish Social Democrats and their labour movement allies decided to take a crucial step beyond the welfare state toward socialism. Their idea was to legislate the creation of what was called a "wage earner fund." The fund would take the form of a payment to workers which would not be paid either as wages or pensions. Rather the fund would be reinvested in the company employing the workers, giving the workers themselves an increasing equity share in the ownership of the company. The implications of the policy were clear enough. As the private sector made profits, a share of those profits would be accumulated so that someday in the future the workers would have majority control of the companies for which they worked.

The corporate sector's response to the idea of the wage earner fund was swift and predictably negative, and it occurred at a time when the social democrats were on the defensive for other reasons as well. The Swedish economy was engaged in a difficult transition in the new global economic atmosphere of the 1980s, and the bargaining power of labour was thus declining. When the Swedish Social Democratic Party lost the election of 1991, ousted by a right-of-centre coalition government, the prospect for a major step toward socialism, embodied in the idea of the wage earner fund, fell by the wayside.

However, the gains made by the Social Democrats over the preceding six decades were too deeply entrenched to be easily rolled back by the new government, and for their part, the Social Democrats returned to power in 1994. The distinctiveness of their societal model was nevertheless diluted still further when Sweden joined the European Union in 1995.

The three crucial cases of Britain, France and Sweden offer a nagging reminder of the limits encountered by twentieth-century social democracy. Indeed, a forceful case can be made that social democracy, which enjoyed a genuine golden age following the Second World War, has been in retreat for the past two decades and now faces the novel challenge of adapting to the transformed capitalism of our era.

CHAPTER 4

THE NEW CAPITALISM AND THE NEW RIGHT

IT has always been the case that layoffs cannot be far behind when companies go bankrupt or suffer significant losses. Today, however, giant corporations announce record profits one week and then proceed to downsize their workforce the next. Early in 1996, the major Canadian banks announced multibillion-dollar profits, then decided to cut the size of their workforces further than ever. Acquaintances of mine who are employed by the banks are constantly wary, watching for the signal that their jobs may be next. Why was that meeting called for our unit today?

There is no question that the new capitalism has an anorexic managerial style. The managers who are in vogue, like fashion models, are the minimalists. The paradox of the high-energy, high-productivity capitalism of our age is that it creates unprecedented wealth for a small minority and stagnating incomes and pervasive insecurity for the majority.

In the United States—from which the trends of the new capitalism wash into Canada—nearly 2.5 million workers lost their jobs as a result of corporate restructuring between 1991 and 1995. According to the U.S. Labor Department, median wages for workers, adjusted for inflation, were 3 percent lower in 1996 than in 1979. (Adjusting for inflation, men were paid almost 9 percent less in 1996 than in 1979, while women were paid 7.6 percent more.) And while household income increased in the United States by 10 percent between 1979 and 1994, 97 percent of the gains in household income went to the richest 20 percent of

households. Moreover, while workers have been experiencing stagnant wages and job insecurity, their bosses have never had it so
good. Top pay for corporate executives has skyrocketed to about
two hundred times the pay of the average worker, compared with
a factor of forty, twenty years ago.[1]

As the name of the system plainly advertises, capital is central
to capitalism. In all types of capitalism, profits are earned from
invested capital and then are ploughed back as new investment in
the quest to generate yet more profit. This process of reaping profits from invested capital and then reinvesting them is the wheel on
which the whole system turns. Everything apart from this central
process of investment and profit making is a means to an end.
This is true of labour, raw materials and technology. Whether a
capitalist is in the business of producing goods or selling services,
the wheel of investment that leads to profit and yet more investment is of primary importance.

The new capitalism that has grown up over the past two
decades has a different twist. While the system still turns on
investment-profit-investment, the realization of this process has
been transformed. Where industrial capital, invested in the production of manufactured goods, predominated in the old system,
financial capital has now taken precedence. "Money" has become
an industry in itself, and other industries, such as automotive
manufacturing or microelectronics, pale by comparison. The
financial sector now enjoys a global freedom of action that has
sharply reduced the authority of the state, of central bankers and
of other sectors of business, including manufacturing and retailing. So when Wall Street and Bay Street are booming, things don't
necessarily feel so hot on Main Street.

In the postwar era, the old capitalism—what we can properly
call industrial capitalism—reached its peak. The proportion of
workers employed in manufacturing industries was the highest it
was ever to be, and traditional "heavy" industries, such as steel,
automotive, chemicals and machinery, were more important than
they were before or have been since. About 30 percent of
Canadians were employed in manufacturing in the mid-1950s,

compared with about 17 percent today. In the mid-1990s, over two-thirds of Canadians are employed in the service sector—in financial services, retailing, wholesaling, advertising, entertainment, personal services, education and health care—leaving a declining minority producing manufactured goods, extracting resources, farming and fishing.[2]

In the old industrial capitalism, the so-called "Fordist" age of production, the emphasis was on the capacity to produce large quantities of identical products. Compared with the situation today, organized labour was in an advantageous position, because the average rate of unemployment was less than half of what it is in the 1990s. Enormous workplaces, the most famous of which was the immense Ford plant just outside Detroit, were the great economic cathedrals of the age. The mammoth manufacturing establishments of the 1950s fitted with the expectations of theorists of the left who believed that working-class solidarity was a likely outcome of this kind of industrial system.

The transition from the old capitalism to the new was sharply punctuated in the spring of 1979 when Margaret Thatcher, a more uncompromising Conservative than her predecessors, led her party to victory in Britain. A few weeks after Thatcher's win, I was in London, where I conducted a television interview with Michael Foot, one of the Labour Party's most renowned intellectuals and militants. Foot had always been one of my heroes, and I was thunderstruck when he said that "the golden age of social democracy was the period from the end of the war to the early 1970s."[3] I hadn't got used to the idea that social democracy was in decline. But here I was, face to face with the clearly discouraged Michael Foot, at the dawn of the Thatcher era. Foot, who was later to lead Labour into its dismal defeat against Thatcher in the post-Falklands election of 1983, went on to say that the twenty-five years following the war had been the age of Keynesianism, full employment and the rising welfare state.

During the postwar era, social democracy seemed to hold the key to the future. It espoused the virtues of the so-called mixed economy, in which the public sector would play a crucial role in tandem with the private sector, at a time when the budget of the state was increasing as a proportion of the economy as a whole. This fit well with the insights of Keynesian economics in an era when it was in vogue to set countercyclical fiscal policies, in which governments spent more during times of economic downturn and less during times of boom. Social democrats spoke on behalf of labour at a time when trade unions were at the peak of their power. Most of all social democrats were the leading advocates of the extension of the welfare state during the quarter-century when the most critical social programs were being created. During its golden age, social democracy was regarded as the sane alternative to unfettered free enterprise, with all its attendant inequities, and to state communism, with its suffocating centralism and absence of political freedom.

The new capitalism has been emerging from the chrysalis of the old for a quarter of a century. The old capitalism, though, centred in giant manufacturing establishments, operated within the restraints of clearly delineated national economies. But the powerhouse of the new capitalism is the financial sector, and the world is truly its oyster. To figure out who was dominant in the old capitalism, you needed to know how much steel and how many autos a country produced. In the new capitalism, you need to find out how many of the world's leading banks are located in a country, and how strong it is in microelectronics. Virtually everywhere, the old capitalism was much more successful in achieving the full employment of its workforce than the new capitalism has been.

By the early 1970s, the transformation had gathered sufficient force that we can say that the shift to the new capitalism was decisively under way. Like any vast historical change, this one involved elements that were geopolitical, economic, ideological, technological and social.

The onset of the geopolitical change—from a bipolar world centred on two superpowers, to a world of multipolar capitalism—was pushed along by the Vietnam War, the economic rise of West Germany and Japan, and the challenge to the industrialized world mounted by the Organization of Petroleum Exporting Countries (OPEC). While the Vietnam mobilization was at its peak, the combined demand for munitions and consumer products created supply bottlenecks in the United States. The American economy became overheated, and this made it an easier target for foreign exporters. This provided an ideal opportunity for West Germany and other European countries, as well as Japan, to rapidly close the productivity gap with their American competitors.

Another fateful consequence of the war was the generation of a new level of inflation in the United States, which was quickly transmitted throughout the industrialized world. In large measure the new inflation was a result of the Nixon administration's unwillingness to choose between funding the war and keeping the U.S. consumer economy going at full throttle. The consequence was the monetization of the public debt, through a rapid expansion of the money supply. In other words, instead of paying off the debt with real tax revenues, the government printed new money to make up the shortfall. As American trade deficits with other countries mounted steeply (the consequence of America's declining competitiveness), the quantity of U.S. dollars held by foreign central banks skyrocketed.

Faced with a deteriorating trade balance and a looming current account crisis, President Richard Nixon acted unilaterally to change the rules of the game. On August 15, 1971, he addressed the world from the Oval Office to announce that the U.S. was severing the link between the dollar and gold, so that the dollar would no longer be redeemable at thirty-five dollars per ounce.

This was a radical departure from the Bretton Woods international economic regime—so called because it was designed at Bretton Woods, New Hampshire, under American leadership in the summer of 1944. The hub of the Bretton Woods system was the U.S. dollar, which was designated as the reserve currency of the international economy. The dollar was pegged to gold at thirty-five dollars per ounce, so that, theoretically, the dollar was redeemable in gold at that rate—and the currencies of other countries were positioned against the dollar at *fixed* rates of exchange.

One of the most important ways the United States helped relaunch the postwar economies of West Germany and Japan was by agreeing to fix the deutschmark and the yen at artificially low levels of exchange against the dollar. Low exchange rates for their currencies strongly encouraged the growth of export-centred industrialization in the two countries.

As West German and Japanese exports to the U.S. took off during the 1960s, the holdings of U.S. dollars by foreign central banks mounted explosively, to the point where they came to exceed the value of the American gold supply. This effectively nullified the notion that U.S. dollars could be redeemed for gold.

Nixon's announcement that the U.S. would no longer redeem dollars for gold was a flagrant repudiation of the conditions under which foreign central banks had run up their vast holdings of U.S. dollars. Quite literally, the unilateral move left foreign central bankers holding the bag—stuck with U.S. dollars worth potentially less. It showed that while the United States was an economically wounded superpower, it was a superpower nonetheless, and other countries had no choice but to go along with its decisions.

In addition, Nixon imposed a temporary 10 percent surcharge on U.S. imports—a special tariff, whose goal was to reduce American imports and thus to counter the country's rising trade imbalance. Over the next few months, the Nixon administration forced a downward revaluation of the U.S. dollar in relation to the currencies of the country's leading trading partners. Within two years of the emergency Nixon program, the Bretton Woods system of fixed exchange rates, with the U.S. dollar as the global reserve currency, was replaced by a new nonsystem of *floating* exchange rates.

The challenge to American industrial supremacy from Europe and Japan, the beginning of the new global inflation and the collapse of the Bretton Woods exchange rate system were followed by another crisis: a quadrupling of the world price of oil from about three dollars a barrel to over eleven dollars a barrel.[4] The oil price shock in 1973–74—and a second shock following the Iranian

Revolution in 1979—subjected industrial economies to serious new strains. The huge increase in oil prices added dramatically to the inflation that had already been unleashed by the American response to the Vietnam War. The oil shock slowed the growth of industrial economies, pushing them into recession, while simultaneously hitting them with a major increase in prices. The combination—slower growth and higher prices—resulted in the combination of stagnation and inflation that came to be known as "stagflation."

The onset of high inflation in a world of flexible exchange rates undermined the pursuit of the "demand management" policies of Keynesianism. Governments that followed Keynesian policies managed their economies by manipulating fiscal (tax) and monetary (money supply) policies so as to keep the economy on an even keel. When the economy was slumping, Keynesians favoured tax cuts and increased government spending as a means of augmenting demand so that economic growth could be renewed. Alternatively, when the economy was growing too quickly (which brought the risk of inflation and supply short-ages), Keynesians favoured tax increases and reduced government spending. In principle, over one complete economic cycle, the government's budget would thus be balanced.

In reality, however, the balanced budget became a nearly unat-tainable goal—especially with the introduction of flexible exchange rates. These floating rates encouraged investors to shift their assets from country to country in order to buy the most val-ued currencies. And this meant that whenever governments increased government spending to shore up demand, the value of their currency went down, making it unattractive to financial market investors and speculators. Interest rates then had to be raised to make the currency more attractive on the international market.

On the domestic scene, however, higher interest rates increased the cost of doing business and the real price of houses, automo-biles and household appliances. This would then create a vicious circle by shutting off the economic recovery that the government was trying to promote in the first place. Over time, the rise of currency speculation, promoted by the deregulation that allowed capital to move freely from one part of the globe to another, and the new technology, which made a global financial market technically feasible, heightened this tendency.

Keynesian economics was thus discredited, and its demise opened the door to the powerful and inherently right-wing alternative, monetarism, which although it had been around for decades, had lived in the shadow of demand-management economic policies during the postwar era. Monetarists, such as Milton Friedman, wanted to return to a more classical, less regulated, market system, and were therefore opposed to governments making macroeconomic efforts to promote full employment. They also believed that the size of the money supply determined whether there would be price stability or inflation, and they favoured squeezing the growth of the money supply to kill inflation and thereby ensure price stability.

Monetarism was a recipe for deflationary economics. It was based on the assumption, rejected by Keynesians, that the price of labour was just like the price of a commodity, that it could be made flexible so it would respond smoothly to the law of supply and demand. A properly run market system, they believed, could force workers to accept low wages whenever work was in short supply. While Keynesianism was geared toward the achievement of full employment, and therefore tended to increase the bargaining power of labour, monetarism was centrally concerned with price stability, even if this meant a return to high levels of unemployment, which were bound to have the effect of reducing the bargaining power of labour.

Monetarism seemed to make sense in an era of stagflation, when inflation was ever present. And it was ideologically attractive to new business lobby organizations and think tanks that were forming in the mid-1970s to give business a more powerful voice in public affairs. The public mood accompanying the oil price revolution had set off alarm bells in the minds of corporate leaders.

The public was highly suspicious of global petroleum companies that were announcing record high profits at a time when consumers were facing huge price increases at the gas pumps, and on several occasions during the 1970s, actual shortages of gasoline in the United States. In March 1974, this negative view of the giant oil companies was lamented in an editorial in the *Wall Street Journal*: "On the evening TV news there were those pictures of oil tankers lined up to disgorge their precious loads while the voice-over wondered how there could really be an oil shortage unless those tankers and storage tanks were hoarding fuel against our distress. Sandwiched in were the film clips of this or that Congressman or some instant expert like Ralph Nader inveighing against huge windfall profits."[5]

Concerned that the public in Western countries did not identify with the market system and its goals, key business leaders decided they had to engineer a change in attitudes. In the United States, a new organization, the Business Roundtable, was established. It was a streamlined affair, composed solely of the chief executive officers of major corporations. As Irving S. Shapiro, the chief executive officer of Du Pont Corporation and a mid-1970s chairman of the Roundtable, put it: "The guts of the Roundtable is the fact that the chief executive officer is the man who participates."[6] And membership in the Business Roundtable was by invitation only. Its role would be to prepare probusiness positions on all major public policy issues and to lobby government. And when it came to influencing government and working with conservative think tanks to sway public opinion, the Roundtable was much more effective than the traditional business lobby organizations—the chambers of commerce and the American Manufacturers Association.

In Canada, the Roundtable formula was soon cloned with the creation of the Business Council on National Issues (BCNI). The BCNI was also an invitation-only organization whose members were the chief executive officers of major corporations, both foreign and domestic, operating in Canada.

So secretive was the BCNI that it didn't make its existence known to the public until April 1977, even though it had then been in the process of forming for two years. The choice of founding cochairmen revealed where the centre of gravity in the new lobby organization lay. They were: W.O. Twaits, who had been Mister-Big-Oil in Canada, the former chief executive officer of Imperial Oil (the subsidiary of American-owned Exxon Corporation) and Alfred Powis, the chief executive officer of Noranda Mines Ltd. Both of these men were heads of giant resource-extracting companies. Including 140 other chief executive officers, who headed big banks, big manufacturing establishments and more big resource producers, the BCNI was the unparalleled voice of the largest corporations in the country. Cochairman Powis was blunt about this in an interview in December 1977: "We formed the Council because a lot of us felt there was no credible, cohesive voice of business. Issues were coming up such as when David Lewis was conducting his campaign about corporate ripoffs, and while some companies replied, most stayed silent.... So now we have what I'd guess you'd call the voice of big, or bigger, business."[7]

Audaciously, the BCNI structured itself as a mirror of government, dealing in its closed door sessions with the agenda items that come before a federal Cabinet—economic strategy, national unity, government spending, social programs—all, of course, from the standpoint of its high-powered, corporate membership. Since its inception, the BCNI has been adept at focusing support for the business agenda among federal and provincial governments and opinion makers. In the debate on the Canada-U.S. Free Trade Agreement (FTA) leading up to the crucial federal election in November 1988, for instance, the BCNI and its president, Thomas D'Aquino, played an indispensable role in marshalling support for the FTA and the Mulroney government.

For two decades, the Business Roundtable and the BCNI have helped drive the trend toward a more market-centred economy. While these lobbies work to maintain a new version of the unpredictability and ruthlessness of the old free market capitalism, the global economy has been further destabilized through the rise of new technology.

Changing technology has always driven capitalism, undermining vast enterprises and putting others in their place, sometimes in astonishingly short periods of time. It is easy to think of great enterprises of the past century and a half that have risen and fallen as a consequence of technological change. Carriage makers that did not make a fast transition to the internal combustion engine were sent into oblivion with the arrival of the motor car. The great railway empires, which were on the top rung of business well into the twentieth century, were reduced to mere fragments of their former selves when they met up with superhighways, long-haul trucking, the automobile and jet aircraft. In the space of fifteen years, the typewriter has nearly become a museum piece, and successive waves of computers have come and gone. As new communications technology takes hold, the daily newspaper, so central to the history of the twentieth century, thrashes to carve out new niches for itself just to survive, its prospects several decades from now highly uncertain. Other long-term implications of the new technology are matters of urgent speculation. For example, will microelectronic technology end the historic need to centralize production in metropolitan centres and launch a new and historic decentralization of production—with immense implications for the future of the city?

Even giant and dominant enterprises have been successfully challenged and replaced by newcomers using new technologies and techniques of production. A critical case, which signalled the passing of American industrial enterprise from the zenith of its power, was the spectacular overtaking and surpassing of the giant American automotive manufacturers by Japanese firms. When Detroit's Big Three were confronted by an invasion of their territory, first by Volkswagen in West Germany and then decisively by the Japanese automakers, the response from top executives at General Motors, Ford and Chrysler was initially one of complacency. They were unaware of how revolutionary the Japanese challenge was.

This challenge was based not only on the superior use of new technology, but also on new techniques of production and a different system of management-labour relations within the industrial process. They pioneered the computer-driven technique of just-in-time delivery of parts and components to plants. And they benefitted enormously from the input of production ideas from workers on the plant floor, something the more hierarchical American industrial corporations were slow to do. Ultimately, the Japanese manufacturers were able to deploy a computerized production system to produce custom-made vehicles—so that each vehicle differed in its particular features from those coming before and after it. For many years, the U.S. Big Three did not even come close to achieving this level of finesse.

It is not that the Japanese manufacturers were the decisive innovators in each of these areas. Taken as a whole, however, they mounted a radical challenge to the Big Three. Their triumph came to symbolize the victory of a new paradigm of industrialism over an old one. The American system of production had grown lazy in its wasteful use of energy, its sloppy management of inventory, its emphasis on minor design changes rather than fundamental improvements, and its regimented conception of the workplace. A more lithe, creative, and intelligent system of production couldn't help but take over the market.

The Japanese triumph in the automotive sector was indicative of the sweeping success Japanese capitalism was enjoying in comparison with American capitalism. From the early 1950s on, Japan pursued a strategy that brought the private sector and the state together to plan for crucial economic breakthroughs. It did not wait for market signals to develop new technology and new products. Instead, the Japanese anticipated where the market would go and where its long-term economic advantage lay. By contrast, in the United States, the notion of setting specific industrial policies to promote strategic breakthroughs in key sectors has always run against the grain of government and business. During the great era of the expansion of American industrial capitalism (from the end of the Civil War in 1865 to the onset of the Great Depression in 1929), the idea of an industrial strategy involving government was anathema. American economic thinking has never escaped from the assumptions of this golden age.

The great exception to this ideologically based antipathy to industrial strategy has been the wide-ranging research and development money made available under the rubric of national defence. Defence spending has provided a massive backdoor route to industrial policy in the United States. In November 1991, for instance, the European Community issued a study concluding that American civilian aircraft manufacturers received "massive systematic support" from the U.S. government in the form of tax benefits and R&D grants from the Defense Department and the National Aeronautics and Space Administration (NASA). In sum these benefits amounted to between $33 and $41 billion during the period 1976 to 1990. Other industries have also received underwriting from defence spending—including the automotive industry, which has itself produced military vehicles whose development costs have assisted in the development of nonmilitary vehicles as well. In the autumn of 1993, President Bill Clinton showed how useful he thought the linkage with the Pentagon could be to U.S. industry when he said he planned to invite the Big Three auto giants to share in the R&D built up by the Pentagon during the Cold War.[8]

In the case of Japan, industrial policy has been front and centre from the first days of the country's economic recovery in the 1950s. Under the direction of the Ministry of International Trade and Industry (MITI) and the Ministry of Finance (MOF), the Japanese state has played a planning and coordinating role in conjunction with the private sector. The Japanese government has largely avoided interfering with competition among firms in particular sectors, and it has not disrupted the framework and assumptions of the market economy. It has, therefore, borne very little resemblance to a command economy like that of the Soviet Union. However, it has certainly been willing to encourage some sectors at the expense of others. The Japanese state has been prepared to anticipate future market breakthroughs in particular sectors and to push them down a path to strategic success.

In conjunction with private firms, including the largest manufacturers, big banks and small business, MITI has set broad goals for the Japanese economy. In the 1950s, the strategic objective was for Japan to make the transition from light to heavy industry. To encourage this transition—a difficult one, which flew in the face of the traditional notion that a country with few resources and an excess of labour should concentrate on light industry—the Japanese state controlled access to raw materials and capital, making it desirable for private firms to pursue the state's objective and nearly impossible for them to maintain the status quo. In the 1960s and 1970s, the objectives were to make Japan a world leader in the automotive and electronic industries. In the 1980s, the goal was to put Japan on the cutting edge of the new micro-electronic technology, both in its techniques of production and in the worldwide marketing of high-tech products.

By the 1980s, Japan's extraordinary achievements were evident to the whole world. In critical industrial sectors, Japanese firms displaced American and European competitors and became the new pace setters. And in mid-decade, Japan surpassed the United States as the world's leading source of new foreign capital. Meanwhile, the United States became a net debtor nation for the first time since 1919.

The transitions in the global economy in the mid-1980s were historic. Japan was eclipsing the United States in important ways at the same time as the nations of the European Community were setting out to transform their own economic and political union. Four decades after the United States had launched the new international economic system at Bretton Woods in the summer of 1944, the system of global economic power had changed beyond recognition. In his book *Head to Head*, American economist Lester Thurow pointed to the importance of this transformation:

• In 1970, the world's 100 largest corporations were based as follows: 64 in the United States, 26 in Europe, 8 in Japan. By 1988 the numbers were 42, 33 and 15.
• In 1970, the world's 50 largest banks were based as follows: 19 in North America, 16 in Europe, 11 in Japan. By 1988, the numbers were 5, 17 and 24.

- In 1990, none of the world's 20 largest banks were American, and 9 of the 10 largest service firms were Japanese.
- In the chemical industry, the three largest firms are now German-based.[9]

Japanese control of global automotive and electronic markets weakened in the 1990s. The country's vastly overpriced land boom has imploded and that has created a serious crisis for Japanese financial institutions. Moreover, scandals involving the ruling Liberal-Democratic Party and major Japanese businesses have undermined the legitimacy of the Japanese government. Since the early 1990s, Japan has experienced little economic growth. That said, Japan remains the leading provider of global capital, and its unemployment rate is at an enviable 3 percent. Moreover, in the 1990s, Japanese firms have been investing tens of billions of yen in the economies of East Asia, including China, positioning themselves to dominate the region that is becoming the centre of the global economy. Japan's recent time of troubles has not erased the gains the country made in the 1980s. Indeed, it is highly likely that the reorganization of Japan's investments abroad will open the way for a further increase in its international economic sway.

If you wanted to mount a tombstone over American economic hegemony, you'd probably inscribe it with the dates 1919–1986. The United States was a net creditor nation during this era, meaning that foreigners owed Americans more than Americans owed them. During the long period of the development of the American national economy, leading up to 1919, the United States had always been a net debtor nation (its principal creditor was Britain). In 1986, the United States became a net debtor nation once again, and this time, the creditor torch was passed to Japan. The net indebtedness of Americans has been growing rapidly ever since, from $144 billion in 1988 to $555 billion in 1993.[10]

At the end of the Second World War, in contrast to its waning position today, the United States dominated the global economy to an even greater degree than mid-Victorian England had a century before. The United States was in an unprecedented position to impose its agenda on the global economy. By the summer of 1944, when the United States met with its allies at Bretton Woods to plan the postwar economy, the defeat of Germany and Japan was already in sight. The United States had constructed the most powerful military machine in history and its industrial prowess was the greatest in the world. Wartime economic mobilization had consigned the dark time of the Depression to the past. It was entirely natural for the Roosevelt administration to feel confident that the lessons Americans had learned in constructing their national economy should serve as the basis for the construction of the postwar global economy.

At its early postwar peak, America had a capital surplus far superior to that of any other country; its industrial capacity was vastly in excess of that of any competitors; its technological prowess was unmatched; and its military reigned supreme. By the late 1980s, the first three of these pillars of hegemony had crumbled, leaving only the fourth, the military supremacy of the United States, fully intact.

The waning of U.S. economic hegemony has left the capitalist world facing the uncertainty of new struggles for supremacy. (Today that uncertainty is exacerbated by the demise of the Soviet Union, whose threatening presence formerly pressured the leading capitalist states into military and political unity.) Power struggles over the future shape of the global economy could endanger the rules and norms that are the legacy of the era of American control. What role, for example, will China and India play in the global economy over the next twenty-five years? What about other potential giants, such as Brazil?

Emphatically, the new capitalism takes different, even divergent, forms in the three major centres of power within the advanced, industrialized world—the United States, Europe and Japan. While capital has gained enhanced power everywhere, the three major subtypes of capitalism within the advanced countries retain their distinctiveness. The American system—which, broadly speaking, is common to Britain, Canada, Australia and New Zealand—is the most market centred of the three. The European system—with Germany and France at its centre—involves a much greater degree of state intervention, as well as the concept of a partnership between government, business and labour. And the Japanese system involves state and business planning of technological breakthroughs much more than the American and European systems do.

In the English-speaking world, with its pronounced insularity of thought, the supposed virtues of the American economic system are regarded as axioms, and they are rarely compared with the other two systems. One of those axioms is the supposed virtue of free trade as a route to economic development. British historian Eric Hobsbawm has made a droll point of this in a reference to the work of economic historian Paul Bairoch: "For the nineteenth century it is at least arguable that, contrary to the classical model, free trade coincided with and was probably the main cause of depression, and protectionism was probably the main cause of development for most of today's developed countries."[11]

As U.S. domination eroded, vast changes were simultaneously occurring between the private sector and the state, and within the private sector.

New technology was one reason for the economic changes referred to under the ubiquitous label of globalization. Developments in microelectronics enhanced the ability of firms to operate on a global scale, so that sourcing of raw materials, production of machinery, parts, components and end products, industrial research and marketing could be done in different parts of the world. For example, in the first half of the 1990s, United Technologies eliminated 33,000 jobs in the United States and created 15,000 jobs in other countries.[12]

While automobile interiors could be made in Mexico or in a low-wage Asian country, automotive capital equipment was designed in the U.S., Germany, Japan or Sweden, and the automobile itself was assembled in places like Oshawa, Ontario. In the financial services sector—without a doubt the locus of capitalist power in our age—microelectronics opened pathways for global transfers of capital on an unprecedented scale. The technical capacity to run the global financial market on a twenty-four-hour basis, transferring assets instantaneously from Tokyo to London to New York, was inconceivable in the age before microelectronics.

But the enhanced status of financial capital had nontechnological causes as well. The multicentred capitalism that evolved after the Nixon-era collapse of the Bretton Woods system helped free the financial sector from state regulation. After the demise of fixed exchange rates in the 1970s, the Eurodollar market—a market strikingly independent of government controls—was born. The movement for deregulation of capital flows within the major capitalist states has led to a vast expansion of speculation and investment through an ever-larger, unregulated market. In addition, particularly in the United States, deregulation contributed to the emergence of a "casino"-style capitalism, in which a surge in takeovers was triggered by devices such as junk bonds—whose purpose often was the stripping of assets by new owners who had no real interest in the production of goods and services.

The hallmark of the new global capitalism at the end of the twentieth century is the novel freedom and dominance of the financial sector in relation to all the other sectors of business and with regard to the state and society in general. The ability of those who control large pools of capital to move assets freely and to acquire and sell firms at will has given them immense new economic and political leverage.

Global capital markets have acquired an independence from the state to a degree never before achieved by segments of business. Decision makers in the financial sector have gained such power that it is not unrealistic for them to seek to impose their agendas on nation-states. One consequence of this heightened leverage is that business is now able to shift production to jurisdictions where labour and environmental standards are low.

In labour-intensive manufacturing industries, such as auto parts and electronics, there has been a pronounced drive to invest in low-wage countries with weak or nonexistent unions. The quest for a low-wage workforce was a major reason American business supported free trade with Mexico through the establishment of the North American Free Trade Agreement (NAFTA). Similarly, Mexico was a country with minimal environmental regulations and a reputation for hardly enforcing those it had. In an era in which governments point with pride to new international environmental accords, multinational corporations actively seek out countries where they can pollute virtually at will. And the fact that economic growth has been slow in the advanced countries in recent years should not blind us to the planetary scale of industrial activity and its grave implications for the world's ecosystem. As the World Commission on Environment and Development reported in 1987: "Over the past century, the use of fossil fuels has grown nearly thirtyfold, and industrial production has increased more than fiftyfold. The bulk of this increase, about three-quarters in the case of fossil fuels and a little over four-fifths in the case of industrial production, has taken place *since* 1950. The annual increase in industrial production today is perhaps as large as the total production in Europe around the end of the 1930s."[13]

A further sign of the global power of the financial sector has been deregulation in most countries, which has vastly reduced controls that formerly existed to limit where money could be invested, domestically and abroad, and which limited the role banks, trust companies, insurance companies and other financial institutions could play. Deregulation has opened the doors so wide that restrictions on sending capital abroad and on the functions specific kinds of financial institutions can perform have been dramatically reduced. The consequence has been a huge rise in the clout of bondholders—those who have lent capital to finance both the public and the private debts of the world.

Who are the bondholders? *New York Times* columnist Louis Uchitelle, writing about them from an American perspective, has aptly described them as "a loose confederation of wealthy Americans, bankers, financiers, money managers, rich foreigners, executives of life insurance companies, presidents of universities and nonprofit foundations, pensioners and people who…now buy shares in mutual funds."[14] Not surprisingly, what bondholders care about is the rate of return on capital. They have a morbid fear of inflation, since loans repaid in inflated currency aren't worth as much as those repaid in stable currency. At the merest hint of inflationary trends, they sell bonds, and when bond prices drop, the inexorable consequence is a rise in interest rates. Higher interest rates slow economic growth because they increase the cost of investments, and they increase the price of houses, cars and appliances. Moreover, higher interest rates vastly increase the burden of the national debt. (For example, if interest rates are at 10 percent, the government has to pay out $10 billion a year to carry a debt of $100 billion. At 5 percent interest, the government has to pay out only $5 billion a year.) A slow-growth, noninflationary economy is precisely what bondholders want—even though this is a virtual guarantee of high rates of underemployment. And underemployment does two things to make decent social programs unaffordable: it pushes more people onto various forms of social assistance and it shrinks the tax base that supports the programs.

High rates of economic growth, on the other hand, push suppliers of basic commodities—steel, plastic, lumber, parts and components for use in manufacturing, etc.—up against the limits of their capacity. When that happens, prices rise, companies are forced to expand their capacity through new capital investments and new jobs are created. This, in turn, creates a greater demand for labour, thus increasing the bargaining power of workers and giving an immense impetus to their demands for higher wages.

But all of this growth carries with it the risk of the resumption of inflation. Indeed, periods of rapid economic growth have historically been accompanied by inflation. What is different today, however, is that the locus of power within capitalism has shifted to give those who have a huge vested interest in limiting that process sufficient mastery within the system to substantially change the outcome. The bondholders' fear of inflation acts as a very effective brake against a resumption of sustained, rapid economic growth. The surest sign of the power now exercised by bondholders is that real interest rates have been at an historic high for the past ten years—in comparison to real interest rates in the postwar decades.

For bondholders, the key agency of the state is the central bank, but in recent years, and not accidentally, more and more steps have been taken throughout the Western world to insulate central banks from national governments. In *The Agenda: Inside the Clinton White House*, Bob Woodward recorded the immense frustration experienced by President Bill Clinton because of the capacity of bondholders and Alan Greenspan, the chairman of the Federal Reserve Board, to play havoc with his economic policies. Here was Clinton, supposedly the most powerful man in the world, seeing himself as a captive of the thirty-year bond rate.[15] In Germany as well, the president of the Bundesbank has long been the head of a virtual government within the government, with a sometimes shocking freedom to criticize the policies of the chancellor on fundamental issues of economic and taxation policies.

Recently, the mandate of the Bank of France has been changed to make it more similar to that of the Federal Reserve Board and the Bundesbank—to narrow its responsibility to sustaining the value of the franc and to reduce its commitment to the pursuit of other economic objectives and its ties to the government of the day. And while the Bank of Canada remains theoretically subordinate to the federal government, and specifically to the minister of finance, the pressures felt in other countries have been felt in Canada as well. Virtually the only power the Canadian government dares to exercise is to replace the governor of the Bank with someone more to its liking, as the federal Liberals did after coming to power in November 1993, when they refused to renew John Crow's appointment and replaced him with Gordon Thiessen.

In *Shooting the Hippo: Death by Deficit and Other Canadian Myths*, Linda McQuaig has exposed the role played by the Bank of Canada in keeping real interest rates high: "Since Crow [John Crow, governor of the Bank of Canada] began tightening monetary policy in earnest, real interest rates in Canada have gone up to historic levels." During the 1960s, the real interest rate averaged

3.2 percent in Canada, while in the 1970s, a decade when inflation was much higher, it dropped to 1.2 percent. In the 1980s, McQuaig shows that "as the Bank of Canada tightened its monetary policy in response to inflation, the real interest rate shot up to an average of 6.6 percent. But under Crow's extreme tightening during the 1990–92 period, the real interest rate went all the way up to 8 percent." Real interest rates in Canada have also been exceedingly high in comparison to those in other advanced countries. McQuaig concludes that "for the financial community, the war against inflation means high real interest rates, which are very desirable...."[16]

The lesson from the behaviour of central banks is clear. In the new capitalism, monetary policy is too important to be left to democratic governments. The greater power of the financial sector has had negative consequences for other sectors of capital, but the consequences have been especially negative for labour. While there is controversy on the subject of income distribution in Canada, the broad picture is plain enough. For the past two decades, the incomes of individual salary and wage earners, adjusted for inflation, have stagnated, in sharp contrast to the substantial increases of the post-war decades. While family incomes, on average, have risen somewhat in the past twenty years, this has been due, in large measure, to the rise of the two-income family.[17]

Not only have the incomes of the majority failed to rise as they did in the post-war decades, the problem of unemployment and underemployment has grown ever larger. In each decade since the 1950s, the average rate of unemployment has increased in Canada and the United States.

Anyone who imagines the economic restructuring of recent years has been beneficial to the majority of Canadians should consider this information from Statistics Canada:

• In 1992, 42 percent of workers were employed part-time, worked full-time on a temporary basis or were unemployed for part of the year. Forty-six percent of those with full-time, permanent jobs earned less than $30,000 per year.

- Only 20 percent of working women held full-time, permanent jobs that paid more than $30,000 per year.
- Taken as a whole, only 31 percent of all workers had full-time, year-round jobs that paid more than $30,000 a year.[18]

The long-term rise of unemployment and underemployment has been the direct cause of the crisis of the welfare state. In Canada in the 1990s, roughly 25 percent of the workforce is unemployed or underemployed—including the roughly 10 percent who are classified as unemployed, the approximately 5 percent who have dropped out of the hunt for jobs (the so-called "discouraged" workers) and the 10 percent—at least—of the workforce who are employed in part-time jobs but who would prefer full-time work. The crisis of the welfare state is a direct function of the changing nature of capitalism and of the inability of present-day capitalism to foster full employment.

The social impact of rising unemployment and underemployment has been to undermine support for the welfare state and social democracy and to promote divisiveness within the ranks of salary and wage earners. Instead of inspiring a new social movement dedicated to transforming or transcending capitalism, the new capitalism has been successful in dividing its opponents and sowing despair in the ranks of social democrats. Indeed, the social divisiveness of the new capitalism goes far beyond such divisiveness in the past, both because of the global scope of the new economy and because of the heterogeneity of contemporary society. Today unemployed and underemployed workers can be played off, not only against other workers in their own country, but against workers in other developed and developing countries as well. In the context of both regional and global trade agreements, workers have lost much of the solidarity formerly provided them by a national economic context.

There is nothing mystical about the failure of governments to pursue economic strategies that would create jobs. First and foremost, governments throughout the industrialized world are serving the interests of the dominant capitalists—the big banks and the bond market. And the world's creditors are just not interested in job creation. Indeed, as we have seen, their interests directly impede job creation. The problem is not that governments could not figure out ways to create jobs if that was their top priority. Historically, there are plenty of examples of governments creating jobs, both through public sector hiring and through policies that stimulate the private sector to create jobs.

In the 1930s, for instance, the Roosevelt administration created jobs with the New Deal; during the Second World War, the government's drive to produce armaments led to a return to full employment in both the United States and Canada for the first time since the onset of the Great Depression in 1929. And in the postwar decades, governments throughout the industrialized world created jobs when they expanded social programs, extended public education, and improved infrastructure by building highways, airports and telecommunications systems. Moreover, in the postwar decades, governments pursued fiscal and monetary policies whose purpose was to increase economic demand and thereby to promote job creation by the private sector.

The effects of large-scale job creation are equally predictable. If, for example, half a million new jobs were created in Canada, the production of goods and services would increase by nearly $30 billion, and about $12 billion would be generated in additional tax revenues for the three levels of government. In addition, of course, the savings to unemployment insurance and the public purse would be enormous. Double that to the creation of a million jobs, and the fiscal crisis of the state would be resolved. The reason such policies are not pursued is not that no one is capable of thinking them up, but that the dominant interests are opposed to them. The problem is political, not technical.

As they have lost the solidarity formerly reinforced by national borders, workers find themselves in a society that is much more heterogeneous than in the past. It is only a small exaggeration to say that in 1944 when Tommy Douglas and the CCF won power in Saskatchewan, their task was to convince the adherents of the

United Church to support them. There was a very close fit between the social gospel protestantism of the day, most strongly situated in the United Church, and the ideas of the CCF. Moreover, there was a high degree of homogeneity in economic tradition and in the conceptions of culture and society among those who voted CCF. While solidarity is never easily achieved among the broad mass of the population, it came much more easily in 1940s Saskatchewan than it can be expected to today.

As the source of immigration has shifted over the past two decades from Europe to the Caribbean and Asia, the ethnic and racial mix of Canadian society has altered. Racial tensions have increased in the major cities—particularly in Toronto and Vancouver. The racial discrimination experienced by nonwhite populations has introduced a dynamic into Canadian society that was previously absent, at least on this scale. Racial differences have become fodder for politicians whose stock-in-trade is the promotion of fear and exclusionism. As in other countries where political parties of the far right have deftly turned concerns about racial differences and fear of immigrants into live political issues, the Reform Party of Canada plays on concerns about heterogeneity to improve its political fortunes. In Canada, the incidence of violent crime in general and the homicide rate in particular have actually been declining, and yet concern about crime has risen markedly. Indeed, there is a widespread public perception that crime is dramatically on the rise. And when fear of crime is linked in the public imagination to the presence of racial minorities, the result is a weakening of social solidarity.

The new right has been highly adept at playing on the tensions created by heterogeneity. For the new right, the so-called "hot-button" issues of crime, welfare, race, sexual orientation, and the role of men and women in society have been useful substitutes for a genuine critique of the new capitalism. The problem, the right insists, is the rise of a so-called "victim" culture, in which women, racial minorities, welfare recipients and the disabled insist on making the case that they have been hard done by. The right-wing answer to the obvious problems of social division is to insist on the harsh assertion of the mainstream culture. If everyone would just stop complaining, pull together and work harder, all would be well, they proclaim.

For the right, whose fundamental purpose is to ensure that social solidarity against the bondholders is not established, backlash politics is a ready weapon. California's Republican Governor Pete Wilson demonstrated the potency of the backlash weapon in his campaign for re-election in 1994, when he promised that he would cut off social and educational services to illegal immigrants. In a state where business hires hundreds of thousands of illegal Mexican immigrants and pays very low wages, the issue was a winner for Wilson, who has moved sharply to the right over the course of his career.

The politics of backlash also played a role in the Newt Gingrich-led Republican success in winning control of both the U.S. House of Representatives and the Senate in the fall of 1994. Gingrich's victory and that of the Ontario Conservative Party in the provincial election of June 1995 depended heavily on the issue of drastically changing the welfare system. Gingrich and Mike Harris were highly successful in selling the notion, developed by Charles Murray, that welfare dependency rather than unemployment is the problem, and that it is best addressed by cuts to welfare, and mandatory workfare.

Important segments of the media persistently stir the pot, keeping the antagonisms of heterogeneity before the public. Many newspapers present only an incomplete summary of the news, and feature sensationalized accounts of crime as their daily fare. On private radio, commentators often have a daily opportunity to air views unabashedly of the political right.

With the collapse of the communist system in the Soviet Union and its satellite states, capitalism has become nearly global for the first time since 1917. (The assumption is made that China is quickly being converted to a new and dynamic form of capitalism, despite the label still used by the country's governing party and its aging leadership.) Even though one could truthfully affirm that the Soviet system was nothing but a counterfeit socialism for decades, it nevertheless represented a supposed alternative to capitalism and was therefore an important social and political fact in the West. Indeed, the existence of the Soviet Bloc materially aided Western workers in their struggles for full employment, better working conditions and improved social programs, and its disappearance has reinforced the tendency of business and conservatives to turn their backs on the needs and aspirations of the working class. While the new capitalism is revolutionary in some of its features, in other ways what we are seeing today is a reversion to a very old capitalism. Indeed, its attitude to the mass of the population would have been all too recognizable to the people of the 1920s, or even those of the Edwardian era.

At the heart of the new capitalism is the flight of the upper classes away from the idea of citizenship and the social commitments it implies. One measure of the effectiveness of this revolt is the declining proportion of taxes paid by corporations. In 1983, corporate taxes accounted for 13.0 percent of federal revenues in Canada. By 1992, the percentage had dropped to 7.6 percent. Over the same period, the proportion of federal revenues derived from personal taxes jumped from 47.8 percent to 61.9 percent.[19]

The major accomplishment of the right in the 1990s is that it has achieved ideological hegemony. At the very centre of the right-wing system of thought is the notion that society is comprised of individual actors, not collectivities, and that, accordingly, nature itself dictates that private decision making is superior to public decision making. Following from this central proposition is the conclusion that private enterprise is superior to public enterprise. For right wingers, this last notion is accepted without any need for it to be demonstrated empirically. How could a private enterprise, motivated by the drive for profit, fail to outperform a public corporation, whose goals have been established, at least in part, to achieve public policy ends?

Connected with this assumption is the idea that in all realms of existence, private space is superior to public space. Indeed, one of the most important victories of the right has been its success in dismantling public institutions and thereby denying to millions of people notions that once prevailed about what was appropriately public. This privatization process has gone far beyond the privatization of government corporations, although that has been a crucial aspect of it.

In Canada, for many decades, it was accepted that public sector corporations would play a key role in transportation, communications, energy, culture and specific industrial sectors such as petrochemicals and nuclear energy. Traditionally, Canadian conservatism allowed public corporations to play a large role. Indeed, it was conservatives, more often than liberals or social democrats, who constructed the strong Canadian state and who brought key sectors under public ownership, at both federal and provincial levels. One of the considerable ironies of the policies of the Mike Harris government in Ontario is that the Common Sense Revolution promises to roll back public ownership precisely in sectors where former Tory governments were responsible for establishing crown corporations in the first place. Ontario Hydro, TV Ontario, and the Liquor Control Board of Ontario (LCBO) were all created by former Conservative governments and are leading candidates for privatization under Harris.

The toryism linked to the active state contributed not only to the Canadian political tradition, but to its cultural tradition as well. Today, that toryism is an endangered species, lingering only in a few individuals still associated with the Conservative Party. Dalton Camp, for one, manages to hold aloft the banner of a toryism which is not neoconservative, but his is not the ascendant voice among Canadian conservatives.

In the ranks of Canadian conservatism today, neoconservatives like David Frum, author of *Dead Right*,[20] are all the rage, while red Tories like Huey Segal, perennial adviser to federal and provincial Conservative leaders, are seeing their influence slip away. For David Frum, who thought Ronald Reagan's great failing was that he didn't go far enough in reducing the size of the welfare state, traditional Canadian conservatism, with its predilection for having the state play a major role in the economy, is a monstrosity.

Always contemptuous of the historic Tory tradition in Canada, Frum's goal is to educate Canadian conservatives to subscribe to the wisdom of the American right. Especially among young conservatives in Canada, it is Frum and not Segal who is the hero of the day. Contemporary neoconservatives are seeking nothing less than the banishing of the public realm and the enshrining of the private realm, so that individualism can be exalted. And that radical quest puts neoconservatism on a collision course with traditional conservatism, whose fundamental characteristic is the quest for stability.

What we are seeing is no less than a cultural war being waged by the right. The objectives of their campaign extend far beyond the debate over which corporations should be privatized. It is being fought in the cultural arena, where the right is committed to the sharp reduction, or even elimination, of state support for the arts, for reasons that extend well past the drive to reduce public sector deficits. For the right, public sector support for the arts is seen as coddling and sustaining artists, filmmakers, writers and others who would not otherwise be able to support themselves. Today's conservatives hold that artists who cannot make it in the marketplace don't deserve to make it at all.

This *kulturkampf* is designed to marginalize nonconservative voices. Newt Gingrich, Republican speaker of the U.S. House of Representatives, is a master of cultural warfare of this variety. In a speech in 1995, he charged that too many reporters disseminate "liberal propaganda," that the *New York Times* is "gradually drifting off into irrelevance" and that the city of New York itself is "an enclave of elitist values."[21]

In Canada, the populist right-wing attack on nonconservative media has long focused on the Canadian Broadcasting Corporation and its supposed bias in favour of the left. The assault on the CBC has been pushed by such advocates of free trade and neoconservatism as John Crispo, professor of management studies at the University of Toronto. After his outspoken criticism of the political balance of its programming, the Mulroney government appointed Crispo to the CBC's board of directors. Besieged by an increasingly hostile ideological environment, CBC's managers lean on producers and story producers to limit left-wing voices on the air. The consequence is that the CBC often presents the views of right-wing think tanks, business specialists and corporate representatives as though they are simply conveying "objective" information. The CBC also generally treats spokespersons for the C.D. Howe Institute and the Fraser Institute as though they were neutral investigators of what is happening in the economy. In truth, they are front-line proponents of a strongly right-wing agenda. They promote cuts to social programs, ever closer economic ties with the United States, privatization of crown corporations and the slashing of government budgets.

Several times a day, CBC radio features reports on daily business from people who work for big financial institutions or the *Globe and Mail's Report on Business*. The content of these reports is at least as much ideology as it is fact. One morning, for example, while I was driving through downtown Toronto, I heard a report from an investment dealer with Scotia McLeod on CBC's *Metro Morning*. It was a very cold morning in early February and street people were huddled over heating grates in the sidewalks. The investment dealer was feeling feisty—"Never felt better," he said, because the Toronto 300 had pierced the 5000 barrier.

This feature is on every morning. The analysts are different, but their perspective is always the same.

On Wednesday mornings, the CBC radio program *Morningside* always has a panel on business right after the nine o'clock news. The three panelists are business cheerleaders, who may disagree about how to analyse a particular event, but whose take on the world is monotonal. The very idea that *Morningside* could have a weekly panel with three labour or antipoverty spokespersons, without having right wingers to balance them off, speaks volumes.

The CBC is a survivor from an earlier era of Canadian experience, and would never be created today, if it did not already exist.

Within the public sector it is not just broadcasters who have had to respond to the ideological power of the right. Educators at the secondary and postsecondary levels are being subjected to immense pressure to conform to the demands of today's corporate agenda. In universities and community colleges, funding cutbacks have been especially harsh in disciplines that are not seen as having a direct market application. Instead of fostering high levels of scholarship and liberal education, governments are pressuring universities to become high-level training schools. In secondary schools, cost-cutting pressures have also opened the door to corporate influence as schools receive payments from soft drink manufacturers to stock their products exclusively. As schools purchase computers, they find their choices of educational software limited, and usually have to rely on large American corporate sources.

The cultural war is waged in a wide variety of other arenas as well. Even public spaces are being privatized, thus weakening the very concept of community. Where once everyone had access to downtown shopping streets, today the retail marketplace has shifted toward privately owned malls. Security guards at malls have wide latitude to decide who may or may not be on the premises, which means that particularly for suburban youth, the notion of public space has been significantly limited. Similarly, over the past few decades, access to public beaches on Canadian lakes has declined significantly as the interests of private cottage owners has predominated over the interests of the general public. And in 1996, the Ontario government decided to turn a number of provincial parks over to the operation of the private sector.

From the French Revolution to the decades following the Second World War, citizenship was at the centre of a vast societal impulse toward greater egalitarianism. The French Revolution swept away the conceptual barriers to the idea of equality, replacing them with the idea that human beings share an essential sameness of condition, rooted in their common mortality, and that they are imbued with rationality. The notion of citizenship was the counterpoint to the inherited privilege of the *ancien régime*.

The advance of the idea of citizenship, so that it came to feature first political and later economic and social rights, was closely linked to the rise of the nation-state. The nation-state grew in importance and capacity from the end of the eighteenth century, reaching its zenith in the decades following the Second World War. For many decades, the nation-state was understood as the instrument for opening a space for the development of a national economy. In Canada, the main business of the federal state, from the time of the National Policy of the late nineteenth century on, was "nation building"—the development of the financial, transportation and communications sinews needed to establish a transcontinental economy. In the decades following the Second World War, the nation-state then became the social state, responsible for setting up health care, unemployment insurance, welfare, old age pension and educational programs—all of this dedicated to the achievement of social equality. As we have seen, this vast movement toward greater equality, in both Europe and North America, was bound up with a particular stage of industrial development and with the sociopolitical alignments that were the product of the Second World War.

The new capitalism and the sociopolitical alignments of the new right have fostered a vast impulse away from equality, and as a consequence, away from the idea of citizenship. Along with the nation-state, the concept of citizenship has withered, for at the heart of the new right is a new and insistent emphasis on the invigorating value of inequality. The old solidarity associated with citizenship in the nation-state has given way to the uncertainties of a heterogeneous society and a reduced role for the state. Inequality and a wider gap in power and wealth between the social classes are the hallmarks of the new capitalism.

Such inequality in a class-divided society is the fundamental condition against which social democrats have always battled. The way they have done it, though, has changed dramatically over the decades.

CHAPTER 5

TOMMY, DAVID AND THE BIRTH OF THE CCF

IN the spring of 1963, at the climax of his second long and gru-
elling federal election campaign within a year, Tommy Douglas
addressed a giant rally at Maple Leaf Gardens in Toronto. Fifteen
thousand people had packed the hockey stadium to hear the former premier of Saskatchewan, who had become the first federal
leader of the New Democratic Party in 1961. I was twenty-one
years old, and it was the first time I'd seen Tommy Douglas in
person. Everywhere in the arena were the banners of NDP riding
associations in Toronto and the surrounding region. As Douglas
made his way to the platform, there was a prolonged, emotional
standing ovation; the air was electric. This had nothing to do with
everyday politics. When the clapping settled down and Douglas's
distinctive, high-pitched voice filled every corner of the Gardens,
there was a sense among the people in the crowd that they were
part of a national movement to remake Canada. And there was no
mistaking the key message of the address. When Tommy Douglas
called for the creation of "a prepaid medicare program for every
man, woman and child in Canada," the cheers nearly drowned
out the country's greatest orator of the day.

Medicare was not a partisan issue, but one that touched every
family: parents with children, adults with elderly parents, anyone
facing the prospect of serious surgery. People would no longer have
to fear that they could not afford medical care if they fell sick. And
when Tommy Douglas talked about medicare, he did not seem to
be outlining a political platform. He was speaking what felt like

the plain truth. Why should those unfortunate enough to fall sick be made to pay as a consequence of their suffering? Was it not right that we should share the burdens of our brothers and sisters? Medicare was more than health insurance. It represented a new kind of citizenship. Canada would be a different country, and Canadians would have a new relationship with each other.

That night in Maple Leaf Gardens, it appeared that nothing could stop Tommy Douglas's crusade for a more caring society. To walk out into the street after the rally, surrounded on all sides by people who had been stirred by his message, made a tremendous impression on me. We were the many, not the few. What we stood for made sense. Our cause was that of greater equality, simple justice. Only the rich and the hopelessly selfish could possibly be opposed to the plan.

I had no inkling at the time that this was high noon in the golden age of social democracy, not only in Canada but in the industrialized world. The drive to extend the welfare state had reached its crest. And yet, even at the crest, the going was far from easy for reformers like Tommy Douglas. Although almost no one in the audience knew it at the time, the night Douglas addressed the giant rally at Maple Leaf Gardens, a spectator stormed onto the platform and assaulted him. Douglas, who had been a bantam-weight boxer in his youth, met the attack with greater aplomb than others might have. Nonetheless, the incident was symbolic of the difficult two years Douglas had endured since becoming the first federal leader of the New Democratic Party.

For Tommy Douglas, the battle to establish medicare began as soon as he led the CCF to power in Saskatchewan in 1944—the first time a social democratic party had ever won office in North America. Before the Douglas government was ready to introduce provincewide medicare in Saskatchewan, it set up an experimental program in the Swift Current region, the poorest part of the province. Data collected from that trial run was invaluable for the 1962 provincewide launch of medicare and for the federal Liberal government of Lester B. Pearson when it established a nationwide system in 1967.

The next move was to establish a tax-supported hospitalization plan in 1947—the first one in Canada. This meant that henceforth the cost of stays in hospital would be funded by the province. After the federal Conservative government of John Diefenbaker subsequently established a national hospitalization scheme in 1957, providing funding for provinces to establish programs such as the one in Saskatchewan, the CCF felt ready to move forward to full-scale medicare. When Tommy Douglas called a provincial election for June 1960, he declared that he was seeking a mandate to implement medicare across Saskatchewan. With its fifth consecutive electoral victory—the CCF won two-thirds of the seats in the legislature—the government was ready to proceed toward its full goal.

The CCF was about to learn a painful political lesson: an electoral mandate is not much to rely on when great social forces are in contention. A mandate gives a government a passive green light to pursue reform, but little more than that. In Saskatchewan, the Douglas government was up against the power of the continental doctors' lobby, which focused its ample resources on crushing what it called "state medicine."

By the early 1960s, when the doctors mobilized to confront the CCF, the politics of the province had also shifted. A hard-edged opposition to the Douglas government had emerged within the Liberal Party, eventually making itself the instrument of anti-CCF opinion in the province. In an atmosphere of growing confrontation between the government and the Saskatchewan College of Physicians and Surgeons, a special session of the legislature passed the Saskatchewan Medical Care Insurance Act on November 17, 1961. The act was to go into effect the following spring, but by the time the Saskatchewan legislature had adopted the Act, Tommy Douglas had stepped down as premier to take over the federal leadership of the newly formed New Democratic Party, the successor to the CCF.

In 1962, the medicare crisis built steadily, with the Saskatchewan College of Physicians and Surgeons adopting a belligerent stance against the implementation of medicare. Woodrow Lloyd, Douglas's replacement as premier, made a tactical error when he delayed implementation of medicare from April 1, 1962, for a period of three months. The delay, which had been intended to conciliate the doctors, instead gave them extra time to organize their opposition, and when the plan went into effect on July 1, Saskatchewan doctors promptly went on strike. Many doctors simply packed up and took their families on vacation.

During the tense days that followed, the people of Saskatchewan were not wholly without medical services. Two hundred of Saskatchewan's usual roster of 470 doctors stayed on duty—but to provide emergency service only. Thirty-four of the province's 148 hospitals remained open.

Although the strike was never total, emotions ran extremely high. Charges and countercharges were launched; the province was completely polarized. Sensational news stories dramatized the death of a baby whose parents had driven ninety miles because they were unable to find a doctor any closer. Anonymous vigilantes threatened doctors with violence if they did not return to work. Large and angry demonstrations, initiated by an antimedicare movement called the Keep Our Doctors Committee, were held in front of the provincial legislature in Regina. There were reports of demonstrators physically threatening medicare supporters. To alleviate the shortage of doctors caused by the strike, the provincial government recruited doctors from England, and predictably, the newcomers were often resented as strikebreakers. On occasion, they were denied hospital privileges in the communities to which they were assigned.

The struggle in Saskatchewan had national, even continental, significance, and media attention focused on the province from across Canada and the United States. A *Globe and Mail* editorial underlined the importance of what was happening when it said that the leaders of the strike "supported, it must be suspected, by the Canadian and American Medical Associations, are fighting not this particular medical insurance plan, but any form of government health insurance anywhere on this continent."[1]

In the end, the doctors' strike and the Keep Our Doctors Committee did not prevail. Throughout the conflict, medical practitioners had not been wholly united; an important minority of them supported the introduction of medicare. With the aid of a Labour Party member of the British House of Lords who served as mediator, an agreement was struck between the College of Physicians and Surgeons and the government, bringing the three-week strike to an end on July 23.

The essential principles of the medicare scheme were retained and within a few years, the principles at the heart of the Saskatchewan scheme were embodied in a national medicare plan that was established by the federal government but administered provincially. And in time, medicare became an enormous success, redefining the very meaning of Canadian citizenship. It won the support of the vast majority of people in every part of the country. In an era when Canada was beginning to fragment regionally and along linguistic lines, medicare became, in effect, a new pillar of Confederation.

The depth of the transformation brought about by medicare can be seen in the way rhetoric changed after it was implemented. During the doctors' strike in Saskatchewan, opponents of medicare used whatever means they could to frighten the population. People were warned that the government would choose their doctors for them, and would intervene between doctor and patient in determining what medical treatment they would receive. Women were even told that the government could take their babies away from them to raise them as wards of the state. Much was made of the almost sacred nature of the doctor-patient relationship and the grave danger that would follow if the government were allowed to interfere with it. It was said that "state medicine" would make doctors lose their entrepreneurial drive and would reduce them to mere civil servants.

This kind of rhetoric, which was as common in 1960s Canada as it is in 1990s America, virtually disappeared once medicare was established. This is not to say that political battles over the financing of medical care were a thing of the past in Canada—far from it. The Canada Health Act of 1967 laid down the basic principles of medicare, stipulating that if provinces enshrined those principles in their medicare schemes, they would be eligible for federal funding. Provinces that have failed to live up to the principles in the federal act have periodically been threatened with the withdrawal of a portion of federal funding. (The Alberta Conservative government, for instance, has risked a reduction in funding from Ottawa because it has allowed the operation of private clinics. The former NDP government in Ontario similarly ran afoul of the federal government when it cut the rates for Ontarians requiring hospitalization outside Canada from four hundred to one hundred dollars a day.) Battles over extra billing (billing by physicians in excess of the medicare fee schedule), opting out (the right of physicians to opt out of the medicare system and to bill their patients privately) and the right to set up hospitals and clinics outside medicare, which bill privately, have all posed threats to medicare.

In the 1990s, medicare has faced a host of new threats. As medical costs have soared as a result of technological advances, an aging population and the problems of the fee-for-service billing system, in which costs are driven by physicians' billings, the financing of medicare has become a major political issue. Provincial governments have been forced to pay an ever higher proportion of the costs of the medical system as the federal government has capped its own contributions. Although the present fiscal crisis has added to funding problems, medicare has been so popular with Canadians that it has not been possible to attack it directly. Instead, the political right has used the fiscal crisis to launch a potent indirect assault that may lead medicare to suffer the death of a thousand cuts.

While the Reform Party carefully asserts that it would not decrease Ottawa's contribution to health care, even though it would slash virtually everything else, leader Preston Manning has made it clear that he would not object to provinces setting up their own medicare rules. This means that the Reform Party would allow the emergence of a checkerboard health care system in Canada, in which some provinces allowed user fees and enabled doctors to extra-bill or even to opt out of the medicare system altogether.

A further threat is posed when provinces like Alberta allow private clinics to be established. Under the terms of NAFTA, once private clinics are permitted, U.S. commercial medical firms would have to be allowed equal access to Canada to provide the same services. Private clinics, where the ability to pay replaces universal access, represent the thin edge of the wedge in the creation of a two-tier health care system: a private system for the affluent and a public system for the rest. Once a two-tier system is created, the affluent can be expected to withdraw their support from the public system, which can then be expected to deteriorate. (This process has been at work in the undermining of the British National Health Service since the Conservatives were elected in 1979.)

The CCF-NDP government that established medicare in Saskatchewan was defeated in the subsequent provincial election in 1964. After two decades in power, after winning five consecutive electoral victories, having introduced an epochal and largely popular social reform, the only social democratic government in Canada lost power. The province Tommy Douglas had governed elected the most right-wing provincial Liberal party in the country. Its leader, Ross Thatcher, was himself originally a CCFer. Elected federally in 1949 and 1953 as a CCF MP, Thatcher was increasingly at odds with his party. In Ottawa, he found soulmates more to his liking among Conservatives and Liberals than among fellow CCFers.

Thatcher's Liberals came to office armed with a rhetoric that was highly antagonistic to that of the defeated CCF. The new premier championed a brand of rugged individualistic capitalism, as against what he depicted as the "collectivist socialism" of the CCF. He attacked the crown corporations that had been set up by the CCF and promised a radical free enterprise alternative.

In the 1964 election, the CCF had failed to match the energy and political imagination of its past campaigns. The introspective Premier Woodrow Lloyd was principled and idealistic, but he was no Tommy Douglas. He lacked the oratorical firepower of his predecessor, and his government made a number of significant strategic errors before the campaign—among them an ill-explained extension of financial support to Catholic separate schools. The party platform was also a disappointment. There was little new in it to capture the imagination of the electorate.

Even in its hour of defeat, however, the CCF-NDP had managed to win a higher percentage of the total vote—by one percentage point—than its Liberal opponents. But the party that had come to power in 1944 promising to preserve the family farm had lost the support of many rural constituents, and on election day, the province gave the governing mandate to the free enterprise Liberals.

In some ways, the CCF had paid the price for its own initial successes in rural Saskatchewan. In the years that followed the government's emergency measures to prevent banks from foreclosing against farmers, most family farms regained a measure of prosperity—although many farmers continued to leave the land, a process that had by then become universal in the industrialized world. Ironically, as farmers grew more prosperous, they also tended to become more conservative, and many of them turned their backs on the social democratic party that had saved so many of them during the difficult years.

Many epitaphs were written for Saskatchewan social democracy after the defeat of 1964. Don McGillivray of Southam News wrote a column which he called "a requiem for a government which in its best days stirred the blood and the idealism of the people of Saskatchewan...it's the end of an era for Saskatchewan and for Canada."[2] In a more negative vein, the Saskatoon *Star-Phoenix* editorialized: "After twenty years, the Saskatchewan voters made a tremendous decision to cast out socialism. They have become very weary of the diaper service provided for them by the Welfare State. After twenty years, Saskatchewan breathes freely once more."[3] Despite the epitaphs, however, the new Liberal government was hesitant to attack the CCF reforms. During its seven-year life, before it, in turn, was defeated by a revitalized NDP, the Thatcher government imposed so-called deterrent fees for medical visits, supposedly to prevent the misuse of medicare by a segment of the population. But despite its right-wing ideology, the new government did not dare to tamper with the essentials of medicare.

Right-wing politicians have always been hesitant about making direct attacks on medicare. The reason is that medicare has been such a seminal reform that it has proven difficult to reverse, even by governments hostile to its underlying philosophy—the proposition that health care is too fundamental a social need for its provision to be entrusted to the marketplace. That idea challenges the right-wing view that capitalism can combine justice and equity with efficiency in meeting a basic human need. Medicare, in other words, advances the case for a set of values that is at odds with the values normally encountered in a capitalist society.

First of all, medicare rests for its justification on a social democratic conception of equality that is quite different from the liberal conception of equality. In North American liberalism, the idea of "equality of opportunity" is so commonplace that its meaning is seldom examined. Equality of opportunity embodies the notion that in an individualist, capitalist society, every person should have a fair chance at financial and social success. It is the slogan of the American dream, of the populist urge of the ordinary person to have a shot at self-realization. In that sense, equality of opportunity is a crucial, democratic concept.

The social democratic conception of equality is different. In place of equality of opportunity, social democrats espouse equality of condition. The emphasis is on the right of people to have a fair share of what they produce in common. And that emphasis arises from the conviction that society is composed of collectivities or communities, not simply of the individuals that populate the liberal imagination. This view of equality is reflected in the principles enshrined in the Canada Health Act: health care must be universal—available to all; accessible—there are no user fees or

extra billing; comprehensive—all medical treatment is fully covered; portable—valid in all provinces; and public—a not-for-
profit system.

The ethical justification for medicare can vary from one person
to another. But for Tommy Douglas, its ethical basis was to be
found in social gospel protestantism, in the belief that it is wrong
that people who are unfortunate enough to be sick should have to
bear this burden on their own. An episode during his boyhood
helped shape his views. As a young child, Tommy Douglas developed osteomyelitis, which afflicted his leg close to the knee cap.
Many operations were performed on the stricken leg, and by
chance, when he was in a Winnipeg hospital, his problem came to
the attention of a distinguished orthopaedic surgeon. The surgeon
decided that the case could be useful for teaching purposes and
offered to operate on Douglas, whose own working class family
could otherwise never have afforded his services. The operation
was a great success, and the young boy, who had faced the
prospect of having his leg amputated, was so improved that he
became a noted athlete. The experience could not help but influence his thinking about medical care. As he told his biographer,
"When I thought about it, I realized that the same kind of service
I got by a stroke of luck should have been available to every child
in that ward...."[4]

If personal experience, religious conviction and a socialist conception of equality shaped Tommy Douglas's views on medicare,
others have focused on the greater rationality and effectiveness of
a public system. They have pointed out that Canada's public
medicare system costs less, as a proportion of Gross Domestic
Product (GDP), than the private system in the United States.[5]
And while the Canadian system covers everyone, the American
system leaves thirty million people entirely uninsured and millions of others with inadequate coverage, so that a person with a
serious illness could be ruined financially. Huge numbers of
Americans have to think carefully not only about what medical
treatment might be best for them, but also about what medical
treatment they can afford. For many, deciding whether to move to

a new job involves considering whether this would mean the loss of their existing medical coverage.

The arguments about effectiveness are vitally important, but without the resonance of social democratic values in Canada, there would have been no medicare. Despite the fact that so much of our political thinking and popular culture have American origins, social democratic values are much more pronounced in Canada than in the United States. The paradox of a powerful social democracy in Canada, alongside a virtually nonexistent social democracy in the United States, has long been a matter of note. At its 1956 Convention, the CCF received a tribute from the American Social Democratic Federation which read, "Comradely greetings from the weakest socialist organization in the Western Hemisphere to the strongest one, the CCF of Canada. It is a comfort to have a big strong brother next door to us."[6]

The story of why social democracy is so much stronger in Canada than in the United States takes us to the heart of the political cultures of the two countries. In Canada, social gospel protestantism combined with the political outlook of a labour movement inspired by the British example to create a distinctly Canadian form of social democracy. On the other hand, in the United States individualist values have prevailed from colonial times, to the extent that the U.S. is the only advanced industrialized country with no significant social democratic or socialist movement.

During the last decades of the nineteenth century, an era of rapid industrialization and rising urban squalor radically altered the physical and philosophical environment of Europe and North America. In response to this, one wing of protestant thought diverged from traditional Christian beliefs in its approach to the new social conditions. Throughout the English-speaking world, in Britain, the United States and Canada, thinkers and religious and social activists were up against the new realities of growing factory towns, where people were forced to work long hours in appalling conditions. And there was the problem of those who fell between the cracks—the children, the jobless, the alcoholics—those who were unable to cope with the changing world.

The protestant ethic, a product of the early capitalism of the centuries following the Reformation in the sixteenth century, held that each individual is responsible for his or her own salvation, and approaches God on his or her own. Protestants were also preoccupied with the question of how one was to be assured of being among the "elect." The prevailing and stern view was that no one could ever be sure of being in this position, but that there were important clues. Success, material and personal, especially when it could be considered the fruit of one's own efforts was considered to be a promising sign. Failure was a bad sign. In the age of early capitalism, with its emphasis on saving, planning, thrift and enterprise, those who worked hard and were rewarded were the paragons of protestant sensibility. The poor, the wretched, the unsuccessful and those who could not live up to the demands of an ethic of delayed gratification were the fallen. The goal of protestant evangelism was to win the sinners back to the path of righteousness, and it was the task of evangelists to show them the way. In the end, though, it all depended on whether or not the individual chose to see the light.

In the late nineteenth century, as society was transformed by industrialism, this ethic appeared grotesquely inadequate to a growing body of thinkers. How could the individual cope with the enormous forces of an inhuman industrial machine that could make or break lives in ways that were so obviously capricious? The literature of the period is replete with reflections on the horrors of industrialism and how the natural world had been replaced with an unnatural, human-made environment. It would have been surprising indeed, under such circumstances, if there had not been major changes in the way society was perceived.

The social gospel was one response to the new industrialism. Rejecting the emphasis on individual salvation as having little to do with the new societal reality, social gospellers concluded that the path to salvation must be social as well individual in character. Just because one person is a success in material terms while another is a failure, proves little, the social gospellers insisted. The successful person may have benefitted from a highly favourable environment—wealthy parents, a good education, social connections—while the person who failed may have experienced a negative environment—poverty, illiteracy, illness.

For social gospellers, the Christian life and purpose had to include efforts to transform society so that those who were suffering could lead decent lives and thereby could return to the path of righteousness. Salvation, then, was no narrow, individual matter. It entailed struggle for social change. True religion was therefore about much more than the preparation of people for the hereafter—it was about the realization of a society that embodied Christian values in this world. This explains the great resonance social gospellers and social democrats found in the hymn that proclaimed: "We will build Jerusalem in England's green and pleasant land."

One way that the new ideas were given practical application was through the establishment of settlement houses, whose purpose was to cater to the needs of the poor in the most destitute sections of cities. This movement was the catalyst that politicized the man who was to become the first national leader of Canadian social democracy, J.S. Woodsworth.

At first glance, James Shaver Woodsworth was an unlikely figure to lead a political movement. Born in 1874 on a prosperous Ontario farm, he was the son of a Methodist minister of loyalist stock. J.S. Woodsworth, as he was invariably known, was an austere, aloof, even patrician individual, who developed an enduring reputation, even among opponents, for putting principle ahead of personal convenience.

After studying in England, where he was absorbed by the problems of poverty and social inequality—and gained first-hand experience working in a London settlement house—Woodsworth returned to Canada. At the turn of the century, he was ordained a Methodist minister, but the conventional life of the cloth was not for him. The social activism he had discovered in England remained paramount, and he was soon the central mover in setting up the All People's Mission in Winnipeg. In the years before the First World War, his mission lent a helping hand to scores of poor immigrants who were settling in the Canadian West.

During the war, Woodsworth and his family moved to Gibson's Landing in British Columbia, where Woodsworth, though a frail man now in his mid-forties, worked as a longshoreman. He became involved in union organizing and joined the Federated Labour Party, the largest socialist organization in B.C. As his political ideas matured, he endured a growing tension between his convictions about society and the views and practices of the Methodist Church. He became more and more critical of the institution—which he saw as compromising unduly with the wealthy and the socially pre-eminent. Finally, having become a committed pacifist, he resigned from the church in 1918 because of what he regarded as its undue support for the war. He had became convinced that political action was required to achieve the social reform his understanding of the gospel now demanded.

In 1919, Woodsworth went on a speaking tour that brought him to Winnipeg at the height of the Winnipeg General Strike. A cataclysm that pitted the major social forces of a rapidly industrializing Canada against one another, the Winnipeg strike laid bare the workings of the country's social and political system as no event had done before. It was the only time in Canadian history that a major city was completely polarized along social class lines. A strategically located city, Winnipeg was the railway hub of the West. The strike was provoked by the high stakes that came into play when employers refused to engage in collective bargaining with the city's rapidly organizing workforce. Members of the Building Trades Council and the Metal Trades Council went on strike in May 1919. With the support of the Winnipeg Trades and Labour Council and of other unions in the city, the strike grew to the status of a general walkout, with thirty-five thousand workers staying off the job.

The city was sharply divided between the supporters of the General Strike Committee, made up of representatives of all the unions involved, and the largely middle-class opponents of the strike, who together with the business elite established the so-called Citizens' Committee of One Thousand. As tension grew in the city, all three levels of government and the Royal North-West Mounted Police were closely involved with the Citizens' Committee in planning how to put down the upheaval.

The strike broke out at a time of immense historical uncertainty and high drama. Canadian troops were coming home after demobilization at the end of the war. The economy was experiencing a short, but sharp, downward turn. Moreover, in the spring of 1919, the Canadian political and economic establishment was easily spooked by anything that vaguely resembled the Bolshevik Revolution, which had occurred in Russia only a year and a half before. And a general strike was bound to be disturbing because such a crisis inevitably raises the issue of who runs society, even if those involved in the strike have no wish whatsoever to challenge the authority of the state. When a strike becomes truly general, it shuts down so many parts of the economy that daily life threatens to grind to a halt. Who is going to provide milk, bread and other food? Who is going to run the public transit system? Who is going to police the streets? Because a general strike raises these basic concerns, the strike's leaders are forced, by the logic of their situation, to assume some of the decision-making responsibilities of the government.

Faced with such pressures, the Winnipeg General Strike Committee decided to endorse the provision of certain basic services in the city, making it clear that those providing them were not strikebreakers. Milk wagons making deliveries were decked out with signs that read "Permitted by Authority of Strike Committee." Such signs, which could be interpreted as civic-mindedness on the part of strike leaders, were seen as deeply sinister by their opponents. As far as the authorities were concerned, the signs were evidence of an intention on the part of strike leaders to take over the functions of the state. In the fevered mood of the struggle, they were inclined to think darkly that the strike leaders were intent on setting up workers' state institutions along the lines of the so-called "soviets," which had been established by the Bolsheviks during their seizure of power in Russia.[7]

Woodsworth, who commanded great respect in Winnipeg dating back to his days in the mission there, addressed a giant outdoor rally in support of the strikers. And when the editor of the *Western Labour News*, a prostrike newspaper, was arrested, Woodsworth took his place and was himself arrested two days later. During his subsequent trial, he was accused of seditious libel on the grounds that he had published the following passage in the paper from the Book of Isaiah: "And they shall build houses and inhabit them; and they shall plant vineyards, and eat the fruit of them. They shall not build, and another inhabit; they shall not plant and the other eat; for as the days of a tree are the days of my people, and mine elect shall long enjoy the work of their hands."[8]

In the end, the strike was violently suppressed by the North-West Mounted Police. On June 21, armed with guns and baseball bats, special municipal police and the RNWMP attacked a parade organized by the strikers. One man was killed and thirty others were injured.[9] Although the goals of the strikers were not realized, the strike left a permanent mark on Winnipeg and on Woodsworth. In 1921, he was elected to the Canadian Parliament by the riding of Winnipeg North, long to remain a bastion of the left.

A storm of protest was blowing across western Canada the year Woodsworth was first elected. In 1921, sixty-five Progressives won seats; they were representatives of the agrarian protest movement, which was then reaching its zenith.[10] The movement expressed the alienation of Western farmers from the historic Tory National Policy, whose tariff and railway policies favoured central Canadian bankers, industrialists and railway barons, at the farmers' expense. The election was historic in that it ended the virtual monopoly of federal politics by the Liberal and Conservative parties, though over the next half-decade, the storm of Progressive protest was to blow itself out. Most of the Progressives were successfully absorbed by the Liberal Party of William Lyon Mackenzie King—not so J.S.Woodsworth. Leading the so-called Ginger Group, which for years consisted of himself and one other member of Parliament, Woodsworth became the central figure around whom disparate labour and socialist groups began to coalesce. In 1926, Woodsworth was able to bargain his two votes in a House of Commons closely divided between Liberals and Conservatives to win a pledge from Mackenzie King to establish old age pensions in Canada.

In 1932, it was natural that Woodsworth should become the pivotal figure at a Calgary meeting of labour, agrarian and socialist groups, the purpose of which was to establish a new national political party. The following year at Regina, the new party was founded. It was the CCF, the Co-operative Commonwealth Federation, and it moved Canadian social democracy from the fringe to a position where it became a vital and significant aspect of Canadian life.

At the founding convention, delegates adopted the Regina Manifesto as the program of the CCF. The manifesto, which acquired an almost religious significance among CCF adherents in the years to come, was largely the work of intellectuals, grouped together in the League for Social Reconstruction (LSR), its chief author being Frank Underhill. The LSR was modelled on the Fabian Society, an intellectual group with close ties to the British Labour Party.

The Regina Manifesto was written at the very depth of the Great Depression. It advocated immediate measures to deal with the disastrous economic and social crisis and to initiate the long-term replacement of corporate capitalism with a "cooperative commonwealth." To achieve the goals of social equality and social security, aims which made the new party authentically social democratic, the manifesto called for a planned Canadian economy, in which large corporations in the key sectors would be nationalized and operated under public ownership.

The manifesto did much more than present a platform for a political party. It was a clarion call to the supporters of a political movement whose goal was the radical transformation of Canadian society. The philosophical break with liberalism could not have been clearer. The manifesto proclaimed that the goal of Canadian social democrats was to "replace the present capitalist system" with a new social order in which class exploitation was to be ended and unregulated private enterprise was to be replaced by national economic planning.[11]

J.S. Woodsworth was chosen as the first leader of the CCF. Charismatic and revered, he was depicted as a saintly figure, a prophet in politics. It is not uncommon for metaphors like this to be applied to Canadian social democratic leaders. Because the adherents of Canadian social democracy have often undertaken what has appeared to be a long journey into the political wilderness, they have depended heavily on strong leaders—men and women of impeccable character who have served as prophets, models and strategists. J.S. Woodsworth was the first of these larger-than-life personalities, and his prophet-like austerity was a personal watchword. As he travelled about the country by train, he invariably went by coach, not availing himself of the comforts of a sleeping car.

Woodsworth's personal example and charisma could carry the CCF only so far, however. The new party would also need organization, and a strategy for survival and growth in a largely alien political landscape. Those elements were fortunately available in the person of a great figure, who was to complement Woodsworth and be crucial to the development of the party for decades to come: David Lewis.

For me, social democracy is always associated with the steadiness, the sternness and the political vision of David Lewis. I knew him best in the late 1960s and early 1970s during the battle between the youthful Waffle movement (about which more later) and the party establishment, whose pre-eminent figure was Lewis. Even though he was in a very real sense a political opponent, he was also a political hero, for whom I had immense respect. As I saw him during those years, it was not at all unreasonable to think that while David Lewis lived, Canadian social democracy would never founder. It would always be a critical presence in Canadian life, forcing the country's not very enlightened establishment to pay heed to the needs and aspirations of working people.

Although David Lewis deeply respected J.S. Woodsworth, in background, personality and political formation, he could not have differed more from the leader of the CCF. For David Lewis, social democracy was grounded not in the protestant social gospel, but in the great model of the British Labour Party and its organic relationship with the trade union movement.

Lewis was born in Poland in 1909. His father was a socialist and a strong anti-Bolshevik, and this heritage would prove crucial for the young Lewis, who emigrated to Montreal with his family in 1921.[12] As a young man in Montreal, Lewis had his first experience of Canadian socialism, and it was there that he attended McGill University. When he won a Rhodes Scholarship, he moved to Oxford, where he first made contact with the British Labour Party. Before winning the Rhodes Scholarship, however, Lewis had to appear before a committee which included, among other notables, Edward Beatty, the president of the Canadian Pacific Railway. When Beatty asked the young Lewis what he aspired to do in his life, Lewis, completely unfazed, replied that he wanted to be the first socialist prime minister of Canada. "And what would you do as prime minister?" Beatty asked. "I'd nationalize the CPR," the young man shot back.

In spite of his frankness, Lewis won the scholarship and went to Oxford, where he became the first Canadian president of the Oxford debating union. There he honed the formidable parliamentary skills he was to display in his later career in Canada. He also developed close and lasting ties with leading figures in the British Labour Party, a tutorship that was to be crucial in the development of his views on the proper political direction for a social democratic party. In the winter of 1971, I flew to Sydney, Nova Scotia, with Lewis where we were to appear in one of the debates for NDP leadership candidates—we were both candidates to succeed Tommy Douglas as federal NDP leader. Lewis told me that in the late 1930s, Stafford Cripps, then a renowned figure in the British Labour Party, had been urging him to run as a Labour candidate in the U.K.'s upcoming general election. In those days, Canadians were eligible to participate in British politics, and I have no doubt that Lewis would have become a brilliant figure in the postwar Labour government had he chosen to stay in the United Kingdom.

Instead he returned to Canada, and in 1936 became National Secretary of the CCF, a job he held until 1950. The effort he made, at a starting annual salary of eighteen hundred dollars, was close to superhuman. In an organizational sense, he virtually "was" the national CCF. His years as national secretary coincided with the rise of industrial unionism in Canada, most of which occurred within the framework of American-based, international unions. These were the great days of the creation of the two major industrial unions that were to play an enormous role in the future of Canadian social democracy, the United Steelworkers of America (USWA) and the United Auto Workers (UAW). In the Canadian sections of these unions, which were affiliated with the Congress of Industrial Organizations (CIO) in the United States, there were sharp, bitter political struggles between communists and social democrats. David Lewis played a pivotal role in motivating and assisting the social democratic leadership within these unions, both to draw them into an ever closer relationship with the CCF and to block the communists from acquiring power in the unions.[13]

Lewis believed that Canadian social democracy would endure only if it was linked to the organizational muscle and practical politics of the labour movement. When the Canadian Labour Congress (CLC) was formed in 1956 out of a merger between the Canadian Congress of Labour (CCL) and the Trades and Labour Congress (TLC), Lewis saw an opportunity to tighten the tie between labour and the CCF.

It was chiefly at his urging that the party adopted a new statement of principles, the Winnipeg Declaration of 1956. For "true believers" in the CCF, there was a strong suspicion that any move away from the Regina Manifesto could only mean a weakening of basic values, so the new declaration never achieved the authority of the original manifesto. It did, however, mark an important ideological turning point for the party. The new declaration abandoned the quasirevolutionary rhetoric about eradicating capitalism and undertaking sweeping nationalization. "Private profit and corporate power must be subordinated to social planning," the declaration read, retaining a critical perspective on capitalism and keeping it firmly in the social democratic tradition of the CCF. Gone, however, was the idea of replacing capitalism root and branch. In a 1955 lecture to the Ontario Woodsworth Memorial Foundation, Lewis signalled his vision of the party's new course and tackled the thorny issue of public ownership, stating: "Public ownership in a democratic society and under a democratic socialist government will never cover more than a part of the economy…. The time is long overdue when this should be frankly stated without qualification and without apology."[14]

Lewis believed the new statement of principle was the ideal vehicle for moderating and updating the doctrine of the party. This, he hoped, would tighten ties to labour and possibly, in the years ahead, even prepare the ground for a new political party that would have a broader base than the CCF. The Winnipeg Declaration emphasized creating a society where greater equality of condition would be attained through full employment and the extension of social programs. To realize full employment, the government would use fiscal and monetary policy to guide the economy's trajectory. In the Winnipeg Declaration, the overriding focus of Canadian social democracy shifted to the redistribution of benefits within the economy and away from the functioning of the productive system itself. In this important sense, the document pointed the CCF, and later the NDP, to the course they would take until the end of the 1980s. David Lewis had managed to reorient the party in the direction he thought was necessary, if it were to become a successful labour party. Ironically, this occurred on the eve of what proved to be the great crisis in the history of the CCF.

In 1957, as Canadians went to the federal election polls, they passed judgment on a Liberal Party that had been in power since the Depression days of 1935. At the time of the election, the Canadian people were fed up with the arrogance and remoteness of Louis St. Laurent's government, steered as it was by the iron hand of C.D. Howe. John Diefenbaker, the Prairie populist with the personality of a small-town crown prosecutor, led the Conservatives to power, though with a minority of seats in the House of Commons. With the Liberals in disarray, the CCF was also able to make gains in the 1957 election, increasing its total number of seats in the House of Commons to twenty-five.[15]

The following year, however, the CCF was plunged into electoral disaster. Under their new and inexperienced leader, Lester B. Pearson, the Liberals moved a motion of nonconfidence in the Diefenbaker minority government, suggesting that the Conservatives were incapable of governing and that they should resign. Diefenbaker used the opportunity to call a snap election. At the end of a whirlwind campaign, he emerged with the largest parliamentary majority in Canadian history. With 208 out of 265 seats taken up by the Conservatives, the Liberals were reduced to a mere rump, and the CCF had managed to acquire only eight seats and a disastrous 9.5 percent of the popular vote.[16]

The electoral defeat was interpreted by CCF leaders as undeniable evidence that the party was going nowhere, and that its direction, ideas and political strategy had to be completely rethought if it was to avoid eventual extinction.

What ought the CCF to do under the trying circumstances? David Lewis, the architect of the Winnipeg Declaration, thought he knew the answer. His aim had always been to ensure the long-term survival of Canadian social democracy by building a strong organizational link between the labour movement and the CCF. Now that the CCF was in serious trouble politically, the way to achieve that aim was clear—it was to create a new party, which would arise from collaboration between the labour movement and the CCF.

The defeat in 1958 was thus both a warning for the future and an opportunity. The warning was that unless the CCF managed to communicate with a larger number of Canadians, the party would slowly wither and become a mere vehicle of protest. Alternatively, the CCF could renew itself, refurbish its doctrines and establish an institutional link with the labour movement, which would help it to survive setbacks like the disastrous 1958 election.

But for David Lewis, the idea that a new party should be established had developed well before the 1958 defeat. He had always wanted to set up an organic link with the labour movement, and had seen that possibility from the moment the Canadian Labour Congress was created in 1956. He viewed the unified national trade union organization as the ideal partner for the CCF in forming a new social democratic party.

The process of renewal within the ranks of Canadian social democracy took three years and effectively involved a very large number of people. At the highest level, negotiations between the CCF leadership and the CLC prepared the ground for the future affiliation of trade unions to the NDP. Conferences were held, social democratic doctrine was reconsidered and the relationship of social democracy to liberalism was debated. As the process went on, the new party actually began to take shape even before its founding convention. So-called New Party clubs were set up, and the new party managed to elect its first member of Parliament, Walter Pitman, in Peterborough, Ontario, not only before the party had been officially launched, but even before it had chosen a name for itself.

In terms of ideology, David Lewis had already established the ground for the new party in the Winnipeg Declaration of 1956. To that body of doctrine was added the idea that an institutional link with the labour movement was essential. The other new concept that became prominent during the period of rethinking was that the new party must reach out to so-called "liberally minded Canadians."

The desire to attract a broader constituency to the new party showed how much the CCF leadership wanted to use the opportunity of restructuring to move somewhat closer to the centre of the political spectrum. Canadian political culture had historically been predominantly "liberal" in its values, but with the Regina Manifesto, the CCF had mounted a radical assault on liberal assumptions. The Second World War and the conditions of the 1950s, however, had altered the CCF in two important respects. First, during the war a broad political consensus had developed in favour of governments playing an active role in the economy and in the establishment of social programs; this helped legitimate the more moderate goals of the CCF. Second, the Cold War promoted a mood of intense anticommunism, which made the more radical aspects of the CCF program appear highly suspicious. In one respect, the CCF's ideas were more acceptable than ever before: throughout the industrialized world, this was an era in which enormous advances were being made in the creation of social programs. In other ways, though, socialism was even more suspect than before, more open to the attack that it represented an alien extremism.

For David Lewis, de-emphasizing public ownership went hand in hand with embracing Keynesian economics. The "demand-side" economics of Keynesianism had become the bread and butter of social democrats. The idea was that through the use of fiscal and monetary policies, the economy could be steered away from boom and bust, toward steady growth and full employment. In times of economic slack, government could spend more and cut taxes, thereby increasing demand and priming the economy for more consumer spending and business investment. Alternatively, when the economy was booming and in danger of overheating, the government could cut back spending and increase taxation to prevent a dangerous bout of inflation. Over the course of each economic cycle, therefore, the goal would be for government spending to be in balance. According to this thinking, there was no reason for the development of a permanent government deficit of the kind encountered almost everywhere in the industrialized world from the mid-1970s on.

Keynesianism was at the heart of the great social democratic compromise of the postwar decades. The bulk of the economy was to be left under the control of the private sector, which would therefore be in a position to determine its investment priorities. On the other hand, there would be a strong emphasis on the achievement of full employment, which by its very nature was bound to increase the bargaining power of labour in wage and salary settlements.

Social programs were also central to Keynesianism. Not only did they provide a safety net for a working class which was for the first time being treated as though it had a legitimate place in the system, but they accounted for much of the increased public spending that was a prominent feature of the postwar economy. And to Keynesians, public spending provided necessary ballast for the economy, offering a source of demand when the economy was weak, and an area where cutbacks could be made during times of boom. In other words, social programs fit perfectly within the logic of countercyclical spending on the part of the state.

In the postwar decades, Keynesianism was not only embraced by social democrats, but was also widely accepted among governments of all stripes and mainstream economists as a means of fine tuning the economy. Liberals in Canada and Democrats in the United States viewed Keynesianism as the new orthodoxy of the postwar era. Even Conservatives in Canada and Britain and Republicans in the United States made peace with the Keynesian model. But for social democrats, Keynesianism was fundamental. It opened the door for them to achieve legitimacy for their social goals, which were to improve the position of labour and to extend the welfare state.

For David Lewis, then, the new social democratic party that would emerge out of the CCF's crisis of the late 1950s was to be a Keynesian labour party. In that sense it would be quite different from the more radical CCF of the 1930s, with its much greater commitment to public ownership of major industries and its greater reliance on the values of social gospel protestantism.

In July 1961, 2000 delegates convened in Ottawa to launch a new social democratic party. One of the questions that remained unanswered at the beginning of the convention was what the new party should be called. Some people wanted to call it the Social

Democratic Party, while others favoured the name Democratic Party, with its overtones of liberalism. In the end, a groundswell of enthusiasm, particularly among the delegates from Ontario, led to the adoption of the name New Democratic Party, and the party was launched with Tommy Douglas as its first leader. If J.S. Woodsworth had been the chief architect of Canada's first social democratic party, the CCF, David Lewis was the chief architect of the New Democratic Party.

CHAPTER 6

THE NDP'S UNCERTAIN JOURNEY

THE New Democratic Party met with greater electoral success than its predecessor, the CCF. While the first and only CCF government held power in Saskatchewan from 1944 to 1964, the NDP eventually won elections in four provinces: British Columbia, Saskatchewan, Manitoba and Ontario. At the federal level, the NDP has also won a higher percentage of the national vote and more seats in the House of Commons than the CCF. Between 1972 and 1974, when David Lewis was federal leader, the party held the balance of power in Parliament and was able to influence the course of Pierre Trudeau's minority government. Ironically, however, the NDP has never been able to equal the CCF in pioneering a reform as fundamental as that of medicare. In part, that was because medicare was a reform that could be pioneered only once. But there is more involved here than a tautology.

In the first dozen years of its existence, the NDP was deeply affected by the political storms of the 1960s and early 1970s—the Vietnam War, the American civil rights movement, Quebec nationalism and the rising tide of Canadian nationalism. In its first general election, in 1962, the NDP won nineteen seats, a marked increase over the eight seats the CCF had won in 1958.[1] Still, it was a disappointing result for a party that had been launched with the hope of becoming a major national force. And the disappointment was made worse because of the personal defeat of Tommy Douglas in his own riding in Regina. Just days before the provincial government was to launch medicare, the former

Saskatchewan premier was crushed by a Conservative candidate in his own seat, by a margin of ten thousand votes. It was a stunning humiliation.[2]

The NDP was by no means alone in having to adapt to the turbulent circumstances of the 1960s. Both the Conservatives and the Liberals were also evolving under pressure. Threatened with the rise of Quebec nationalism, the Liberal Party made a daring change of leadership when it groomed Pierre Trudeau as the successor to Lester B. Pearson. With Trudeau claiming to embrace the notion of a "just society," as he did in the 1968 election campaign, many New Democrats got the uneasy feeling that the Liberal Party had successfully occupied their traditional ground— the advocacy of ever more advanced social programs. In the two years following Trudeau's majority electoral victory in 1968, New Democrats often debated whether it was time for social democrats to "move beyond the welfare state" to a broader concept of economic democracy, which emphasized self-government for wage earners in the workplace.

In fact, what would later become apparent was that in the early Trudeau years the welfare state was nearing the end of its era of expansion. The last great forward step was taken at the national level in 1971 with the broadening and revamping of the Unemployment Insurance (UI) program. In retrospect, the era of the major advances in social programs was not all that long. It had begun with the creation of Family Allowances in 1944, to which was added Hospitalization in the 1950s. Then in the 1960s, the high point was reached with the Canada Pension Plan and Medicare. Once UI had been made more generous in the early 1970s, Canada, along with the rest of the industrialized world, began the transition to the new capitalism with its higher rates of unemployment and slower growth. It would not be long before the advocates of the welfare state were thrown on the defensive.

In spite of the changing times, David Lewis was highly effective as NDP leader during the period of the Trudeau minority government from 1972 to 1974. During a time of rising economic uncertainty, Lewis focused the widespread concern about the control of Canada's economy by U.S. multinational corporations, particularly in the petroleum sector. The seriousness of the problem was symbolized by the strength of the petroleum lobby. In the early 1970s, led by Imperial Oil, which was controlled by Exxon in the U.S., the petroleum companies were lobbying Ottawa for higher oil and natural gas exports to the United States. Then in 1973–74, when world oil prices quadrupled, the Canadian price was held down through government controls, and oil companies applied enormous pressure to raise the domestic price. Ottawa was at an immense disadvantage in dealing with these companies, since all of Canada's vertically integrated oil companies (those operating in all phases of the industry—exploration, production, refining, transporting and retailing petroleum) were controlled abroad. So sentiment grew in favour of the creation of a crown corporation that would give Canada "a window on the industry."

Holding the balance of power in the House of Commons, David Lewis and the NDP helped make the case, which was also being made behind the scenes within the Trudeau government, for the creation of such a crown corporation. Although Petro-Canada was not actually established until after the election of 1974, when the Liberals regained their parliamentary majority, the government committed itself to its creation during the minority period when David Lewis was in a position to apply maximum pressure on the Trudeau Liberals. With provincial NDP governments in Manitoba, Saskatchewan and British Columbia, the social democrats had reached a new height of influence in Canada. But David Lewis, who had given so much to Canadian social democracy, was destined to be a short-lived leader of the NDP. By the time the July 1974 general election was called, Lewis already knew he was suffering from leukemia. He carried on bravely during the election campaign, however, and was to remain intellectually and politically active until his death in the spring of 1981.

While the political landscape had been highly favourable to the New Democrats in 1972, it had become unfavourable by 1974. Economic uncertainty in the aftermath of the global oil price revolution and the legacy of two years of minority government helped prepare the ground for Pierre Trudeau's electoral crusade for a Liberal majority government.

Conservative leader Robert Stanfield made Trudeau's task easier in 1974 when he proposed mandatory wage and price controls as a strategy for coping with the new economic environment of stagflation. Trudeau was caustic in rejecting mandatory controls during the campaign—and by championing job creation and generous social programs in a threatening new economic era, he managed to win people back to the view that the Liberal Party remained the voice of the ordinary Canadian. Trudeau's campaign thus cut the ground out from under David Lewis and the NDP, reducing the party to sixteen seats in the House of Commons. With the loss of his own seat in York South in Toronto, the parliamentary career of David Lewis came to an end.[3]

In his latter years, after he had stepped down as leader of the party, I had the great pleasure of having a number of lengthy, relaxed conversations with David Lewis. Even though it is appropriate to associate him with a particular vision of social democracy in the postwar decades, he was certainly not trapped intellectually within the assumptions of that period. At the end of the 1970s, he was highly alert to the threat posed by neoconservatism and understood clearly the battle that was bound to erupt between them and social democrats.

In 1970, David Lewis and Tommy Douglas were still at the helm of Canadian social democracy. By 1974, their careers, which provided a living connection to the early days of the CCF in the 1930s, had entered their twilight phases. Douglas stayed in Parliament longer than Lewis and remained an inspirational force among NDPers until his death in 1985.

The last time I saw Tommy Douglas was during the federal NDP convention in Regina in July 1983. Threatening black clouds blew in from the west as I was driving back to my hotel from the site of the convention on the outskirts of the city. As I drove along a road, passing only the odd warehouse from time to time, I saw a man walking the same way I was going. There was no other traffic. The solitary figure stopped to pick up some newspapers that were blowing along the road. He crumpled them up, looked around for a moment, then took them over to a warehouse, where he stuffed them neatly behind a drainpipe. As he came back to the road, I saw that the man was Tommy Douglas. I stopped and offered him a ride downtown. As always, he was optimistic, commenting on how well he thought the convention was going. The storm burst before I dropped him off at his hotel. At seventy-nine, Douglas remained what he had always been—unpretentiously dedicated to what he believed in, and cheerful about life.

Following the 1974 election, Oshawa MP Ed Broadbent took over as interim NDP leader. Broadbent had run a disappointing campaign for the NDP federal leadership in 1971, placing fourth at the convention that chose David Lewis. Once he became interim leader, however, he succeeded in winning the support of the same elements in the party that had backed Lewis for leader in 1971. At first, support for Broadbent from the party establishment was lukewarm. In the end, though, when the party and trade union establishments had considered the alternatives, they solidly backed Broadbent at the next party convention, held in Winnipeg in 1975. Initially a somewhat uncertain and even mundane standard bearer, with little of the eloquence of Tommy Douglas or David Lewis, Broadbent grew in stature on the job. Eventually, he made himself the country's favourite New Democrat, a voice for social equality and for the average Canadian at a time when the economic order was tilting away from full employment.

If his rise to the party's top job was less than spectacular, he was to hold it for longer than either of his eminent predecessors, leading the NDP through four federal election campaigns—in 1979, 1980, 1984 and 1988. Fatefully, his career as national leader of Canada's social democrats spanned the period in which a new right wing was established in Canadian politics—a right wing that eventually succeeded in winning the battle for free trade with the United States in the historic election of 1988.

Broadbent's watchword was "fairness." For extended periods of time, voters told pollsters that Broadbent was their first choice for prime minister. Broadbent personified the successful, but still recognizably ordinary, urban Canadian of the day—an image more popular than those of Tommy Douglas, who had the air of the social gospel and Saskatchewan about him, and David Lewis, who appeared to combine the qualities of a labour leader and politician. Raised in the auto town of Oshawa, Ontario, Broadbent had earned a Ph.D. in political science, and it was said that he was the kind of successful son every Oshawa mother wanted.

As leader, Broadbent's great shortcoming was his inability to preside over the rethinking of NDP economic analysis and policy in a period in which fundamental changes were occurring. As research director for the federal NDP caucus in 1982–83, I was deeply involved in the party's effort to reconfigure its economic policies. But Broadbent could not bring himself to move away from the Keynesian perspectives that had become the staple of Canadian social democracy in the 1950s. As the economy was ground down in the vicious recession of 1981–82, he continued to cling to the belief that a combination of tax cuts and increased public spending would give the economy the "stimulus" needed to bring about recovery. These remained the key policies of the NDP at a time when they were appearing increasingly ineffectual, shopworn and politically contradictory.

It was not that Broadbent failed to consider alternatives to the course he was following. In 1982, as his research director, in conjunction with his principal secretary and communications coordinator, I urged an alternative economic approach on him. We were engaged in this at what was, in retrospect, a critical juncture in the evolution of the new capitalism. The most severe postwar recession to date was underway, having been generated by the tight money policies initiated by the U.S. Federal Reserve Board and its chairman, Paul C. Volcker.

The Canadian economy was so closely integrated with that of the United States that if consumer demand was stimulated in Canada through tax cuts and additional government spending, much of that increased demand would be satisfied through purchases of foreign goods and services and even through foreign tourism. The consequence of this kind of "leakage" was that traditional social democratic Keynesianism could easily produce a balance of payments crisis and high interest rates rather than economic recovery.

This left us to grapple with designing a made-in-Canada economic policy that embodied social democratic values at a time when the Keynesian approaches of the past had become highly problematic. The trouble with Broadbent's variety of Keynesianism, which was derived from the social democracy of the preceding quarter-century, was that the measures it relied on to achieve economic stimulus—tax cuts and increased public sector spending—were not workable, by themselves, in the globalized economy of the 1980s.

In the early eighties, Canadian social democracy crossed a critical threshold as far as these issues were concerned. There was no longer value in a political program that had evolved in the postwar era, in which the use of the so-called big levers of fiscal and monetary policy replaced public ownership as the way to achieve a full-employment economy. The NDP program lacked believability. No government, critics suggested, could simply spend its way back to economic recovery, given the propensity of Canadian demand to leak out to the United States.

In fact, in the early 1980s, the issue of the government deficit was taking a critical turn. In the industrialized world, the government that put all others in the shade in running up the public sector debt was the Reagan administration in the United States, where the contradictory monetarist and supply-side elements of U.S. economic policy contributed to a vast deficit increase. The tight-money (monetarist) policy of the U.S. Federal Reserve Board promoted a steep plunge in inflation and dramatically increased the impact of the Reagan supply-side tax cut. Because the drop in inflation prevented Americans from being pushed into higher tax brackets ("tax creep"), the effect of the tax cut in combination with tight money was to reduce U.S. government revenues much more than the tax cut would have done on its own. And on top of the tax cut, the Reagan administration vastly increased outlays for defence.

The unprecedented skyrocketing of the U.S. government deficit in turn contributed to that socioeconomic oddity—the Reagan economic recovery. The porous foundation of the Reagan recovery was the quicksand of two deficits—the U.S. government deficit, and the steeply rising U.S. current account deficit (balance of payments). Their combined effect was to push the U.S. down the road to becoming a net debtor nation for the first time since the end of the First World War, soon to be the world's largest debtor. This development speeded the transition of world capitalism from the era in which the United States was the world's leading creditor nation to the era in which Japan played that role.

The politics of the Reagan deficit was especially significant, involving, as it did, a curious paradox. While the American right wing was clearly responsible for the skyrocketing deficit, it was American liberalism that paid the price for it. The huge deficit had three major political effects: it reinforced the right-wing interpretation that government was out of control and needed to be reined back; it added vast weight to the argument that social spending needed to be cut back to tackle the deficit problem; and in fostering the public's growing disillusionment with government, it added force to the case for tax cuts as the best way to restore prosperity.

This last effect had a twisted logic all its own. While it might have been expected that the rising deficit would improve the case for tax increases as a way to achieve a balanced budget, it actually had the opposite political result. From the standpoint of the core right-wing constituency, of course, tax cuts were always on the agenda, both ideologically, as an essential feature of the downsizing of government, and pragmatically, as a way of currying favour with affluent voters who had much to gain from across-the-board tax cuts. The rising deficit helped build support for tax cuts well beyond the core of the right wing and among the affluent, however. That was because, as it became apparent that Americans had entered an era when government services were deteriorating and an increasing proportion of taxes were being applied to interest payments, general public support for the payment of taxes was bound to deteriorate.

Try as they might to make the right appear shabby as a consequence of the policies that had led to the rising deficit, it was liberals whose strategic position was imperilled. Reagan's deficit helped promote a further realignment of American politics, establishing a de facto electoral alliance that included the ideological right wing, the affluent and much of the working class in support of tax cuts. This alliance, usually depicted as aligning the so-called "Reagan democrats" with the Republicans, cut deeply into the traditional liberal voting bloc.

The politics of the deficit in Canada has followed a similar logic, where the right, both provincially and federally, has been highly effective in using the issue to promote political realignment. As in the United States, Canada's war on the deficit has meant higher taxes and reduced services for the middle class and the working class. The consequence has been an undermining of support for government in general and for governmental provision of services in particular.

The election of the Harris government in Ontario in June 1995 illustrated this with great force. Just under five years after much of the working class and middle class supported Bob Rae and the NDP, a sizeable number of the same people switched to support the hard-right agenda of Mike Harris and the Common Sense Revolution. The vote for the NDP in 1990 aligned much of the working class and middle class with the recipients of spending on social programs and education. In 1995, the Tory message of smaller government, deficit reduction and cutbacks to welfare benefits aligned much of the working class and middle class with business and the affluent. What was clear in the dramatic swing of the Ontario electorate between 1990 and 1995 was the way the deficit issue worked to the benefit of a right-wing political realignment. Whether a shift in values has occurred along with political realignment remains highly uncertain. But by making use of the deficit issue, the right has constructed a powerful electoral coalition.

Ed Broadbent, like many other prominent Canadian social

democrats, failed to recognize the economic conditions behind this realignment, or its political implications for social democracy. He remained wedded to the tried and true formulations of the past, thus helping to ensnare the NDP in the trap of appearing to represent policies from an era whose conditions would never return. Social democrats like Broadbent failed to recognize that the rising deficit was the consequence of an escape from economic and social responsibility on the part of the affluent. Simply continuing to demand what they called "stimulative economic policies" showed that social democrats had no answer to the onslaught of the right—the central, though unadvertised, strength of which was a willingness to allow the state to sink into insolvency.

The late American social critic Christopher Lasch analysed the profound change in American society that led to the political realignment taking place in his country. For Lasch, it amounted to no less than a counter-revolution:

> The privileged classes—the top 20 per cent—have made themselves independent not only of crumbling industrial cities but of public services in general. They send their children to private schools, insure themselves against medical emergencies by enrolling in company-supported plans, and hire private security guards to protect themselves against the mounting violence.
>
> It is not just that they see no point in paying for public services they no longer use; many of them have ceased to think of themselves as Americans in any important sense, implicated in America's destiny for better or for worse. Their ties to an international culture of work and leisure...make many members of the elite deeply indifferent to the prospect of national decline."[4]

The strategic climax of the Broadbent years was the 1988 federal election campaign, which evolved into an historic showdown between the contending social and political forces in Canada. A victory for Mulroney and the Tories would mean that Canada would be embedded in a free trade agreement with the United States—a deal whose implications extended far beyond trade. And since both the Liberals and the NDP were committed to "tearing up the deal," in the words of Liberal leader John Turner, a Tory defeat would mean that free trade would not be implemented.

The opposing sides in the free trade debate were enormously different in terms of societal power and the clarity of their respective visions. Rarely in Canadian history has business—multinational and domestic, large and small—been as united as it was in 1988 on behalf of free trade. Against business was arrayed a much more disparate alliance of nationalists, social activists, trade unionists, farmers, members of the cultural community and intellectuals. Despite their much more limited resources, the opponents of free trade were able to mobilize immense popular support for their case. Victory for the Conservatives would dictate the much fuller adoption of the American socioeconomic model in Canada, and a majority of Canadians rejected this. The implications of victory for the anti-free-trade side were less clear. Certainly, though, the opponents of free trade wanted a made-in-Canada economic strategy, whose primary goals would be job creation and the further development of Canada's system of social programs.

Whether the opponents of free trade would have proven capable of plotting an alternative course for Canada is something we cannot know. What we do know is that the election campaign became a virtual referendum on free trade. And there can be no doubt that the opposition political leader who made it so was John Turner, not Ed Broadbent. Throughout the campaign, Turner put everything he had into the issue. The climactic moment of the entire election campaign came during the English-language leaders' debate on national television. In an episode of high drama, Turner accused Mulroney of betraying Canada in negotiating the free trade agreement with the United States, of gravely compromising the country's capacity to survive as an independent state. Public reaction to the statement was immediate and dramatic. Polls showed Turner's Liberals surging ahead of the

Tories in popular support.

Broadbent's approach to the campaign was different from Turner's. Apparently calculating that the free trade issue would work better for the Liberals than the NDP, Broadbent did not even mention the matter on the day he launched his election campaign. For a politician as experienced as Broadbent, and at a time when the free trade debate had already been highly prominent, it is impossible to believe that this was not a deliberate campaign decision taken by Broadbent and his advisers. The conclusion is clear: the Broadbent campaign team decided to "low-bridge" the free trade issue in 1988.

But after the preliminary phase of the campaign, when it became clear that John Turner had succeeded in making free trade the central election issue, the NDP altered its strategy. During the critical phase leading up to the confrontation between Turner and Mulroney during the leaders' debate, Broadbent joined the Liberal assault on free trade. This combined Liberal-NDP attack on the Tory position turned public opinion polls around and Turner's Liberals gained the lead over the Tories. This was the pivotal moment of the election campaign and Broadbent had a crucial choice to make. Should he keep attacking Mulroney and free trade, or should he also mount an attack on Turner and the Liberals?

Broadbent and his advisers made a strategic decision that was to infuriate key labour leaders like Bob White, president of the Canadian Auto Workers Union. The de facto common front between the Liberals and the NDP on free trade came to an end as Broadbent's campaign posture changed yet again. Insisting on the hustings that a vote for the Liberals was no better than a vote for the Tories, Broadbent was back on the ground he had staked out in his highly effective 1984 election campaign during which he had dubbed Turner and Mulroney "the Bobbsey twins of Bay Street."

Broadbent's attack on Turner in the closing weeks of the 1988 campaign coincided with a virulent assault on the Liberal leader by Brian Mulroney and the Canadian business elite. The gloves came off. This was an election business had no intention of losing, and Turner was pummelled by his one-time Bay Street allies.

In the aftermath of the election, the anti-free-trade forces could boast that they had the majority of Canadians on their side. Between them, the Liberals and the NDP won 52 percent of the votes cast. But the Tories, with 44 percent of the popular vote, had won the war, and their re-elected majority government brought the Canada–U.S. Free Trade Agreement into operation on January 1, 1989.

The implementation of the FTA inexorably placed the core policies of Canadian social democrats under siege. The FTA's "national treatment" provision outlawed special support for Canadian-owned firms, making it a legal requirement that any tax, grant or public procurement scheme established to assist Canadian firms in key sectors be made equally available to American-owned firms. The provision took dead aim at the very idea of a Canadian industrial policy. It gravely compromised the potential for Canadianizing important sectors of the economy and ensured that the historic inequity visited upon Canada as a consequence of the vast ownership of the national economy by American firms would remain an unalterable fact of Canadian life.

By countering the notion of a national economy for Canadians, the FTA drew Canada more deeply into the logic of the American socioeconomic model. And that fact, more than any specific clause in the FTA, was to have important consequences for Canadian social programs. By further blurring the already indistinct line between the Canadian and American economies, the FTA ensured that policy making in Canada would have, as its essential point of reference, the continental economic system, of which Canada was now formally a part.

With free trade, business could play the game of "lowest common denominator" with telling effect. The FTA made it much easier for Canadian businesses to desert jurisdictions with expensive social and environmental programs and better paid workers—and therefore higher taxes—and to seek out those with lower levels of spending. For the first time since the onset of the age of the welfare state, Canadian business was in a position to pose that threat and to be believed. What the FTA did was to tilt the balance against social programs by placing Canada further inside the sandbox of American capitalism, thereby giving Canadian—and American— business increased leverage over government decision making in Canada.

Broadbent's approach to the 1988 election campaign contributed, in its own way, to the failure to stop the FTA. It hurt more than it helped as a means of opposing a change in capitalism that was decidedly against the interests of Canadian workers. Key trade unionists who had fought body and soul against free trade were left with a deep feeling of bitterness. In March 1989, Bob White, director of the Canadian Auto Workers Union and the most prominent trade unionist in the country, submitted a brief to the federal NDP, which included this assessment of the 1988 campaign: "What was and remains an issue, was the style and orientation of the NDP campaign...this reflected a deeper problem: a feeling of disillusionment and drift which threatens to reduce active commitment to passive support... 'Is our party becoming a pale imitation of the other parties? Can we still count on it to stand up for us?'"[5]

White's soul-searching comments reflected the important change within the left that had occurred during the election. While the NDP campaign had been a disappointment to many, the development during the election of a popular opposition to free trade among trade unionists, social activists, Canadian nationalists and members of the cultural community pointed the way toward the movement politics that were to develop over the coming decade.

When Ed Broadbent stepped down as NDP leader in 1989, his was the predominant social democratic voice in the country. The same could not be said for his successor, Audrey McLaughlin, who was to find herself overshadowed by the three NDP provincial premiers in Ontario, British Columbia and Saskatchewan. A former social worker who had sat for Yukon in the House of Commons, McLaughlin came to the job with the intention of offering a different conception of leadership, one of genuine consultation in policy and strategy formulation—both inside the NDP and beyond it. But McLaughlin's emphasis on democratic process was all but lost in the crisis that befell the party during her tenure as leader. There is no question that McLaughlin understood the issues of the day as well as the leaders of other political parties did. At times—such as during the leaders' television debate during the 1993 election campaign—she could be eloquent. For some reason, however, what she said was not perceived as memorable—a deadly problem for a political leader.

McLaughlin presided over the federal party during a period when Canadians faced severe recession, a constitutional crisis and the rise of a populist right that appealed to elements of the NDP's own electoral base. Decisive for McLaughlin, though, were the changing fortunes of the three NDP provincial governments.

The Rae government in Ontario had unusual importance for Canadian social democracy because it held power in the financial-industrial heartland of the country. What began so hopefully with the election of the NDP in September 1990 was to end up as a case study in the futility of postwar-style social democracy in the setting of the new capitalism. Although Bob Rae had come to office in Ontario with only 37 percent of the popular vote, opinion polls in the months following the election revealed that a large majority of Ontarians had a positive view of their new premier. Like other new majority governments, the Rae government enjoyed a honeymoon—his lasted until well into the winter of 1991.

The premier-elect took what turned out to be a fundamental strategic decision on election night, September 4, 1990. In his televised victory speech, Bob Rae pledged to govern on behalf of all Ontarians. Instead of inviting the whole province to consider the merits of the election platform on which he had won office, he began the process of uncoupling himself from that platform and offering himself as the servant of all the people. Shortly after being sworn in as premier, Rae addressed a major business audience, telling them that since business and his government were going to be together for a long time, they ought to try to understand each other, and perhaps get along.

According to those who observed him from within the

Premier's Office, Bob Rae held the view, from the outset, that he was the only one in the government who really understood how the business community operated. He made it his mission to woo business and appeared convinced that eventually he would succeed. This approach eventually led him far from the terrain his party had mapped out in the election campaign. In the end, as he jettisoned long-established positions such as the commitment to a publicly operated system of auto insurance, he set his course toward his own conception of the political centre, which he hoped would place him at the fulcrum of a new consensus in provincial politics.

The climactic event in this political odyssey came in 1993 with the passage by the Rae government of the so-called "social contract," which arbitrarily reopened the contracts of public sector employees and imposed salary rollbacks on them. This measure reduced government expenditures by $2 billion and was part of a three-pronged approach to dealing with the government's steeply mounting deficit. The other two prongs of the approach were a $2-billion increase in taxes and a $2-billion cut in expenditures.

From a political standpoint, the social contract was to have by far the greatest consequences for Ontario's social democrats. The government tried first to make a deal with public sector unions. In early June 1993, however, Bob Rae's negotiator, Michael Decter, told reporters that although "we were very close [to a deal]," "we never got there."[6] Having failed to reach an agreement, the Rae government nevertheless made the momentous decision to press ahead with the imposition of the social contract.

Many New Democrats and public sector unionists felt betrayed by the decision. At the time negotiations broke down, Jill Marzetti, the Ontario NDP's provincial secretary, confirmed that the party had lost about five hundred members who were "specifically saying they [were] critical of the government's policies." In early June 1993, angry public sector workers converged on Bob Rae's constituency office in Toronto to protest the social contract.[7]

In the way it was imposed, the social contract was perceived to be a political assault on the friends of the Rae government. It signalled the inability of the government to make its case to public sector unions, consider their case in return and reach a deal that both could live with. Rae chose instead to impose the social contract, thus dealing more harshly with those who refused an accord than with those who gave way. The social contract became a symbol of Rae's retreat from the social democratic elements in his program. It was vastly disillusioning, because it signalled to proponents and opponents of social democracy alike that the hopes and aspirations of the left were out of keeping with reality.

With the social contract, Bob Rae thought he was en route to a politically advantageous destination—the coveted centre of Ontario politics, and some pundits heralded the arrival of the Rae government at an apparent new realism. *Globe and Mail* columnist Jeffrey Simpson wrote: "From crisis comes opportunity, and the opportunity before the NDP is a weakening of its relationship with the public-sector unions that will cause short-term grief but provide long-term political benefits."[8] But the political benefits never arrived for Rae and his colleagues, for they had flown straight into a hurricane in a political era in which the old compromises of the postwar type were no longer a possibility. In the last year before the provincial election that brought Mike Harris and the Tories to power, Rae's operatives tried to coax life back into the NDP's political fortunes. I remember a long-time party strategist phoning to ask me how I thought the NDP could win back the roughly one in two supporters from the 1990 election who had now indicated to pollsters they were no longer backing the party. Put that way, the government's unpopularity could be made to seem like a technical problem that could be solved if only enough focus groups could be held so the experts could find a formula for wooing back the 50 percent of former supporters who had strayed.

In the end, party strategists did hit on an approach of sorts. It was to portray the premier as a pragmatic man for the nineties, a man who had learned much while in office and who was vastly superior to the leaders of the other two parties. To that approach, the Rae team clung until two weeks before election day; but by that point the die had been cast. In the electoral battle, Bob Rae's standing as an individual did the NDP little good. The middle ground on which he had staked the fortunes of his government turned out to be a middle to which no one else was attracted. Rae's defeat opened the door to the harshest right-wing government in the history of Ontario. It also made it plain that the province's centrist political tradition was a thing of the past. In power was a confrontational government, which boasted that it would implement every promise in its program while remaining steadfastly impervious to any other voices in the province. Would the social democrats, who had been the last defenders of the old centrist tradition of Ontario politics, now accept the fact that the character of politics had decisively changed?

Eight months after the defeat of his government, Bob Rae resigned as leader of the Ontario NDP. For many who had stood by him during the bitter debate on the social contract, Rae's decision to enter a Toronto corporate law firm was perplexing and disillusioning. In a letter to party members announcing his resignation, Rae said his government had "worked in partnership with workers and business to save jobs and communities."[9] He left politics, as he had governed, the advocate of a partnership with a business community that wanted no partnership with him. It was truly the politics of one hand clapping.

The Rae government had been disillusioning to social democrats, not only because it had backed away from long-time NDP commitments, but also because of the way it operated during its nearly five years in office. The Premier's Office, during the Rae years, has been described to me by insiders as chaotic and secretive. Rae and his closest advisers believed that policies should be made at the centre, in the Premier's Office and the Cabinet Office, and then handed over to the ministries for implementation. Some who worked in the Premier's Office came away convinced that no one knew exactly what their job was. The result was a lack of direction, while the key decisions were being taken by Rae and his small circle of insiders. The two most influential insiders were Principal Secretary David Agnew and Ross McClellan, who was in charge of policy. Others joined the inner circle for specific purposes and for limited periods of time. In the end, though, this was a government whose most important decisions were primarily made by three people.

The Ontario election defeat was not the only major development to disillusion to Canadian social democrats. In the months following the demise of the Rae government, the NDP government in British Columbia was twisting in the agony of scandal and cover-up as its mandate neared its end.

Unlike Ontario, British Columbia has experienced polarized politics for decades. In 1951, W.A.C. Bennett, who had been a member of the coalition Liberal-Conservative provincial government that formed to keep the CCF out of power, crossed the floor of the legislature and created a new party, the B.C. Social Credit. The result was the demise of the Liberals and Conservatives as major provincial parties and the rise of Bennett's Social Credit as the major engine of the antisocialist political right. In 1952 the Social Credit won power as a minority government, and the following year, in another provincial election, it won a majority of seats in the legislature.

This win, in the province with the highest proportion of its workforce unionized, underlined the extent of class division in British Columbia. As in other regions of the country, such as northern Ontario, where resource industries—mining and forestry—have predominated, the relationship between labour and capital has been hard edged. In the mining towns like Trail, in B.C.'s interior, few middle-class niceties have moderated the battles between unions and bosses. From the time of the Great Depression on, the CCF acquired a major base both in the lower mainland of B.C. and in the interior.

The Bennett era in B.C. politics was dominated by the rhetoric of free enterprise versus socialism.[10] Bennett bred this polarization intentionally so his party would earn the loyalty of those committed to keeping the CCF, and later the NDP, out of office. This would keep them from straying back to the Liberals or Conservatives.

There was another side to polarization, though. It meant that the only viable alternative to the Social Credit was the CCF–NDP. Eventually, the patronage, scandals and shoddy administration of the province came to count for more in the minds of voters than the socialist "bogeyman." All those years of polarization meant that many people who would have joined the Liberals if they had lived in Ontario, aligned themselves with the NDP.

In 1972, the first breakthrough came with the election of an NDP government under the leadership of former social worker Dave Barrett. The Barrett government lasted just three years, until its defeat at the hands of a rejuvenated Social Credit under the leadership of W.A.C. Bennett's son, Bill Bennett. Under constant attack from a vitriolic media and charged with financial misman-agement, the Barrett government actually managed to hang onto its share of the popular vote as it went down to defeat. In 1975, the B.C. NDP won 39.2 percent of the vote—about the same as the 39.6 percent it had received in 1972. What doomed the gov-ernment was the massive swing of the antisocialist vote back to the Socreds, who obtained 49.2 percent of the vote in 1975, com-pared with 31.2 percent in 1972.[11]

The Bill Bennett government proved to be much more ideo-logically right wing than the old Social Credit regime had been under the elder Bennett. Indeed, many count that government as the earliest neoconservative regime in the country. It lived up to that label by pursuing a program of severe cuts to public spend-ing, laying off thousands of public sector workers. In response, the left and militant sections of the trade union movement (in partic-ular, the B.C. Teachers' Federation) built up a large common front that opposed the government and mounted huge demonstrations.

The Bennett government succeeded in maintaining its hold on B.C.'s antisocialist vote and in keeping the NDP out of power, despite the fact that in the provincial elections of 1979, 1983 and 1986, the New Democrats received a higher percentage of the vote than in 1972, when Barrett had won office. It was not until 1991, when the Social Credit was falling apart in the wake of scandalous allegations involving Premier Bill Vander Zalm, that the NDP again came to power, this time under the leadership of the former mayor of Vancouver, Mike Harcourt.

The central drama in the life of the Harcourt government was its ongoing attempt to deal with the deep split among its electoral supporters between environmentalists and loggers. If the words *social contract* call up the crucial event in the experience of the Rae government in Ontario, *Clayoquot Sound* brings to mind the great struggle that bedevilled the Harcourt government in British Columbia.

At issue were two imperatives: the urgent demand by a powerful environmentalist movement that clear-cutting of old-growth forests be banned and the desire of the province's loggers for work. The confrontation had been long in the making. It pitted an industry that had virtually mined out the province's forests, quickly depleting what should have been a fully renewable resource, against one of the world's most sophisticated and militant environmentalist movements.

After sit-ins and arrests and a global campaign against clear cutting, the government came up with a policy that went a long way toward meeting the demands for a halt to clear cutting of old forests and for a regime of advanced silvaculture in regions where logging was to be permitted. But the resolution did not come without a price. While there was nothing easy about the position in which the Harcourt government found itself, its members floundered for a long time, and in the process, the NDP's standing with the public was seriously eroded.

What furthered the erosion was a bizarre financial scandal and its apparent cover-up by top officials of the provincial party. While not directly implicating the members of the Harcourt government themselves, the scandal involved the siphoning off of funds to the NDP from charitable bingo in Nanaimo. The ham-fisted efforts of the premier, Cabinet ministers and party officials to contain the damage and come clean about what was known when and by whom gravely damaged the government's reputation.

In its last days, the Harcourt government recklessly played the populist card to win back support from the public. In the fall of 1995, it announced a regulation that would make anyone who had not resided in British Columbia for three months ineligible for welfare. This clearly violated the ban on residency restrictions, which was one of the conditions attached to federal transfers of funds to the province for social assistance. In addition, in the aftermath of the narrow win for the federalist side in the 1995 Quebec Referendum, Harcourt acted as though the unity of the country was hardly of concern to him. As far as he was concerned, he said, Quebec would get nothing, including recognition as a distinct society, that his own province did not get. Social democracy in B.C. had been reduced to an unprincipled local-boosterism. In a column in the *Globe and Mail*, Vancouver author Robert Mason Lee made the point succinctly: "Socialism was once a great notion; it is too bad Mr. Harcourt has reduced it to Mike Harris with a heart. Canada was also a great nation; it is too bad Mr. Harcourt has joined the separatists in breaking it up."[12]

In November 1995, the denouement came with Harcourt's announcement that he would step down as premier and as leader of the B.C. NDP. In February 1996, a party convention picked the youthful Glen Clark, a minister in the Harcourt government, as its new leader. Sworn in as premier, Clark was immediately embroiled in fresh charges that B.C. Hydro had provided special favours for NDP insiders in its overseas investments.

Clark rallied from the scandals, however, and tried to put the Harcourt government's less-than-stellar record behind him. The new premier proceeded to initiate a bold strategy to win re-election for the B.C. New Democrats. He drew a line in the sand which differentiated the interests of the working class and middle class on one side from those of corporations and the wealthy on the other. He hoped that class politics would win the B.C. NDP another term in office.

Clark's strategy ran counter to the way politics has been played almost everywhere in North America. It certainly ran counter to how Bob Rae had tried to win a second term for his social democratic government in Ontario. The militant defence of the interests of the nonaffluent was Clark's touchstone, while for Rae the goal had been to cover over divisions within society.

In April 1996, on the eve of the calling of the provincial election, Clark used the east-end Vancouver working-class neighbourhood where he grew up as the backdrop for a paid political address to British Columbians. He told viewers, "I know where I come from and which side I'm on."[13] He was trying to put his leading opponent, Liberal leader Gordon Campbell, formerly a wealthy developer, on the defensive—on the other side of the line in the sand.

Virtually alone among the country's premiers, Clark maintained that increased government investment in human development and infrastructure was the way to go. In his first two months in office, he announced initiatives in health care, education, job creation for young people, a ferry service to Vancouver Island and funding of Aboriginal bands. Admittedly, however, there has been a streak of harshness against the poor in the behaviour of the Clark government. Clark has continued the former Harcourt government's insistence that new arrivals remain ineligible for welfare during their first three months in B.C.

It remained to be seen whether Clark's attack on "banks, developers and corporations" and a defence of "average, everyday British Columbians" could breathe new life into the B.C. NDP government.[14]

In Saskatchewan, the original bastion of Canadian social democracy, Roy Romanow managed to lead his party to a second-term majority victory against a divided opposition in September 1995. Indeed, Saskatchewan is the only province where social democrats have succeeded in making their party the natural party of government over a period of half a century. Since 1944, the opponents of the CCF-NDP have been in office for only sixteen years (the Liberals under Ross Thatcher from 1964 to 1971, and the Conservatives under Grant Devine from 1982 to 1991). It is a measure of the sway of social democracy in the province that Ross Thatcher, a virulent opponent of medicare when the CCF first established it, did not dare eliminate it while in power.

After the Thatcher years, Allan Blakeney led the NDP back to power in Saskatchewan in 1971, and used his mandate to direct the growth of the province's resource economy—particularly in the areas of potash, natural gas and oil. Blakeney's cautious, fiscally responsible variety of state capitalism came to an end in 1982 when Conservative leader Grant Devine rode to victory on a wave of Prairie antigovernment populism in the 1982 election, reducing the NDP to eight seats in the legislature.

Nine years later, the people of Saskatchewan were completely disillusioned with the scandal-ridden Devine government, which had managed to plunge the province into debt, something which the fiscally conservative social democrats had assiduously avoided. In 1991, Roy Romanow, formerly attorney-general in the Blakeney government, led the NDP back to power.

Romanow had always been on the liberal edge of the NDP. In 1970, he had run against Blakeney for the leadership of the provincial party and had been seen as the right-wing candidate in a race in which Blakeney was regarded as occupying the centre position between Romanow and the left-wing Waffle group.

Much to its credit, the Romanow government has successfully held onto its electoral base while cutting government spending and raising taxes moderately. As a consequence of this, Saskatchewan reached the goal of a balanced budget ahead of Alberta, where the Klein government had become the darling of the country's right wing in its quest for the holy grail of fiscal rectitude. Most important of all, the Romanow government, despite hospital closures, was able to keep social programs intact, while the Klein government tore into social programs and education to balance the budget. While the Saskatchewan NDP government was buffeted by the storms loosed by globalization and neoconservatism, it remained intact.

This could not alter the fact, however, that Canadian social democracy was in crisis. It was a product of David Lewis's 1950s vision, in which an expanding welfare state and a mixed economy (including important public sector, as well as private sector, activities) would humanize capitalism. But now social democracy was in retreat—and that retreat included Saskatchewan. Unlike the CCF government of Tommy Douglas which heralded the future with its reforms, the Romanow government was chiefly remarkable for having hung onto a fading vision, while keeping its principles more or less intact.

At the federal level, the NDP chose a new leader to replace Audrey McLaughlin in October 1995. Two years after its disastrous showing in the 1993 federal election, New Democrats gave Alexa McDonough the job of leading the party out of the political wilderness. The diminished party McDonough inherited had steadfastly avoided a fundamental rethinking of its position for many years, in some respects for decades. Moreover, the federal NDP, no longer an official party in the House of Commons, lacked the media exposure it had always enjoyed in the past.

McDonough certainly knew what it meant to face a daunting political challenge. In 1980, she had become leader of the Nova Scotia NDP. And while the party remained far from power during her fourteen years at the helm, she did manage to put it on the map by to holding governments up to scrutiny and forcing changes to proposed legislation. Most Nova Scotians would agree that McDonough was an effective opponent of the patronage and kowtowing to powerful interests that were part of the the age-old way of politics in their province.

McDonough won the leadership of the federal party against former Saskatchewan MP Lorne Nystrom and B.C. MP Svend Robinson (who placed first on the first ballot at the Ottawa NDP convention and then withdrew his candidacy in favour of McDonough). Most of the excitement in the leadership race was generated by the candidacy of Svend Robinson, who managed to attract an enthusiastic following, particularly among the young—the very constituency that was so crucial to the future hopes of the NDP. But, in the end, McDonough won the leadership because she enjoyed the support of much of the party establishment in Ontario and of key affiliated unions like the Steelworkers. Once McDonough placed ahead of Nystrom on the first ballot, it was clear that she would have gone on to win on the second ballot even if Robinson had not withdrawn in her favour. The

Saskatchewan party establishment, which supported Nystrom on the first ballot, did not want Robinson to win and would have turned overwhelmingly to McDonough.

Like the four federal NDP leaders who came before her, McDonough won with the backing of what can loosely be described as the party establishment. In that sense the federal NDP has been unlike the Liberals and Conservatives, where it cannot be claimed that a party establishment has been successful in picking leaders every single time.

The fact that McDonough won with the support of the party establishment may be a disadvantage in this era of the new capitalism. It may hinder her from leading her party to embrace political ideas and strategies that are appropriate to the current confrontational terrain. Certainly, McDonough is her own person and has always kept up ties with people with a range of views in the NDP. And there is no doubt that she has the ability to be an effective leader. The crucial question, however, is whether the NDP is about to undertake a fundamental reassessment of its political analysis and strategy. It is a question that remained unanswered when McDonough was chosen leader.

Canadian social democracy has been living off the insights of the great postwar social compromise for the past four decades. Even though it has tackled such issues as American corporate control of Canada and free trade, the NDP has not changed the way it understands the economy, society and politics for a very long time.

The insights of the Winnipeg Declaration served well enough in the days of the advancing welfare state. But since the transition to the new capitalism, which began a quarter of a century ago, these insights have been of decreasing value. Only at its peril does the NDP continue to postpone the fundamental rethinking that will lead the party to a new strategic approach.

CHAPTER 7

THE WAFFLE: A CHILDREN'S CRUSADE

THIS is the story of a children's crusade which subjected Canadian social democracy to the most wrenching internal debate in its history. As the New Democratic Party faces the possibility of a radical realignment in the 1990s, a look at the Waffle episode could shed some light on how social democrats have handled, or perhaps mishandled, fundamental internal debate in the past.

It was unavoidable that the ground on which David Lewis had placed Canadian social democracy in the 1950s would be contested by the new political movements that emerged in the 1960s. During that tumultuous decade, the American civil rights movement, the Vietnam War, the rise of Quebec nationalism and mounting anxiety about American corporate control of Canada had an enormous impact on Canadian society and politics. It was an era of youth politics, rebellion against established society and anarchistic rejection of the norms of the political process. These profound developments had little effect on the NDP for much of the decade, although the questions involved were not unnoticed, and they were debated at party conventions. It was not until the end of the sixties that the full force of the new left politics of the period collided with the thought and political style of mainstream social democracy.

Before the spring of 1969, the Canadian new left, which was heavily influenced by radical movements in the United States, was only loosely connected with the NDP. This changed dramatically with the formation of the left-wing and nationalist Waffle movement, which brought the concerns of the new nationalist left to the NDP in the form of a manifesto. The movement (which acquired its strange name because a participant at an early meeting is reputed to have said: "I'd rather waffle to the left than waffle to the right") came together out of the conviction that Canadian social democracy was badly out of date on important issues, particularly the issue of the American control of Canada. When Gerald Caplan and I convened a meeting in the spring of 1969 involving about a dozen people in Toronto, our main motivation was to discuss the position the NDP ought to take on American domination.

Over the preceding decade, the question of American corporate, and even political and cultural, control of Canada, had been emerging as a major concern in English Canada. In the Conservative Party, John Diefenbaker's nationalist crusade in the election campaigns of 1957 and 1958 harkened back to the nationalism of Sir John A. Macdonald, but also pointed toward the new nationalism of the sixties and seventies. In the Liberal Party during the late fifties and the sixties, Walter Gordon developed the case for economic nationalism, documenting the extent of American corporate control of Canada and warning of the threats it posed. But while the new nationalism in English Canada was very much a phenomenon of the centre and the left, it was nonetheless profoundly influenced by conservative thinkers such as George Grant, Harold Innis and Donald Creighton. In 1965, philosopher Grant wrote *Lament for a Nation*, a seminal work on Canada's relationship with the United States, and galvanized a generation of Canadian nationalists.

The work of political economists and historians such as Harold Innis and Donald Creighton, dating back to the 1920s, had a powerful impact on the new scholarship of the 1960s in political economy. Political thinkers and economists such as Cy Gonick at the University of Manitoba, Charles Taylor and Kari Levitt at McGill, and Mel Watkins and Abe Rotstein at the University of Toronto were contributing ground-breaking work on the economic and political domination of Canada by

American corporate capitalism. Taken as a whole, this body of work analysed the limitations of the U.S.-dominated branch-plant economy in Canada and exposed the extent to which Canadian sovereignty had been undermined by the American economic takeover.

If the youthful left was influenced by the new currents of nationalism in English Canada, it was also shaped by the world-wide youth culture and radicalism of the era, particularly its American variety. This American version of the new left arose as a consequence of a complex interplay of forces in a volatile histori-cal period. In its narrowest and most political sense, it encom-passed movements that arose to struggle for civil rights for American blacks, to oppose the Vietnam War, and to agitate for democratic reforms in the governance of American universities. Beyond these political points of concentration, however, there was a much wider rebellion of American youth against the status quo. The youth culture, with its music, drugs, sexual mores, alternative lifestyles, and with its critique of the drudgery of middle-class work and life, had great political importance, without being overt-ly political. While there is characteristically some form of youthful rebellion against established values in every era, the youth culture of the 1960s was so widespread, and so open to the values and ideas of the oppositional political movements of the time, that it resulted in a high degree of social polarization.

To a certain extent, the youth revolt of the 1960s and early 1970s had an impact on all parts of the political spectrum. Canadians were on the receiving end of a large-scale transmission of American youth culture into Canada. While much of this was apolitical, American civil rights activists and thousands of American draft dodgers and deserters brought American struggles north of the border, and for much of the 1960s, youthful Canadian political activists took up the American-centred strug-gles as though they were their own. The same placards and slogans were used at Canadian protests against the war in Vietnam as in the United States—almost as if there was no distinction in the minds of the demonstrators between the two countries. Youthful activists sought to politicize the poor in community-organizing programs that were replicas of programs south of the border—as though Canada had no political traditions or unique social characteristics and values.

The Americanization of the Canadian new left meant that for a considerable period of time, youthful radicals in English Canada had little to do with the NDP, despite the existence of a powerful Canadian social democratic tradition. From the mid-1960s on, however, a nationalist tendency developed within the Canadian new left, and it was only a matter of time before this strain of youth radicalism encountered the NDP in a serious way.

That is exactly what happened in 1969, when the Waffle assembled. While those who made up the initial group were NDP members, including some of long standing, the Waffle membership within the party and across the country was drawn mostly from the young and the university educated. Numbering about a dozen people at the start, the conclave initially included future NDP leader Ed Broadbent, University of Toronto economist Mel Watkins (author of the 1967 *Watkins Report* on foreign ownership) and Gerald Caplan, a long-time NDP activist, who was a close personal friend and political ally of Stephen Lewis, soon to be the leader of the Ontario NDP.

At the first meeting, we decided that the best way forward was to write a statement setting out the key ideas that had drawn us together. I wrote the first draft of what was to become known as the Waffle Manifesto, and after a second meeting Mel Watkins was given the task of producing a second draft. Gerald Caplan wrote the third and final version.

Entitled "For an Independent Socialist Canada," the Waffle Manifesto was first and foremost a call to recognize the serious threat posed by American corporate and political domination of Canada. The manifesto argued that Canadian independence could be achieved only through a socialist strategy. Public ownership of large-scale corporate entities, particularly in the resource sector, would be needed to assure Canadian independence and to reverse the growing problem of foreign ownership of the Canadian economy. The analysis that led up to these statements was characteristic of the thinking of left-wing Canadian nationalists of the period. Canada's problem, according to this view, was the domination of the country from the outside—by American capital. For a youthful left, in the era of the Vietnam War, reversing the American ownership of key sectors of the Canadian economy took on an aura of immense moral urgency. To struggle against American control of the Canadian oil and nickel industries was to join a worldwide resistance to American militarism and imperialism. The resulting advocacy of widespread public ownership was not dissimilar to the CCF's Regina Manifesto of 1933, but the rationale was entirely different. The problem of foreign ownership of the Canadian economy had scarcely been mentioned in the Regina Manifesto, and if any concern had been expressed about external domination of Canada, it was the British Empire that had been singled out, not the United States.

The second great issue dealt with in the manifesto was the relationship between English Canada and Quebec. It acknowledged the rising tide of Quebec nationalism as a legitimate force and it proposed an alliance between the two nationalisms on the northern half of the continent.

In two distinct ways, therefore, the Waffle Manifesto parted company with the social democracy David Lewis had been fashioning. First, it put public ownership back on the agenda as the most important way to counter the control of the economy by U.S.-owned multinational corporations. And second, the manifesto went beyond the NDP's recognition of Quebec as a "nation"—a recognition that had already led to serious divisions in the party with those who thought that was going too far—to the assertion that Quebec had the right to "self-determination"— that is, the right to secede from Canada if it so chose.

To the leadership of the NDP, which had been carefully crafting its own version of social democracy, designed to win votes and hold the allegiance of a labour movement still dominated by American-based unions, the Manifesto and the Waffle group posed an alarming threat. Moreover, the leadership of the NDP did not have a clear idea of the exact nature of the threat it faced. Particularly in the 1940s and 1950s, David Lewis had led the fight in the CCF against communist infiltration of the party and, more importantly, against communist factions inside the trade union movement. At times, those struggles had been extremely acrimonious, as in the case of the battle against the communist leadership of the Mine Mill union in Sudbury, Ontario in the 1950s. In that conflict, the CCF leadership aligned itself with the United Steelworkers of America in its bid to oust Mine Mill as the union representing the nickel miners at Inco. One consequence of the bitter struggle, which the Steelworkers won, was a division among the left in Sudbury that did not heal for at least a generation.

The leaders of the NDP and of the international unions saw in the Waffle a threat that bore some resemblance to that formerly posed by the communists. The fact that some, although not many, of those in the Waffle group were sons and daughters of former communists, was seized on by some as evidence of a communist connection. (My father, for instance, was a member of the Communist Party until 1956, when he and many others left in revulsion following the Soviet invasion of Hungary and upon learning of the crimes of Stalinism. The fact that I was fourteen years old at the time and was never a member of any communist-related organization myself, did not free me from the taint of communism in the eyes of some NDP and trade union leaders, who were inclined to see communism as a genetic disorder.) The leadership of the NDP had had a long experience of being on guard against communist and Trotskyist infiltration, and they had a not inconsiderable history of expelling those seen as representing these alien ideologies. This could not help but condition the way the Waffle was seen.

In fact, in many important respects, the Waffle spoke for a political movement that was the antithesis of the communists and Trotskyists. True to the spirit of the new left radicalism of the sixties, the Waffle leaned in the direction of an anarchistic style of democracy. Far from being a centralized organization with a highly developed sense of political discipline, the Waffle was open to anyone who was a member of the NDP. During the time that it was a group inside the party, a wide range of party members, with diverse views, attended its meetings. Decision making in the Waffle was far more chaotic than in the bureaucratized mainstream NDP precisely because anyone, with any point of view, could insist on being heard, often at considerable length.

The Waffle Manifesto became the main issue at the 1969 NDP federal convention in Winnipeg. The convention polarized into two warring camps—the party establishment, led by David Lewis and the top leadership of the trade unions, and the Waffle group. The clash was as visible in terms of lifestyle and culture as it was in the sense of political differences. Young, long-haired and often bearded Waffle supporters could be seen racing from one workshop session to another, being pursued by older, and often paunchy, trade union delegates. The race to pack meetings to produce majorities on specific issues quickly generated hard feelings on both sides.

Many of the young Waffle supporters slept in sleeping bags on the floors of crowded hotel rooms. Among the older delegates, there was often the sentiment that their party had suddenly come under assault by a large, unruly throng who lacked respect for established ways of doing things and had not sacrificed themselves for the organization. The strongly entrenched party establishment had never seen anything like the Waffle before.

The convention ended with the Waffle Manifesto receiving the support of one-third of the delegates. The other two-thirds voted for a statement on the same set of issues, drafted by the party leadership, that was known ever after as "the marshmallow." Despite this disdainful depiction, however, the statement echoed many of the themes of the Waffle Manifesto. On paper, at least, the NDP had moved further than ever before in the direction of the left nationalist analysis of the Canadian political situation, at least partially endorsing its prescriptions for dealing with American domination of Canada.

The Winnipeg Convention proved to be a mere opening round in the conflict between the Waffle and the party leadership. When Waffle supporters met at the end of the convention, they were ecstatic about their success in drawing national attention to their cause. While they hadn't yet worked out the details, they decided to continue to meet and function as a group within the NDP—a decision that was to prove fateful, both for the supporters of the Waffle Manifesto and for the party as a whole. This was particularly true in Ontario and Saskatchewan, the two provinces where the Waffle group was to be most strongly entrenched. The decision to continue as a political entity, indeed to progress to a higher level of formal group organization, was bound to spark antagonism among the party's leadership and from many rank-and-file party activists. In part, this was because there has always been a history of sects and schisms within socialist and social democratic parties. The example of the battle with the communists, and the pesky struggles they had had with small Trotskyist organizations, was very much in the minds of party leaders.

But to those who knew anything about the history of the left, it should have been perfectly obvious that the Waffle was not a threat in that sense. The communist and Trotskyist sects were conspiratorial in their operations, their adherents maintaining a secretive internal discipline, not so much as acknowledging to others that they even belonged to the sect. In marked contrast, the Waffle was notoriously and flagrantly open in everything it did.

In both Ontario and Saskatchewan, and to a lesser extent in other provinces, the Waffle established local groups in major centres. The provincial and local Waffle groups engaged in activist politics, both inside and outside the NDP. Beyond the regular activities of the party, the Waffle mounted its own campaigns on public issues—the main ones having to do with countering American control of key sectors of the Canadian economy, particularly the resource sector. The Waffle played a highly vocal role in advocating public ownership of the major foreign-owned petroleum companies, campaigning for a public takeover of such companies as Imperial Oil.

These efforts actually had a significant effect inside and outside the party. While the NDP leadership had been negative toward advocacy of public ownership of major resource companies, public support of the Waffle campaign motivated them to change their position on this question in 1970. The Waffle's activities also encouraged other more mainstream nationalists to get involved. In 1970, the founders of the Committee for an Independent Canada (CIC)—Walter Gordon, Peter C. Newman and University of Toronto economist Abraham Rotstein—candidly acknowledged that they did not want to leave the nationalist terrain exclusively to the Waffle.

In retrospect, it is evident that the Waffle was only a part of a much wider movement in English Canada to assert Canadian independence from the United States, not only in economic matters, but also in terms of politics, the military, culture and intellectual life. It is not coincidental that the Waffle flowered at the same time that a new school of scholarship in Canadian political economy was burgeoning.

It was inside the NDP and particularly in its dealings with the labour movement that the Waffle was to come to grief. The leadership of the Waffle—and I certainly include myself in this—did not fully realize the extent of the trade union movement's growing antagonism. The group was aware that if they directly advocated the idea of independent Canadian unions, they would provoke the wrath of the leaders of the key international unions affiliated with the NDP. Despite pressure from other nationalists, this was a case where the Waffle actually exercised uncharacteristic caution. Rather than calling for independent Canadian unions, which would have paralleled its insistence on Canadian ownership of major corporations, the Waffle talked vaguely of "autonomy" for the Canadian sections of international unions. But this failed to placate key trade unionists like Lynn Williams of the United Steelworkers of America (USWA) and Dennis McDermott of the United Auto Workers (UAW). Perhaps they understood, better than the Waffle itself did, the extent to which the Waffle's nationalist stance implied an inherent assault on international unions—even if there was no explicit provocation.

If the trade union leaders were gravely worried about the Waffle's nationalism, they were also deeply alienated by its manner of political activity. The Waffle was characterized by a youthful aggressiveness that was a commonplace feature of the radicalism of the era. While the Waffle certainly had coherent views and a leadership that knew what it was doing, it was rough around the edges.

The prominence of the Waffle inside the NDP increased in the year and a half following the Winnipeg Convention, largely as a result of the contest for the leadership of the federal NDP, which was decided at the party's convention in Ottawa in April 1971. After Mel Watkins, the best known figure in the Waffle, and Cy Gonick, the Winnipeg-based editor of *Canadian Dimension* magazine, both decided not to run, I was endorsed as the Waffle's candidate for the NDP leadership.

The campaign took place at a fateful historical moment, beginning in October 1970, just weeks after the Trudeau government had proclaimed the War Measures Act to deal with the "apprehended insurrection" that the government claimed was responsible for the kidnapping of British Trade Representative James Cross in Montreal, and the kidnapping and murder of Quebec's Labour Minister, Pierre Laporte. The great debate that followed established the context for the NDP leadership contest.

Federal NDP leader Tommy Douglas, who had announced his intention to step down as party leader, and David Lewis, the overwhelming favourite to succeed him, led the party's strong opposition to the use of the War Measures Act by the Trudeau government. At the time, the NDP's stalwart fight on behalf of the democratic and civil rights of Canadians won it few friends. The imposition of the War Measures Act was immensely popular. In the circumstances, the ability of Douglas, Lewis and other party leaders to keep the NDP almost entirely united in its opposition was a major achievement.

For the Waffle, the War Measures Act crisis brought to the fore the larger issue of Quebec's relationship to the rest of Canada. The Waffle Manifesto had depicted Canada as a union of two nations, English Canada and Quebec, promoting the view that the two required a close alliance if they were to be truly independent from the United States. The manifesto was clear, however, in its support for the right of Quebecers to decide whether they wished to remain in Canada, and this became the fulcrum of the Waffle's campaign for the NDP leadership. While the NDP had adopted the view that Canada constituted "two nations" in its founding program in 1961, it had never gone so far as to assert the corollary, that Quebec had a right to national self-determination.

When the Waffle outlined its views on Quebec's right to self-determination in December 1970, the effect was dramatic. At a convention held in January 1971, the small but politically significant Quebec NDP elected a new leadership and made the right of self-determination the centrepiece of its program. A series of all-candidates debates were held in many centres across the country during the months before the Ottawa convention. The campaign was soon polarized between David Lewis, the embodiment of the party establishment, and the Waffle, with me, a twenty-nine-year-old with a one-year appointment as a history lecturer at Queen's University, as the standard bearer. Lewis was, of course, not a mere candidate for the party leadership. He was the architect of contemporary Canadian social democracy, the personification of its relationship with the key industrial unions that were affiliated with the party. I, on the other hand, was as much the representative of the Waffle movement's ideas as an actual candidate for the leadership of the party.

The other two serious candidates for the leadership were John Harney and Ed Broadbent. Harney was an academic from Toronto who had run unsuccessfully for a seat in Parliament in the past; Broadbent was a first-term member of Parliament from Oshawa, who'd won his seat in 1968. In terms of campaign organization, Harney and Broadbent were no match either for Lewis, with his powerful trade union connections, or for the Waffle, with its significant presence in many key regions of the country.

Moreover, they were caught in the unenviable position of being in the middle during a leadership campaign in which the most important dynamic was the growing polarization between the Lewis and the Waffle camps.

Once, when I was waiting for a flight with Lewis at the airport in Regina, he told me that while I wasn't really running to be leader, but rather to represent the views of a group, he believed that Harney and Broadbent actually wanted to be leader. And he said he thought it would be "a disaster for the party" if either of them were to win. I told him what I believed, which was that, among the candidates who were running, he would make the best leader. When the time came at the convention for me to make a short speech after I came second to David Lewis, it was ungrudgingly that I proposed his victory should be made unanimous. This was a personal gesture I was happy to make.

Personal gestures notwithstanding, the April convention in Ottawa was suffused with bitterness. Between the youthful core of Waffle supporters and the phalanx of Lewis's industrial union delegates, there was a wide gulf of incomprehension, which had as much to do with lifestyle and culture as with ideology. While, for the most part, delegates were well behaved, there were incidents of jeering and even of pushing and shoving between the supporters of Lewis and the Waffle.

While Lewis's victory at the convention was no surprise, the ability of the Waffle to hang onto its constituency through a five-month leadership campaign did surprise many observers. It took four ballots for Lewis to win. On the last ballot the vote total was: Lewis 1046, Laxer 612.

Just weeks after the convention, the Ontario NDP decided to hold a public educational conference in Toronto on foreign ownership in Canada. The conference, which featured speakers from the Waffle as well as from the mainstream of the party, was highly successful, drawing an audience of six or seven hundred people for most sessions and receiving enthusiastic reviews from those who participated. Relations between the Waffle and the party leadership began to thaw.

It was a false spring, however.

Within months, tensions resumed again. Although the Waffle had been highly successful at the Ottawa convention among delegates from NDP riding associations, it had, not surprisingly, won very little support from trade union delegates. Indeed, when I received 37 percent of the leadership vote on the final ballot against David Lewis, that represented a virtual dead heat among riding association delegates, where Lewis's margin of victory was based on his overwhelming support among union delegates. Concluding that the effort to change the party required a different relationship with trade unionists, the Waffle worked hard to create a dialogue. It was moderately successful in involving dissident members of the United Steelworkers of America and of the United Auto Workers.

In both cases, Steelworkers and Auto Workers who were attracted to the Waffle were drawn to its militant position on Canadian independence. Among the Steelworkers who gravitated to the Waffle were leading figures in Local 1005 at Stelco in Hamilton. In the past, some of them had even been disciplined by the union as rebels involved in an effort to create an independent Canadian union. In the UAW, those who became involved with the Waffle included left wingers and nationalists who had been opposed to the Canada–United States Auto Pact during the 1960s. Instead of integrating its auto industry with that of the U.S., they believed Canada should establish its own industry, designing and manufacturing automobiles from start to finish in Canada. Their slogan had been "An All-Canadian Car."

The fact that dissident Steelworkers and Auto Workers were becoming involved with the Waffle was highly alarming to the regional and national leadership of the USWA and the UAW. Previously, that leadership had often accused the Waffle of being a collection of academics and students who were out of touch with the aspirations of the working class. Now they feared the Waffle might be gaining a foothold in their very organizations.

This fear came to a head in January 1972, when the Waffle sponsored a highly successful event in the heart of UAW country on an issue that was of critical importance to members of the United Auto Workers. The Waffle organized a major public conference in Windsor, Ontario, on the Canada-U.S. Auto Pact and the future of the Canadian automotive industry. The conference was cosponsored by the heads of the major auto union locals in southern Ontario, from Oshawa to Windsor, and attended by four hundred people, most of them Auto Workers. The mayor of Windsor was also present. On the Monday following the conference, the *Windsor Star* printed a banner front-page headline announcing that the Waffle's goal was an all-Canadian car.

The Windsor conference was the last straw. Key trade union leaders were convinced that the time had come to dispose of the Waffle. In fact, by the time of the auto conference in Windsor, the effort to get rid of the Waffle had already begun at a much lower level. In the fall of 1971, a resolution was passed by a riding association in Hamilton, Ontario, calling for the group's dissolution.

Both at the highest level, in closed-door discussions between the top trade union leadership and the leadership of the Ontario NDP, and through the Hamilton riding association initiative, the final crisis between the Waffle and the party was at hand. In the spring of 1972, at a meeting of the Ontario NDP's provincial council, provincial party leader Stephen Lewis launched a passionate denunciation of the Waffle. In his leader's report to the council, Lewis depicted the Waffle as a "party within a party." He spent some time detailing the nature of the Waffle group's organizational structure, making the case that the Waffle was an elaborate body with its own committees and public activities, and as such was completely inappropriate within the framework of the NDP.

Following the Stephen Lewis attack, which received major attention from the media, the party established a three-person task force to make recommendations to the party on how to deal with the problem of the Waffle. The task force members were Party President Gordon Vichert; Gerald Caplan, a close confidant of Stephen Lewis who had originally supported the Waffle but had left the group following the federal NDP convention in

Winnipeg; and long-time party activist John Brewin.

After holding meetings around the province, the task force produced a report that was harshly critical of the Waffle, even going so far as to compare its political tone to the stridency of former Alabama Governor and segregationist George Wallace—a metaphor for new left Canadian nationalists that was so extreme as to ultimately undermine the credibility of the task force.

During the weeks following the task force report, the Waffle fought a provincewide campaign to salvage its legitimacy within the party. Debates were held across Ontario by riding associations and groups of riding associations. Behind the scenes, a few efforts were made to find common ground between the Waffle and the party leadership. At one point, Stephen Lewis asked me to have dinner with him, and the pleasant evening we spent discussing the future of the party gave me a false sense of hope that compromise could be possible. Similarly, I retained close ties with my friend Gerald Caplan. Indeed, we would travel together, have dinner and then participate on opposite sides in the debate about the Waffle's right to exist.

Some leading party members who were identified neither with the Waffle nor with the leadership tried to fashion compromise proposals that would allow the Waffle to remain within the party while restricting its right to function as publicly as it had in the past. But there was to be no compromise, no middle ground. The Ontario NDP held a provincial council meeting in Orillia in June 1972. A party executive resolution, embodying the position of the party leadership and that of the top leadership of the affiliated unions, threatened that if the Waffle did not disband, its adherents would be expelled from the NDP. Speaking passionately in support of the resolution, Stephen Lewis asked the party to rid him of this "albatross" around his neck. At the end of a long day, the members of the council voted by a wide margin to support the resolution.

Politically neutered and left with no legitimate political ground on which to stand, the Waffle was finished in the NDP. Soon enough, it would be finished altogether. Its supporters met a few weeks after the Orillia council meeting, near London, Ontario, where the majority of them decided to establish a new organization, the Movement for an Independent Socialist Canada. In this new form, the Waffle survived for another two years, as an organization separate from the NDP. Indeed, this reformed Waffle was highly successful in organizing large-scale public educational courses in political economy. But when it decided to run three candidates in Ontario in the 1974 federal election (I ran in York West riding in Toronto), it was much less successful. The candidates received only about 1 percent of the vote where they ran. Shortly after that, the Waffle disbanded.

In the summer of 1994, years after the Canadian region of the United Auto Workers (UAW) had split off to form the Canadian Auto Workers (CAW), the CAW held a crucial policy convention in Quebec City. One of the discussion papers, which had been prepared by the top leadership of the CAW, reviewed the history of the labour movement in politics—in particular, its relationship to the NDP. The discussion paper, which took a decidedly nationalist position, was highly critical of what it saw as the role of the Steelworkers and the Auto Workers in driving the Waffle out of the NDP. "It should be pointed out," the paper stated, "that the economic nationalism and movement politics advocated in these labour critiques [current CAW position papers] echoed arguments made in the early 70s by a group within the NDP, the Waffle. The Waffle was ultimately thrown out of the party for these views. Ironically both the USWA (United Steelworkers of America) and the CAW, concerned with the Waffle's criticism of international [American based] unions were very instrumental in that decision."

CHAPTER 8

SOCIAL DEMOCRACY AND CANADIAN SURVIVAL

EVERYWHERE in the world, multinational business has launched a frontal assault against the state. The objective of the global campaign is to win the maximum freedom to produce anywhere, to sell everywhere and to keep corporate taxes low by threatening to shift investment out of any country that tries to restore them to the higher rates of the postwar decades. The capitalist "international" polices the world today to ensure that its writ runs everywhere.

Some states are immensely more vulnerable to the assault than others. Canada is one of those states.

Canada is not an inevitable country. It does not tax the imagination to concoct historical scenarios for the northern half of North America that are quite different from what actually happened. More than is the case for many other countries, the survival of Canada depends on the active pursuit of national policies to offset the centrifugal forces that are a constant feature of Canadian existence. The United States and Britain, the countries in which antistate ideology has been strongest, will survive the era through which we are passing. Canada may not.

In the United States and Britain, there are definite limits to how far antistate ideology is allowed to go. The ruling classes in those countries are prepared to demolish the welfare state and public education. They are not, however, prepared to give up the sterner features of state power that have always been crucial to their careers at the centre of global empires. Antistate rhetoric in the United States and Britain never extends to criticisms of these states as nuclear powers.

What limits the antistate position of business in the U.S. and Britain is that the capitalist class in both countries has a nationalist outlook. This certainly does not mean that American and British businesses hesitate to shift investments out of their own countries or to speculate against their own currencies. But it does mean that, despite their bottom-line orientation, business in both countries operates consciously and unconsciously within the worldviews of their nation-states. Although they take advantage of globalization to further their prosperity, the American and British capitalist classes remain patriotic. They identify, and not in a merely perfunctory way, with the place of their nations in the world. Being American or British comes naturally to them, as does their parochialism and chauvinism toward the rest of the world.

Canadian capitalists are different. To enlist in the great odyssey of globalization, they have had to put aside whatever nationalism they ever had. Canada is too small a pond for them, and the affection they express for Canada is artificial and hollow, as shrill and empty as local boosterism. Canada is the country they have abandoned so as to take up residence in an extended American cultural and social space. Canadian capitalists actually believe in the borderless world, while their American and British counterparts believe in it only if the world remains Anglo-American while borders are being erased. In the United States and Britain, antistate ideology on the part of business never reaches such a pitch that it threatens the survival of the country itself (which is not to say that it cannot gravely undermine social stability).

While American and British capitalists have retained their sense of identity, Canadian capitalists have allowed themselves to become so disoriented that they are in danger of doing themselves, not to mention the rest of us, immense harm, as the disoriented characteristically do.

So what has led contemporary Canadian business to lose its sense of self?

Historically, the Canadian state has worked actively with business to overcome obstacles to creating a transcontinental economic space on the northern half of the continent. There have been periods when the federal government consciously acted to promote economic development. At other times, antigovernment ideology—periodically a powerful force in Canada—has prevented the state from playing such a role.

It is a considerable irony that the business class, with its reputation for hard-headedness, has so often had such a clouded understanding of where its own best interest actually lies. Business has always needed the state, whether to protect property or to enhance the environment in which business is conducted. Yet the Canadian state is now under assault—the assumptions that underlie its development have never been more in doubt. To understand why this is so, and the strategic role now occupied by social democratic thinking in relation to the Canadian state, we need to consider how and why the Canadian state first came into being. Only then can we appreciate that it has always been like the proverbial bicycle—unless it continues to move forward, it is constantly in danger of falling over.

Canadian existence has rested on two enduring realities. One of them, of course, has been the presence of anglophone and francophone national societies within Canada. The other has been the fact that English-speaking Canada has had a dual character in its own right. It has been an integral part of American civilization from the very start, and yet has also had its own national character, formed in large measure as a consequence of its deliberate rejection of the United States.

Canada, it is worth reminding ourselves, was a product of the counterrevolutionary eddies of the eighteenth century. Because of the British Conquest of 1759, French Canada missed the French Revolution. And English Canada was born out of the civil war within the English-speaking world that was the American Revolution. The Church in French Canada and loyalism and the British connection in English Canada were the essential reference points for the societies that were to become Canada.

From the Conquest to the late 1840s, the British North American colonies existed within the strategic and economic setting of British mercantilism—a closed economic system, in which it was thought desirable to restrict most commerce to the British Empire itself. It was the age of the Industrial Revolution, and Britain was transforming itself into the world's first industrial power. By the 1840s, industrial Britain had no further use for mercantilism, since it was economically strong enough to buy and sell everywhere. When Britain repealed the Corn Laws and Navigation Acts late in that decade, the British preference on which Canadian merchants had relied was ended, and Canada was thrown rudely into the new world of Victorian free trade.

Canadian merchants felt betrayed by the end of British preference and even by the granting of responsible government, which came at the same time. Many of the colony's leading merchants were involved in drawing up the Annexation Manifesto of 1849, which called for the Province of Canada to become a part of the United States. Instead of annexation, however, Canada was to get reciprocity with the United States by 1854—a free trade deal negotiated by the British, under which Canadians sold primary products to the U.S. and bought back an array of imports, including a rising volume of manufactured goods. This arrangement did provide Canadian merchants with a special economic relationship to replace British preference, but reciprocity did not end the travails of Canadian capitalists.

In the 1860s and 1870s, greatness was thrust upon them. What changed everything was the American Civil War and the complete reordering of strategic realities on the continent that accompanied it. As a consequence of the American Civil War and the tensions it engendered between the United States and Britain, the U.S. abrogated reciprocity with British North America.

Having been pushed out of special economic relationships with Britain and now with the United States, Canadian business and the nascent Canadian state were forced to contemplate an alternative economic and nation-building strategy, this one focusing on the integration and development of British North America itself. Between 1864 and 1879, the critical decisions were taken. First, through Confederation and the establishment of a Canadian

state, the new country had a much greater capacity to oversee economic development than had been the case for the former
Province of Canada.

There was much truth in the quip by the Quebec Rouge who
was an opponent of Confederation that Canada was a "railway in
search of a country." The new Canadian state was designed as an
engine of development, an instrument that could be used to further the plans of the leading bankers and railway promoters of the
day. Without the newly fashioned Canadian state, the idea of a
transcontinental railway with Montreal as a metropolis would
have been unthinkable.

The activist conservatism of John A. Macdonald provided the
worldview that brought all the elements together for Canada's
late-nineteenth-century development strategy. His was the national outlook that best suited the integration of Canada at the time.
By the end of the 1870s, Macdonald, a colonial-nationalist politician, had understood that the assumptions the British brought to
political economy did not necessarily make sense for Canadians.
In a seminal speech in the House of Commons, in which he made
the case for what was to become the National Policy, Macdonald
argued that the British passion for free trade was self-interested,
and in no way a proclamation of universal truth. By the time the
Napoleonic Wars were over in 1815, Britain had succeeded in
establishing itself as the leading economic power in the world,
Macdonald observed. Therefore Britain stood to gain the most
through worldwide free trade since it had enjoyed a head start
over other nations in its industrialization. Unless other countries,
including Canada, adopted policies to shelter their industries
from all-out competition with stronger nations, they would never
develop their own industry. Macdonald's conclusion was clear—
tariffs were justified as a protective barrier behind which domestic
industry could develop.

Macdonald's willingness to use the state to protect Canadian
industry extended to the critical arena of transportation as well. In
1878, on the need to complete the Pacific Railway, Macdonald
declared: "Until this great work is completed our Dominion is little

more than a 'Geographical Expression.' We have as much interest in British Columbia as in Australia, and no more. The railway once finished, we become one great united country with a large interprovincial trade and a common interest."[1] Whatever its shortcomings, Macdonald's nationalism was the essential worldview that lay behind the consolidation of a transcontinental Canadian economy. Without it, it is easy to imagine that Canada's disparate regions would have been absorbed by the United States in subsequent decades.

The major alternative point of view during the Confederation-National Policy era was that of laissez-faire liberalism. It was represented by the Liberal Party, which fought election after election on a platform of seeking economic union or unrestricted reciprocity with the United States. Only with his last electoral victory in 1891, just before his death, did Macdonald finally ensure the durability of the National Policy. Following their fourth consecutive defeat at the polls, the Liberals, under the leadership of Wilfrid Laurier, made an historic policy U-turn. They dropped their basic opposition to the National Policy, insisting only on minor alterations to the tariff schedule. (Laurier's shift was on a par with that of Jean Chrétien in 1993, who, upon winning power, switched his government's position to full support for the North American Free Trade Agreement (NAFTA), subject only to the adoption of scanty side agreements on labour and the environment.) As a result of this policy flip, Laurier and the Liberals, after they won power in 1896, presided over the rise to fruition of the National Policy. So the first decade of this century saw the high water mark of the effort to create a national economy through specialized interrelationships among Canadian regions. (It is deeply ironic that Macdonald, who breathed life into the National Policy, did not live to see it achieve its full flower.)

The system was bolstered by the new wheat economy of the Prairies. The wheat export and the turn-of-the-century flood of immigration to the West provided the engine for a much wider economic takeoff. The exports paid for the construction of two new transcontinental railways and created a huge new market for manufactured products. In turn, the tariff, which was the central element of the National Policy, motivated Canadians to purchase domestically produced manufactured goods.

Regional specialization within the National Policy was certainly geared to making central Canada its major beneficiary. The banks, the railways and the big manufacturers were all located in Ontario and Quebec, and they were the biggest winners under the policy. That said, the National Policy did what no Canadian economic policy has accomplished before or since. It established an integrated national economy in Canada, and while it existed, the leading elements of Canadian business believed that their particular interests were congruent with the National Policy's conception of the national interest. What makes the National Policy period so seminal in the Canadian experience is that it was the only time Canadian business was nationalist in its outlook—with a vision of the world that was neither British nor American, but Canadian.

To claim that Canadian business displayed a national consciousness is not to suggest the flowering of a national bourgeoisie with a perspective as sophisticated as those in other more economically advanced countries. Most economically advanced countries, with the obvious exception of the United States, were also long established nations, with a strong sense of national particularity. This was true, for example, even in the cases of Germany and Italy which were united into powerful nation-states only in the era of Canadian Confederation. Despite pronounced cultural particularism in parts of Germany and Italy, these two countries were bound together by ancient cultures and common languages.

For its part, Canadian business always retained strong economic, cultural and political ties with Britain and the United States. In that sense, a broadly developed and independent worldview never developed within the Canadian bourgeoisie. In other countries, such as France or Sweden, such an independent worldview is evident within the business class and has resulted in business being much more embedded in the national culture, and in the drive for its preservation, than has been the case in Canada.

In the two decades between the end of the First World War and
the outbreak of the Second World War, Canadian scholarship and
culture achieved heights they had never attained before. The tradition of Canadian political economy, pioneered by Harold Innis,
Donald Creighton and other scholars in the 1920s and 1930s,
constituted a declaration of independence. Instead of conceptual-
izing Canada as a political creation that defied geography, as had
been the previous tradition, the new political economists asserted
that the logic of a Canada separate from the United States was
deeply embedded in geography, resources and technology, and in
the historic web of commercial ties to Europe. For Innis, Canada
was much more than the accidental remnant of a former French
colony to which were added loyalists from the Thirteen Colonies
and, later, immigrants from Britain. Canada was rooted in a political economy of the northern half of the continent, the origins of
which went back to the fishery of the sixteenth century, prior to
permanent European settlement. From this early exploitation of a
staple product, the northern economy developed along a different
path from that to the south, which centred on the export of primary products to Europe.

The work of Donald Creighton furthered this line of analysis.
Creighton's masterful study, *The Empire of the St. Lawrence*, first
published in 1937, drew a sharp line between the northern territory that was to become Canada and the territory of the Thirteen
Colonies. In language that proclaimed the integrity and inspiration of the northern nation, Creighton described the St. Lawrence
and its hinterland as follows: "The dream of the commercial
empire of the St. Lawrence runs like an obsession through the
whole of Canadian history; and men followed each other through
life, planning and toiling to achieve it. The river was not only a
great actuality; it was the central truth of a religion. Men lived by
it, at once consoled and inspired by its promises, its whispered
suggestions, and its shouted commands; and it was a force in history, not merely because of its accomplishments, but because of its
shining, ever-receding possibilities."[2]

The rich tradition of political economy established by Innis and Creighton endures to this day. After the mid-1960s, those who followed their lead were much more likely to be on the left politically than on the right, and they worked to differentiate the Canadian from the American experience and to analyse the nature of American domination of Canada. But while the Canadian political-economy tradition was to provide a basis for nationalist scholarship, there can be no denying the fact that mainstream economists and political scientists abandoned this school of thought to embrace the main themes of American scholarship. As British intellectual influence in Canada declined, American influence increased, so that by the 1960s, when universities were undergoing their great expansion, American approaches to the social sciences and economics had become dominant in Canada.

The division of scholarship into a dominant stream that was compatible with North American continentalism and a lesser, but nonetheless critical, stream that was compatible with Canadian nationalism reflected the division of society into contending continentalist and nationalist forces. By the late 1950s, the schism between these tendencies had become a fundamental aspect of English Canadian politics. Since then, the ideas of nationalist and continentalist "parties" have been felt in every major societal debate, from free trade to industrial and social policy questions.

Canadian economic nationalism developed into a significant force during the 1950s, the decade when American economic control of Canada became paramount. In all three major political parties, nationalist tendencies emerged in response to the American takeover of the Canadian economy.

John Diefenbaker sounded the alarm. During the era when the Liberal Party was the political embodiment of the branch-plant economy, his populist-nationalism first revealed the anxiety Canadians felt about the American takeover of Canada. A small-town Tory nationalist from the prairies, Diefenbaker declared war on Liberal arrogance as personified by C.D. Howe. In his 1957 and 1958 election campaigns, he struck an unmistakably nationalist chord when he talked of a "northern vision," whose central idea was the completion of Canadian nation building by opening up the resources of the North. Once he entered office, however, Diefenbaker did virtually nothing to increase Canadian economic independence—apart from making the first great wheat sales to China despite strong objections from the Kennedy administration in Washington.

Liberal economic nationalism was first promoted during the 1950s by Walter Gordon, who was to remain a nationalist during his years in the cabinets of Lester B. Pearson and Pierre Trudeau, and for years after he left active politics. Gordon was much more systematic in his opposition to American domination of the Canadian economy than Diefenbaker had been. Under his influence, federal government inquiries into foreign ownership were undertaken—resulting in the *Watkins Report* in the late 1960s and the *Gray Report* in the early 1970s. A not inconsiderable program of economic nationalism was then developed in the Liberal Party. Among its accomplishments were: the Foreign Investment Review Agency (FIRA), to oversee foreign investments in Canada and to ensure that they were of significant benefit to Canada; Petro-Canada, the publicly owned petroleum company that was established in the mid-1970s as a fully integrated Canadian presence in an industry overwhelmingly owned by foreigners; new rules for foreign publications, such as *Time* and *Reader's Digest*, to prevent them from soaking up a huge amount of Canadian advertising; and the most controversial of all, the National Energy Policy (NEP) of 1980, whose goal was 50 percent Canadian ownership of the petroleum industry by the year 1990.

A nationalist wing also developed among social democrats, who felt the same impulses that were stirring in the Conservative and Liberal parties in the 1960s. In many ways, these nationalists had an easier time of it in the NDP than in the other two parties, making their eventual problems within the party all the more surprising. Nationalist influences among the New Democrats in the 1960s came from a variety of sources. The editor of the *Canadian Dimension*, economist Cy Gonick, was one of the most vigorous exponents of the new left-nationalist position. Charles Taylor, the McGill University philosopher who was also a political analyst and who was for a time considered a likely future leader of the federal NDP, wrote and lectured extensively on the subject. Economist Kari Levitt wrote a pioneering work, highly influential among social democrats, on foreign ownership and the branch plant economy, *Silent Surrender*. And George Grant's book *Lament for a Nation: The Defeat of Canadian Nationalism* had an unprecedented impact on young social democrats following its appearance in 1965.

Among social democrats, the idea of greater government intervention in the economy to halt or even reverse the rise of foreign ownership encountered no ideological obstacles of the kind encountered among those Liberals and Conservatives who were strongly committed to the concept of the free market economy. There were, however, two important barriers to economic nationalism within the NDP. The first had to do with the prominent position of U.S.-based unions in the party. In the 1960s, the predominant unions affiliated with the NDP were the large industrial unions, the Canadian sections of the United Steelworkers of America and the United Auto Workers. As we have already seen, these international unions had been assiduously wooed by David Lewis in forging the ties which ultimately transformed the CCF into the NDP.

The Canadian leaders of the international unions connected with the NDP were highly sensitive to the criticism that ultimate power in their organizations rested with their parent unions south of the border. A policy against foreign ownership, the branch-plant economy and American control in general would inevitably raise the issue of Canadian unionism. As we have seen, this was an issue they did not want raised in any shape or form.

The other important barrier to economic nationalism in the NDP concerned public ownership. Among the remedies to foreign control of key sectors of the Canadian economy, public ownership had always ranked high. And this tradition of public ownership, whether at the federal or the provincial level, had little to do with social democracy. Tory nationalism had been the crucial spawning ground for public ownership in Canada, and it was the federal

Liberals who in the 1930s took "Tory" initiatives in broadcasting and central banking by firmly establishing the Canadian Broadcasting Corporation and the Bank of Canada as public sector entities. This was followed by the creation of crown corporations by the Liberals during the Second World War.

For their part, social democratic governments did little to increase public ownership. There were experiments in the manufacturing, transportation and energy sectors, the most important of which were undertaken in Saskatchewan. But social democratic governments were much more noteworthy for their crucial initiatives in social policy than they were for initiatives in public ownership.

An important exception to this was the role played by the federal leadership of the NDP in pressuring Pierre Trudeau's Liberal government to establish Petro-Canada. Between 1972 and 1974, when David Lewis and the New Democrats held the balance of power in Parliament, they put pressure on the government to create a crown corporation in the petroleum sector. One reason the NDP made much of the issue was that David Lewis and other leading New Democrats had felt enormous pressure from the party's left-wing nationalists to advocate public takeovers of major foreign-owned petroleum companies. (In the end, the Trudeau government transformed Petro-Canada into a reality only after the election of July 1974, when the Liberals regained a majority in the House of Commons.)

The position of the NDP leadership on public ownership had already been set in the period before economic nationalism became a force to be reckoned with. When the CCF adopted the Winnipeg Declaration in 1956, it made the issue a much less important part of policy than it had been in the Regina Manifesto. The doctrinal change was understood by David Lewis, its chief proponent, as crucial to formulating policies that would appeal to labour. But to long-time social democrats, it was also seen as a shift toward the political centre. Within the ranks of Canadian social democracy, debates about the place of public ownership in economic policy were seen as discussions about how left wing or centrist the party ought to be. So as a consequence of the ideological trappings associated with public ownership, the debate about it in the CCF and the NDP was quite removed from the broader Canadian consideration of the issue.

It always struck me as a little curious that the most virulent denunciations of public ownership I ever heard were at NDP conventions. In a country in which the policy played an important role in transportation, communications, energy and even some manufacturing, it seemed strange that the idea of extending public ownership was regularly denounced at social democratic conventions as puerile leftism. At times, in debates in the early 1970s about public ownership in the petroleum sector, I felt as though Canada and its urgent problems with foreign control of a critical industry had been left behind in favour of an abstract ideological tangle.

The debate between the left nationalists and the mainstream party leadership of the NDP dramatically increased the profile of the issues of foreign control and industrial strategy within the NDP. Party leaders made frequent public pronouncements on foreign ownership, the limitations of the branch-plant economy and the implementation of an industrial strategy. But despite the increased visibility of these issues within the NDP, the underlying social democratic analysis of society and the economy did not change. Although the foreign ownership issue, by its very nature, raised questions about who ran the economy and to what ends, Canadian social democracy stayed within the postwar Keynesian paradigm, in which fiscal and monetary policies were the big levers and enhanced social programs were the chief goal. If social democracy can be thought of as a train, then economic nationalism was just an additional boxcar added on at the end, with no real thought about how it affected the rest of the vehicle.

The nationalists in all three parties had a major impact on the thinking of Canadians. But the continentalists, with their close ties to business, were also gaining in ideological coherence. This was due, in part, to the Americanization of the mainstream branches of economics and the social sciences.

Mainstream economists believe that Canada is, and always has been, an illogical economic entity, one whose very existence is an affront to principles of the free marketplace. It is no exaggeration to say that as a profession, Canadian economists have been dedicated to ending the very notion of a national economy that is separate from that of the United States. (If it is traitorous to plan for the demise of one's country, then Canadian economists taken as a whole have been guilty of treason. But since the very concept of treason is a nonmarket construct, economists would respond to this critique by regarding it as an hypothesis that is not quantifiable.)

Beginning in the mid-1970s, a potent new combination of forces advocated free trade with the United States and, later, the adoption of a conservative "globalization agenda." These forces were to include two key probusiness think tanks, the C.D. Howe Institute and the Fraser Institute, as well as the business media, (led by the *Globe and Mail*) and the Business Council on National Issues. These voices of Canadian capitalism became the country's most powerful advocates of the neoconservative agenda developed in the United States and Britain. In these countries, which spawned the new conservatism, the movement aimed at tearing up a domestic postwar social contract. In Canada, the focus was different.

The long march of Canadian capitalism to the promised land of the new conservatism involved a two-stage revolution. During stage one, Canada would be won over to the acceptance of a comprehensive free trade regime with the United States. In the second stage, Canadian economic, social, cultural and educational policies would be harmonized to fit within the American mould. The revolutionaries who carried out the campaign understood that they must not confuse the two stages, that they must deny during stage one what they had in mind for stage two.

In fundamental respects, Canadian neoconservatism was a hand-me-down from abroad. Only in its strategy for a two-stage revolution did it display originality. During the great free trade debate of the 1980s, the promoters of free trade developed a mantra for dealing with the question of what effect economic union with the United States would have on Canadian social and cultural policies. Repeatedly, they denied that there was any connection between the two. There was no reason, pro-free-trade academics like John Crispo and Richard Lipsey liked to say, for increased trade with the United States to force Canada to harmonize its social policies with those in the United States. For the opponents of free trade to suggest such a consequence, they insisted, was to engage in scare tactics.

Although he was an unlikely leader to bring this ideological crusade to fruition, Brian Mulroney became the political front man for the great changes that the new forces of the right had in mind. (Before he became the chieftain of the free trade crusade, he had gone on the record as saying that he did not favour a comprehensive free trade deal with the United States.[3]) In another era, Mulroney might have been quite content to stick with the traditional position of his party on a great issue such as free trade. And, of course, the traditional position of the Conservative Party, dating from the era of Sir John A. Macdonald, was opposition to free trade with the United States. It was only in the circumstances of a vast transformation of the very definition of conservatism in Canada—from the nationalism of the past to the continentalism-globalism of the 1980s—that Brian Mulroney could become the instrument for an initiative so deeply antagonistic to the traditions of his party.

The Canada-U.S. Free Trade Agreement (FTA) dramatically altered the environment for Canadian economic decision making. In effect, it became no less than a fourth level of Canadian government. Indeed, as a treaty signed with a superpower, it became a fundamental law of the land, a kind of second Canadian constitution. For instance, under the doctrine of "national treatment" as spelled out in the FTA, American firms gained the right to be accorded identical treatment to that meted out to Canadian firms. This effectively abolished the right of Canadian governments to pursue an industrial strategy centred on the development of domestic firms. In an economy in which American multinationals occupied a uniquely strong, historically entrenched position in the manufacturing and resource sectors, the national treatment provision in the FTA dealt a severe blow to the very idea of Canadian economic nationalism.

As we have seen, the 1988 federal election resulted in a decisive victory by the continentalists over the nationalists. Even though in that election 52 percent of voters supported the Liberals and the NDP, both committed to tearing up the FTA, the Conservatives won a majority of seats in Parliament with 44 percent of the popular vote.

Since the FTA entered into force on January 1, 1989, nationalists have been in a quandary about what they should advocate. The electoral debate about the extension of free trade to include Mexico in the North American Free Trade Agreement (NAFTA) was a small affair in comparison with the debate of 1988. By the time of the next federal election in 1993, Jean Chrétien had replaced John Turner as leader of the Liberal Party, and Audrey McLaughlin had replaced Ed Broadbent as leader of the NDP. While the NDP continued to espouse the abrogation of the FTA and remained opposed to NAFTA, the Liberals changed their position dramatically.

During the 1993 federal election campaign, the position of the Liberals on the FTA and NAFTA was very much like that of Liberal Prime Minister William Lyon Mackenzie King on conscription during the Second World War. The Chrétien Liberals advocated free trade if necessary, but not necessarily free trade. According to their platform—the famed Red Book—the Liberals would endorse free trade only if significant improvements were made to the deals that had been negotiated by the Mulroney Tories. For most Canadians, the free trade era had begun on January 1, 1989, with the implementation of the FTA, so the NAFTA debate never really caught fire, and the tepid and equivocal position of the Liberals on the issue was never subjected to any serious scrutiny.

The Liberal election victory was quickly followed by capitulation on NAFTA, a capitulation only slightly covered over by the fig leaf provided by the side deals negotiated by U.S. President

Bill Clinton on labour and the environment. For years, the Liberal Party had fought the Tory free trade agenda, a fight that reached its crescendo in John Turner's brave battle in the 1988 election campaign. But the dispute concluded with a whimper when Jean Chrétien ratified a trade deal that was virtually unchanged from the one negotiated by Brian Mulroney.

Where were the nationalists to go, after this dispiriting denouement?

So far, the answer to this fundamental question has been uncertain. The greatest victory won by the right in the implementation of free trade is the conviction among Canadians that, indeed, a new age of world history is at hand, that globalization is an unstoppable, inexorable force, and that the sovereignty of the nation-state is a thing of the past.

Faced with this apparent turning of an historic page, the nationalists and the left were faced with rethinking both their analysis of the world and their political strategy. How were progressive Canadians to understand the new global age? Were they to accept the idea that the nation-state was inexorably in decline and that progressive politics now had to move simultaneously to the local and global levels, with the national level inevitably rendered less important?

Since the implementation of the FTA and NAFTA, there has been, for the most part, a great silence on this subject. Beyond day-to-day battles in defence of the eroding welfare state, workers' rights and the environment, the nationalists and the left have so far not developed a renewed strategic vision. Without one, or the prospect of one, the right remains entrenched on the strategic high ground.

In working out a post-free-trade strategic position, the left has to begin at the beginning—the condition of Canadian capitalism on the eve of the twenty-first century. The establishment of the FTA and NAFTA does not mean the end of the battle between the "parties" of nationalism and continentalism. It helps to realize that NAFTA was not a product of American strength, but of American weakness. One of the most potent arguments among legislators in Washington in favour of NAFTA was that if the United States did not make a trade deal with Mexico, Japanese business would become predominant south of the Rio Grande. In the postwar years, when the United States held unquestioned hegemony, such arguments would have been ludicrous, but not so today. The American socioeconomic system has entered a period of chronic malaise, and Canadian business and the Canadian state have thrown in their lot with this declining superpower to an extent unparalleled in the past. It is a fact of crucial importance for Canadians, indeed for the very survival of Canada.

What is the nature of the society to which we have linked our destiny?

The broadest measure of the American decline in economic power in comparison with its competitors is that in 1945, the U.S. accounted for 50 percent of global economic output, while half a century later, it accounted for only 20 percent.[4] The enormous shift in relative economic weight is evident when we note that the European Union now has the largest economy in the world, and Japan, with a population half the size of that of the U.S., has an economy that is *more* than half the size. This broad shift in economic weight has been accompanied by crucial qualitative shifts. Japan has replaced the United States as the world's leading net creditor nation, a position the U.S. had sustained from 1919 until the mid-eighties. In the decades following 1960, American industry was also overtaken by European and Japanese industry in a long list of sectors—machinery, chemicals, automobiles, microchips and the deployment of computer-driven technology.

In terms of relative sizes of GDP, status as a creditor nation and industrial prowess, the United States has experienced a sharp decline in relation to its leading competitors. This decline has been paralleled by increasing strains within the American social environment, which have come ever more to the attention of analysts in other countries. Several examples of European concern about the direction U.S. society is taking were cited in a column written in Paris by William Pfaff for the *Los Angeles Times*.[5] In the spring of 1995, Pfaff writes, Sir Michael Howard, a British historian, told members of the French Institute of International Relations that the internal problems faced by Americans "are quite literally terrifying," a view shared by a Brussels-based analyst, Philippe Grasset, who argues that the United States is gripped by what Pfaff calls "a solipsistic individualism in society and economy which is deeply subversive of America's own social and economic stability." These analysts are referring to America's problems with race, underclass and violence. Pfaff concludes: "Today the United States is widely perceived as having, in important respects, set itself upon a dangerous new course, which it does not fully understand. Others find this disquieting, even rather frightening. The American condition now is seen by them as a threat rather than a promise."[6]

At the heart of the American societal crisis is a division between rich and poor that is wider than in any other advanced industrial country, and a division between black and white that adds an element of caste to the character of American social class. This societal crisis has been gravely exacerbated by the fact that the United States is the site of the most extreme free enterprise regime in any advanced country. The crisis has now become so visible that it requires willful blindness to continue to regard the United States as a healthy, functional society. Nonetheless, exactly this kind of willful blindness is evident among American and Canadian elites in their discussions of the American socioeconomic model.

The idea that the American model is the best in the world is continually and explicitly proclaimed by American corporate and political leaders. In Canada, the acceptance by similar elites of economic union with the United States through free trade amounts to their implicit acceptance of the American model. In fact, as economic and social integration with the United States proceeds, Canadian elites have grown ever more adamant in their willingness to identify with the goals and modalities of the American model. A previous generation of Ontario elites would never have sat back and accepted a hard right government like that of Mike Harris, whose sensibility is that of a country-club Republican from the American Midwest.

The continentalism of Canadian business calls into question the ability of Canada to endure in more than nominal terms over the long run. As we have seen, the support of key business sectors was indispensable to the viability of the National Policy. Laurier's reciprocity deal with the United States was defeated in the election of 1911 because the banks, the railways and major manufacturers organized to oppose it. On the other hand, in the 1988 election, free trade was victorious because Canadian business—foreign as well as domestic corporations in Canada, and small business as well as big—fought hard to make sure the Mulroney government was re-elected.

Now that business has gone over to continentalism, could a coalition of other social groupings serve as a viable basis for the rebirth of Canada?

The potential for such a coalition of interests was certainly displayed, if briefly, in the election campaign of 1988. Such a demonstration of the ability of the nonbusiness elements of the country to come together was suggestive, but falls short of proving that a basic alternative is actually possible. Only those who have not bought into the neoconservative conception of state and society can be the source of the values on which a new option might be established. And that focuses the spotlight squarely on social democrats.

With their nonmarket values, social democrats have already played a crucial role in defining Canada since the Second World War. In an era when national institutions and national standards have been disintegrating, medicare, beleaguered though it now is, has become a pillar of Canadian identity. Without doubt, universal health care is the greatest contribution that social democrats have made to Canadian society. Medicare is both substance and symbol. It guarantees high-quality health care to Canadians, who have only to look to their neighbours and friends across the border to see an alternative system that costs more and leaves tens of millions of people with no coverage and many millions of others with inadequate coverage.

In a dark time, medicare is a beacon from the past that symbolizes caring and compassion and reminds us that Canadians have been capable of doing important things together in the past. If we look further into the past, beyond medicare, we encounter the tradition of Tory nationalism, the indispensable outlook from which transcontinental Canada was constructed. While Tory nationalism has all but disappeared from the landscape, with the honourable exception of voices such as that of Dalton Camp, social democracy remains a powerful current in Canadian society. Alone among the major political perspectives in contemporary Canada, social democracy provides a rationale, integral to its own logic, upon which Canadians can do important things together in the future.

Emphatically, that extends to the relationship between English Canada and Quebec. One consequence of the rise of the new right has been to undermine the will to seek a new partnership to renew the Canadian federation. Historically, English Canadians and Quebecers understood that living together in one country made both of the "solitudes" more capable of surviving next door to the United States. The right-wing drive for free trade and globalization has cut away at the very idea that the peoples of the northern half of the continent are capable of making common arrangements that matter. The right rejects the notion of a "Canadian economy" separate from that of the United States, and it attacks the idea of Canadian social policies which differ substantially from those south of the border.

While the unfettered market leads inexorably to the end of Canada, a new left can only make progress toward its societal goals as long as it is dedicated to the survival of Canada.

CHAPTER 9

TWO SOCIETIES

THROUGHOUT the industrialized world, two societies coexist with one another, or to put it more accurately, two societies coexist, one within the other. The values of the two societies are discordant, and the rising conflict between them points the way toward social transformation.

The first of the two societies, highly visible to everyone, is the dominant decision-making order. It is market-centred and run by those who are imbued with corporate values, whether they make decisions in the corporate sector or in government. These decision makers have developed a characteristic, if remarkable, tunnel vision, which allows them to focus on what they regard as important and to shut out all else. And what they regard as important is entirely predictable. Economic return or cost-effectiveness is not the main thing according to this mindset, it is the only thing. Television or newspaper reports of economic decisions have become monolithic in reflecting this ethic as the sole intelligent basis for both private and public sector decisions.

As an example, the federal government decides to privatize the Canadian National Railways system, which has been in the public sector since the latter days of the First World War. Why? First of all, the deficit-conscious government is desperate for cash, so it doesn't mind disposing of capital assets, even though such short-term stratagems will make no long-run contribution to solving the debt problem. On the running of the CNR itself, it is argued that privatization will draw in fresh capital, to rebuild the railway at a time of fiscal constraint. Beyond that, privatization is seen as a way to offload the nonmarket responsibilities that have historically been an important aspect of the CNR. Chief among those responsibilities has been providing a freight transportation system for small and relatively remote communities, many of them in the Prairies.

Privatization is what a government turns to when it has locked itself into short-term economic return as its only significant yardstick. In the past, national and regional development and the well-being of communities would have weighed heavily in determining the fate of a national carrier such as the CNR. Today, such factors carry little weight with the federal government, which has determined that the only criterion truly worth considering is the overall competitiveness of the Canadian rail system as compared with the American rail system. (Ruefully, we could remark that if these critical yardsticks had been applied in the late nineteenth century, there would never have been a transcontinental Canada.) Vanished from the calculus of the government is the idea of long-term investment of capital to broaden the capacity of the economy, improve its infrastructure and, rhetoric notwithstanding, improve the productive skills of the labour force.

In the private sector, decisions are also taken with a ruthless eye to the bottom line; scant thought is given to the impact of decisions on employees or jobs. Indeed, in contemporary capitalism, the corporate executives who receive the highest praise from their peers are those who are particularly merciless in downsizing. In February 1995, the *Financial Times* named Victor Young of Fishery Products International Ltd. its chief executive officer of the year. Looking like a very fit senior naval officer, Young's smiling photo graced the *FT*'s cover page. In making its choice, the *FT* explained that Victor Young had completely turned his ailing company around. In the process, the *FT* said, "nearly three of every four FPI employees—more than 6,000 in all—were laid off, most of them residents of single-industry Newfoundland towns."[1] Although the *FT* said not a further word about the fate of the 6,000 who lost their jobs, the story had a happy ending. FPI has been restructured, much to the benefit of shareholders.

That one man could be seen as an exemplar and that six thousand could be sacrificed so blithely takes us to the heart of the new capitalism. There is nothing unusual about the story of FPI. Indeed, in many cases companies are laying workers off at the same time as their profits are increasing, as the following cases from 1995 illustrate: General Motors Canada, profits up 36 percent, decrease in employees 2,500; Inco, profits up 3,281 percent, decrease in employees 1,963; CP Rail, profits up 75 percent, decrease in employees 1,500; Bank of Montreal, profits up 20 percent, decrease in employees 1,428; Canadian Imperial Bank of Commerce, profits up 14 percent, decrease in employees 1,289; Shell Canada, profits up 63 percent, decrease in employees 471; Imperial Oil, profits up 43 percent, decrease in employees 452; and Toronto-Dominion Bank, profits up 16 percent, decrease in employees 354.[2]

In the tunnel vision of the new capitalism, there are two humanities: the private sector players and all the others. The private sector players include corporate executives, entrepreneurs both large and small, as well as those affluent enough to acquire substantial amounts of capital—and this last group includes many highly rewarded professionals, such as doctors, lawyers and accountants. The political goal of the leadership of the private sector players is to continue to shift societal decision making away from the state and a host of public and quasipublic institutions to the private sector. To an overwhelming extent, the state at all levels is now in the hands of those who share this vision and whose top decision makers aspire to a comfortable place for themselves within this societal order.

According to the ethic of the new capitalism, it is the private sector players alone who are fully human; everyone else on the planet is at best a means to an end, or at worst a problem to be managed. The six thousand Newfoundland workers who lost their jobs at the hands of Victor Young were useful to the company once upon a time. But when they were no longer useful, that was that. The financial—if not the long-term societal—interests of the stockholders had to prevail. Calling this ethic into question always provokes the wrath of the defenders of the system. I have watched them ask, in righteous indignation: What should the company do, sacrifice its shareholders on behalf of its workers? And of course, given the rules of the game they are playing, it's a perfectly good question. If one company were to play by a different set of rules, its executives would quickly be abandoned by shareholders, and its competitors would soon take advantage of its deviation from the strict dictates of the market.

The problem is not with the rules, but with the game—a game that reduces economic decisions, and the treatment of the vast majority of the population, to a dreary and inexorable utilitarianism. Jobs, lives and communities are treated as though they are nothing more than byproducts of the system, mere means toward the satisfaction of ends that lie elsewhere. And those ends are never in doubt. They are the maximization of profit for company shareholders and the assurance of skyrocketing levels of remuneration for high-level executives, the only pertinent issue being how best this can be achieved. Even decisions with apparently humane overtones—to treat employees with consideration, to solicit their input, to show concern for the environment, to contribute to charity and the arts—are seen as means toward the same end.

Ironically, the reduction of major economic decisions to a dreary utilitarianism has been sapping the moral fibre of the West ever since its triumph over Soviet communism. Particularly in North America, economic and political culture has been reduced to a single myth—that the market system is the most efficacious way to make major decisions. In place of religious and humanistic ethical systems, which bring subtlety and complexity to societal questions, there has been a reduction of morality to the single pole of marketplace utility. For a civilization with immensely rich ethical and philosophical traditions, this reduction of the basis for decision making to a late-twentieth-century version of "might is right"—with corporations standing in for nineteenth-century armed states—has delivered us into an ethical wasteland.

During the Christmas season in 1994, I had lunch with fellow political scientist Stephen Clarkson in the Great Hall at Hart

House at the University of Toronto. During my undergraduate years at that university, I spent countless hours in the reading rooms, coffee shop, dining room, and athletic facilities of this extraordinary building, which was constructed through a donation from the Massey family at the end of the First World War. What is noteworthy about Hart House is its enduring character, its abundant evidence of quality for the sake of quality, of the aesthetic for the sake of the aesthetic. Hart House was conceived by one of the leading families of Canadian capitalism, yet no market-driven tunnel vision prevailed here. As Clarkson and I lunched in the nearly deserted Great Hall, we shared a sense of an era whose time had passed, of a society that had come and gone—indeed, of a country that had come and gone. Today's dismal utilitarianism will leave few monuments behind it to capture the imagination of the future; its private and public decision makers will build nothing beautiful, will undertake nothing uplifting and will do very little for the sake of people that is not justified on the basis of measurable market benefits.

Fortunately, the story does not end there.

Another society exists within the exo-skeleton of the one just described. And that society is not subject to the tunnel vision of dismal utilitarianism. It is all around us, although when we analyse great economic and political questions, it is scarcely visible.

The other society is made up of communities based in every region of the country that have formed around churches, trade unions, schools, cultural bodies, associations of various kinds, and sporting and recreational societies. The values system within these communities is vastly at odds with the global, market-driven economy of the late twentieth century.

The values of this second society can be felt in any of the tens of thousands of decent public schools in the country. I think of the case of the French-language public school my children attended in Toronto. For months, the grade six class prepared a musical play for the evening of their graduation. Under the supervision of teachers, they fashioned costumes and theatrical sets, chose music, learned their lines, developed song and dance routines and then staged it all in front of family members, friends and others close to the school, including those who drove their schoolbuses. I was impressed by the dignity and effectiveness of the teachers and the fine self-possession of those who were graduating (from grade six) and who already had many of the qualities of young women and young men.

What accounted for the energy, vitality and creativity of all those who participated in the event? Certainly, it was something other than dismal utilitarianism. Those who put huge amounts of energy into the project were not being paid overtime to do so; career benefits would have been minimal at most. And yet, here was an outpouring of initiative and creativity that had nothing at all to do with the profit motive or the bottom line.

Clearly a different ethic was at work from the one that dominates the decisions of major business and state institutions in our society. We can call it a human-centred ethic, whose end is the personal development and fulfillment of a group of people. What clearly distinguishes this moral system from that which prevails in business or in the major decision making of the state is that within it, human beings are ends in themselves rather than the means to some other end.

How is it that the supposedly dominant ethic in our society can be so easily put aside in favour of an alternative, human-centred ethic?

Alternative value systems have always existed cheek by jowl within capitalism. In earlier times, the proportion of people involved directly in the market economy was much smaller than at present. Subsistence agriculture and lower levels of participation by women in the paid workforce meant that the "nonmarket" realm of economic life was significantly larger than it currently is. Indeed, the rearing and education of children, rudimentary though it may have been, provided an essential basis for the very existence of the market economy. Without an enormous output of unpaid labour, the development of a workforce and of a market for the capitalist economy would have been impossible. In terms of ethics, those participating in the unpaid realm were working to sustain themselves and their families, their goals having to do with those around them.

Without the existence of unpaid labour and of the human-centred ethic on which it was based, the profit-oriented ethic of capitalism would have been an utter failure. It has always been the case that the individualist ethic so prized in capitalism, and the competitive economic model, would have been unsustainable without the social cohesion provided by a cooperative, human-centred ethic in other, essential realms of life.

The system of unpaid labour remains indispensable today. Without this labour (most of it still done by women, whether or not they also have jobs), children would not be raised to become available to capitalism as full-fledged consumers and labour force participants. Efforts to quantify the value of such unpaid labour in market terms are subject to inherent limitations, but recent Canadian attempts to do so have put this work in the range of 35 or 40 percent of the size of the formal market economy.

Today, the nonmarket portion of society has burgeoned far beyond the unpaid labour of the household to include the myriad communities mentioned earlier. Never in history has the nonmarket portion of society been as well informed, articulate and clear about its values as it is today. And that fact is of immense importance as the crisis of the dominant order plays itself out.

If these two societies and two ethics coexist, there is no doubt about which one of them occupies the strategic position and has the initiative. The initiative is in the hands of the corporate and political leadership of the new capitalism. And although that leadership is not monolithic, for the most part it is closely linked to the new right.

Today we are in the midst of a vast transformation of capitalism. The mould of societal relationships set in the postwar decades has been decisively broken in a global offensive by business. Those who are propelling capitalism along its new course—corporate executives, investors, fund managers, bankers—want the market to make ever more of society's decisions, and are determined to strip away the decision-making power of democratically elected governments. Private decision makers are using their control of capital to subordinate everyone else to their will, determining in the process whether regions prosper or decay and people work or are unemployed.

The neoconservative assault, the most pronounced feature of the politics of the new capitalism, is partly a response to the perceived weakness of the political left and centre, and partly a response to what are seen by neoconservatives as the necessities of life for contemporary capitalism. And as its offensive has rolled forward, in an effort to tear up the great compromise of the postwar decades, the right has learned how to divide its opponents.

In the new capitalism, social heterogeneity has worked for the right and against the left. During the postwar decades, when full employment was the rule rather than the exception, the principally white and male working class achieved a fairly high degree of solidarity. Because almost everyone who wanted to work had a job, labour enjoyed considerable bargaining power. It was one of the few times in the history of capitalism when there was no large reserve army of unemployed from whose ranks new and cheaper labour could be recruited. While there was huge immigration in the postwar decades, immigrants were absorbed relatively quickly into the employed workforce, and few people lived for long periods on social assistance. It was not so easy then to fan flames of resentment among those who had jobs toward those who did not.

And because national economies were much less open to outside commerce and capital flows than is the case today, while companies could and did close their doors, and could and did move from region to region, the ability of business to play off labour in one country against labour in other parts of the world was much less pronounced. By and large, workers and their union leaders did not have to think about comparative wage costs from country to country in their negotiating strategy, as they certainly now must.

In today's society, with its multiracial character, diverse lifestyles, changing gender relationships, and its permanently high level of unemployment and underemployment, the cleavages, and potential cleavages, within the wage and salary earning classes are enormously greater than they were in the 1950s and 1960s. One feature of social heterogeneity is the so-called "new class." Not only has employment in manufacturing declined dramatically in favour of employment in the service sector, but a highly educated technoprofessional "new class" has developed on a scale that was unimaginable several decades ago. Made up of university and college professors, technicians, accountants, lawyers and others doing knowledge-based work, this large cohort has derived its relative well-being from its educational credentials. The members of this group have a complex relationship with the capitalist class, some associating more or less with the capitalist class and others identifying more with the working class. Those who service business, such as lawyers and accountants, tend to identify with business and take on its political outlook. Others, such as educators, are much less closely aligned with the attitudes of business, and often identify with other social elements.

Despite the societal transformation of recent decades, the fundamental fault line in contemporary capitalism remains the division between business and the rest of society. Throughout the history of capitalism, there have been episodes in which the gap in power between capitalists and the working class has widened profoundly and then narrowed. These episodes are both political and economic, for the relationship between social classes is neither a purely economic nor a purely political phenomenon. It is the outcome of both aspects of what should properly be analysed as a single system.

Social scientists have often attempted to reduce social class to quantifiable factors such as income, education and type of employment. But the living essence of social classes is far from being captured in such statistics. As British historian E.P. Thompson revealed in his epic *The Making of the English Working Class*,[3] social classes are cultural and political, as well as economic, entities. They develop traditions that deeply affect their ability to respond to new challenges to act cohesively. Just because autoworkers in Paris, Turin, Oshawa and Detroit all face similar circumstances, working for similarly massive auto companies, does not mean that they respond to these circumstances in anything like identical ways. The way they adapt to novel pressures is open to a wide range of possibilities.

Historically, capital has always taken the initiative to widen the effective terrain on which business operates, when opportunity or necessity has presented itself. New technologies and the rise and fall of economic competitors prompt changes in how primary products are extracted, in the location of production facilities and in the marketing of goods and services. And when business takes the offensive to reorganize its regime in the face of such pressures and opportunities, labour is thrown on the defensive and rendered less capable of promoting its own interests. But typically, while the development of new techniques of production and the widening of markets initially throw labour into disarray—resulting in new rifts within the working class, of which capital can take advantage—the working class has historically adapted quite effectively to the challenges, forging new alliances and refashioning its politics and even its culture in the face of the new challenge. The pattern has been long established: capital breaks the mould of society and politics as it reinvents the scope of capitalism, and then, in time, labour rethinks its politics and creates new alliances to counter the power of capital. The pattern has repeated itself ever since the original Industrial Revolution in the late eighteenth century.

The periodic widening and narrowing of the gap between the power of capital and the power of labour is analogous to the historic relationship within warfare between offence and defence. As offensive weaponry advances, warfare that exhibits a high degree of mobility gains the advantage. A period of this kind is characteristically followed by gains on the defensive side, which alters the balance yet again and which results in a period of more stationary warfare. If the railway and the rifle opened the way for a warfare of mobility and offence in the mid-nineteenth century, the subsequent development of the machine gun favoured the defence;

later still, the development of the tank once again shifted the balance—this time in favour of the offence.

Capital's offensive in the 1990s is aimed at using its advantageous position in the new global economy to attack the gains made by the rest of society during the postwar decades. Throughout the industrialized world, the offensive features what we can call the "debt game." The game derives from the enormous power of the bond market and financial institutions in the new capitalism.

The essentials of the debt game were exposed in Linda McQuaig's book, *Shooting the Hippo*.[4] McQuaig showed how the Bank of Canada has served the interests of bondholders at the expense of the vast majority of Canadians. Since 1988 the policy of the Bank of Canada has been to achieve price stability, or "zero inflation," as the policy is known. As a consequence, in the early 1990s Canada ended up with the highest real interest rates in any G-7 country. While the price stability policy is associated with John Crow, the governor of the Bank of Canada who initiated it, the policy continues under Crow's successor Gordon Thiessen. The result of high interest rates was that businesses couldn't afford to borrow to expand, consumers were pushed out of the market for big ticket items such as automobiles and appliances, and the housing market was crushed by excessive mortgage rates. Crow's policy played a huge part in driving Canada into the most serious recession experienced in the G-7.

As for Ottawa's deficit, McQuaig concluded that the Bank of Canada's punitive monetary policy vastly worsened it. She wrote that, in 1992, "Close to two-thirds of the entire deficit was actually caused by the recession which the Bank of Canada played a major role in creating. And much of the remaining one-third of the deficit was due to the excessively high interest rates, also generated by the Bank of Canada."[5] A sporting analogy sheds further light on the debt game. If you were playing hockey and every time you got close enough to score a goal, the other team shifted the goal posts, you would object. Well, that's what happens in the economy of the industrialized world, where public sector debts are concerned. Everyone is familiar with the object of the debt game. To win, a country has to slash government spending to eliminate its deficit and then pay down the debt. If a country fails to do this, creditors push up interest rates, which has the twin effect of slowing the economy and steeply increasing the interest payments on the debt. But suppose a country does exactly what the world's creditors—the banks and the bond market—want it to do. What happens then?

In Canada, if Preston Manning were prime minister and all the premiers were clones of Mike Harris, the policy at all levels of government would be to make very deep cuts to public spending. As Linda McQuaig has argued, fighting the debt has given the right a highly effective weapon, one that enables it "to justify dismantling what is arguably the most admirable aspect of our society—our ability to collectively create strong public institutions and programs that serve us all."[6] But cuts to public spending, in addition to eliminating social programs, directly generate cuts to economic demand. If you cut public sector spending by—let's say—2 or 3 percent of Gross Domestic Product (GDP), that would easily be sufficient to throw the country into a serious recession.

Those who favour deep cuts to public spending as the way to pay down the debt like to draw an analogy between the economy and a household's income. They argue that if a household spends more than its income year after year, the result will be bankruptcy. To solve its problems, the household needs to reduce its spending, pay down its debt and live within its means. But when the leap is made from the household to the economy, one crucial unstated assumption is made: that the household's income will not be reduced when it cuts spending. Therefore, the ability to pay down the debt is unaffected. However, in the case of the economy, the unstated assumption does not hold. When government spending is cut, unemployment increases, the tax base is narrowed and economic demand declines, in turn prompting a reduction in the production of goods and services. While a household's income does not decline as it repays its debts, when government spends less, the actual size of the economy shrinks, which makes the repayment of debt much more onerous.

If Preston Manning were prime minister and leaders of a similar persuasion held office in the provinces, draconian cuts to social programs would be the order of the day. Ironically, given the immense hype this option has received from the business press and probusiness think tanks, the full Preston Manning prescription would not achieve the repayment of the public debt. On the contrary, it would provoke a huge wave of business bankruptcies and would seriously narrow the tax base. Despite all the pain that undoubtedly would be generated, the fiscal crisis would remain unresolved.

The neoconservative prescription for paying down the debt is a variation on the hopeless economic prescription that prolonged the Great Depression of the 1930s. The neoconservative cure makes most people worse off. But one thing it certainly does not do is eliminate the problem of the debt. The only way to actually do that is to increase economic growth, create jobs and broaden the tax base. That's because, if your actual goal is to pay down the debt and reduce interest payments on it, a broadened tax base is indispensable.

In principle, increased economic growth could happen in one of two ways: Canada could benefit from an extremely powerful surge of exports to the United States (don't hold your breath) or the government could take steps to stimulate the domestic economy. (Remember, the flat domestic economy has been at the heart of our economic woes for years.) But even if rapid economic growth could be successfully launched, there's still a catch. Counterintuitive though it may appear, bankers and bond market managers are highly alarmed by rapid economic growth, fearing that it will open the door to a resumption of inflation—and inflation is what money lenders dislike above all else, for the simple reason that it cuts into their rate of return.

Today, creditors are in a stronger position to impose their will on the global economic system than ever before. In the early postwar period, an era of greater government financial regulations and of fixed exchange rates, creditors enjoyed no such capacity to reduce growth. Indeed, rapid economic expansion proved to be the way countries paid down the massive debts they had accumulated during the war. Today, however, the bond market uses its power to protect its rate of return whenever economic growth gathers steam. As soon as the economy begins to grow robustly, the bond market falls, and that pushes interest rates up. The consequence is to restrain economic growth, which prevents the overheating that creditors fear. And, of course, what that does is to prevent the broadening of the tax base, which is the necessary precondition for paying down the debt and reducing the interest rate burden under which the public sector labours.

Under the present rules, only the bankers and bond market can win at the debt game. Indeed, the most powerful forces within the new capitalism are happy with the game just as it is. Their real goal is not to pay down the public sector debt, but to go on profiting from the high public sector, corporate and personal debts that are such a prominent characteristic of the contemporary economy.

Canadians are already running very fast on the treadmill in an effort to outpace their accumulated debts. For one thing, on the programs it delivers, the government of Canada has actually been running a surplus in most recent years. For another, once the federal government's planned cuts, announced in its budgets in 1995 and 1996, are fully implemented, Ottawa's programs will account for only 12 per cent of Gross Domestic Product (GDP), their lowest level as a proportion of GDP since the late 1940s.[7] Meanwhile, spending to pay down the debt continues to rise.

The debt crisis faced by Canadians has been analysed in a penetrating study undertaken by Dr. James Stanford, an economist with the Canadian Auto Workers. Dr. Stanford concludes that it is the combination of high interest rates and slower rates of economic growth that has caused the national debt to skyrocket. He estimates that 83 percent of the post-1981 growth of the debt-to-GDP ratio has been a consequence of higher rates of interest and lower rates of economic growth than prevailed prior to 1981. Had pre-1981 interest rates and economic growth rates prevailed, Canada's national debt would total only 30 percent of GDP, instead of the 72 percent it has now reached. Dr. Stanford's conclusion is stark: "To bring the current debt-to-GDP ratio of 72 percent down to just 50 percent over the next ten years, given current conditions, Canadian taxpayers would have to contribute operating surpluses—tax payments over and above the cost of government programs—totalling more than $470 billion."[8]

Those in Canada and abroad who hold the debt and are extracting usurious rates of interest on it need reminding of what happens when indebted societies are pushed too far. Today the whole of the industrialized world is strapped with a combined governmental, corporate and personal debt that has grown astronomically over the past two decades. In *The Future of the Market*,[9] Elmar Altvater, an economist at the Free University of Berlin, reminds us that most of the great debts in history did not actually get repaid. Altvater shows that the major turning points in modern history—the French Revolution, the American Civil War, the two world wars, and the Bolshevik Revolution—led to the repudiation of vast debts.

Even in less extreme circumstances, public debts have gone unpaid. A number of U.S. states repudiated their debts during the nineteenth century. And U.S. President Richard Nixon staged what amounted to a daylight robbery of foreign central banks in 1971 when he unilaterally announced that the United States would no longer redeem its dollars with gold. That left foreign central bankers holding tens of billions of dollars of inflated U.S. paper.

Will the present combined government, corporate and personal debt of the industrialized world actually be paid off? Altvater's conclusion makes it seem improbable: "Defaults and state bankruptcy have occurred so often that it is debt crisis rather than orderly repayment which seems to have been the norm."[10] So what is the fate of the debt? Will it continue to sit atop industrial societies, whittling away at social programs, widening the gap between rich and poor, and denying the young their right to work and take their place in society?

Just as the debt problem was created by the shifting balance of power within the new capitalism, its elimination as a central fact of our existence will undoubtedly be the consequence of further shifts. Just what changes in power relations would alleviate the debt crisis? Three types of developments are highly likely to play a part.

Rivalries and policy divergences among the leading economic powers are likely to feature prominently in breaking the hold of the debt on industrial societies.

The economic decline of the United States relative to Japan and Europe has made it vastly more difficult for the leading industrial powers to arrive at a unified approach. Divergences among the major powers have been evident since the collapse of the Bretton Woods fixed exchange rate system in the 1970s—despite the creation of the G-7.

Competition among the three leading economic powers—Japan, the U.S.A. and the EU—has tended to push them all, to a certain extent, in the direction of what can be called "competitive deflation." According to this strategy, governments in each trading bloc encourage business to cut costs (e.g., by reducing wages), so they can take advantage of export opportunities in the other blocs without incurring the disadvantages of reflating the bloc's economy. (When reflation—the stimulation of an economy—is achieved through tax cuts and increased public sector spending, there is a risk of trade deficits against those who have not stimulated their own economies and a probability of long-term balance-of-payments deficits. The United States experienced this in the 1980s, when the other powers took advantage of the Reagan reflation and ran up huge trade surpluses against the United States.)

Despite the pressures toward competitive deflation, there are also potent counterpressures. In each of the major economic blocs, important segments of business have a strong interest in reflation and a resumption of robust economic growth. Moreover, political leaders, under pressure from an electorate that has suffered from austerity, tend to favour policies that promote growth as elections draw near.

If one of the major blocs succeeds in achieving robust economic expansion, this will put enormous pressure on the other two to follow suit. Rapid growth in one of the blocs would shift economic influence away from bondholders toward other segments of business—manufacturers, retailers and the providers of many kinds of services. The example of such a shift in influence within business in one of the blocs will create pressures for similar shifts in the others.

Austerity policies, which have taken a heavy toll on the working and middle classes throughout the industrialized world, are generating pronounced political volatility. As political leaders, from conservatives to social democrats, preside over governments dedicated to austerity, they are watching their base of political support disintegrate.

Large segments of the working and middle classes have shifted their support from the political left to the right, and sometimes back again to the left. In France, the United States, in various regions of Canada and in the very different socioeconomic setting of Eastern Europe and the countries that make up the former Soviet Union, there are already abundant signs that governments that pursue austerity policies face the prospect of losing their legitimacy in a short period of time.

In the late autumn of 1995, a political earthquake in France was provoked by the Chirac-Juppé regime's proposed cuts to social programs and public services, leading to scenes highly reminiscent of the historic upheavals of 1968. For three weeks, hundreds of thousands of workers and students marched in the streets each day, bringing the country's transportation system to a halt and seriously affecting the national economy. In the tradition of direct working-class political action over the past two centuries, the crisis made it clear that conservative regimes can only press so far in taking back the employment and social policy gains workers have made, without provoking an immense political response. And it should not be forgotten that the great upheavals of the past in

France have served as important examples to political movements in other countries.

Also in late 1995, the sharply negative attitude of Americans to Newt Gingrich, Republican speaker of the House of Representatives, was a signal that the mood of working- and middle-class Americans had changed dramatically in the year since Republicans had won control of both Houses of Congress for the first time in four decades. Gingrich, the architect of the right-wing Contract with America, was now paying the price, not only for the questionable ways he had promoted himself, but for the growing perception that his route to a balanced budget would hurt the average citizen.

In Calgary in the autumn of 1995, hospital laundry workers did what was said to be impossible—they made Conservative Premier Ralph Klein blink. A casually broken promise to poorly paid workers who had taken a pay cut to secure their jobs turned public opinion against the Klein government. Polls showed that Albertans didn't trust Klein on health care, and believed that his cuts to the province's health care system had gone too far.

Meanwhile, in Quebec, sovereignists were appreciably aided during the 1995 Referendum campaign by the reaction of Quebecers against what was perceived as a business-centred federalist agenda. Scare talk from Liberal Finance Minister Paul Martin and other authorities about the "realities" of the new global economy turned people off. For his part, sovereignist leader Lucien Bouchard did what Prime Minister Jean Chrétien utterly failed to do—he appealed to the aspirations of the Quebec working class, making much of his rejection of the politics of cutbacks which was sweeping the rest of Canada. (Once installed as premier of Quebec in the winter of 1996, however, Bouchard had no trouble putting these rhetorical flourishes behind him as he embarked on a policy of steep cuts to government programs.)

In the very different setting of Eastern Europe and the former Soviet Union, the Harvard gurus who had been showing former communist countries the way to free enterprise had outstayed their welcome by the mid-1990s. Ordinary citizens were coping with falling living standards, joblessness, shattered health care and educational systems, rampant crime and official corruption. Their response? To throw out gung-ho capitalist regimes and to elect governments headed by former and born-again communists. There was certainly no nostalgia for Stalinism in this political trend, just a disgust for hard-line capitalism.

These developments mark a clear break from the early 1990s, when it appeared that people were more or less prepared to put up with austerity as a fact of life about which they could do little. Working-class opposition to cutbacks seems destined to grow as the shock value of the neoconservative political assault wears off and as the divisions among wage and salary earners are overcome.

Divisions within the capitalist class are bound to play a role in challenging the power of the bond market and the banks.

Manufacturers, retailers and many businesses operating in the service sector are negatively affected by the stranglehold the financial sector has imposed on the economy. Glacial rates of economic growth and frequent lapses into recession have pushed business bankruptcies to record levels. In 1995, as government cutbacks by both federal and provincial governments coincided to drag down Canada's economic performance, personal and business bankruptcies reached an all-time high, surpassing even the number recorded in the dismal year of 1992.[11]

There is great irony in the fact that many of those heading businesses that ended up bankrupt were fervent supporters of the right-wing governments whose cutbacks were often the final cause of their own demise. Those blinded by ideology are slow to learn, as the mesmerizing hold of the financial sector over all other elements of business has eloquently shown. The proprietors of small businesses have often gone to their own extinction all the while spouting the verities of the bond market.

But even this form of loyalty has its limits, as the rising hostility toward the Canadian banks has shown. While a stark polarization of views between the financial sector and other segments of business is unlikely, so too is unthinking solidarity within the ranks of business. Pressures for policies that allow for expansion are bound to come to the fore from vulnerable sectors of business and are bound to play a role in shifting the balance of power within capitalism.

Taken together, it is highly likely that the combination of forces and pressures just discussed will result in further shifts of power within capitalism, shifts that will in turn limit the stranglehold of the bond market. Friction among the major global powers, within the ranks of business and between business and the rest of the population is likely to lead eventually to the resumption of at least moderate levels of inflation. Without a decrease in the real burden of the combined public sector–corporate–personal debt that inflation would bring, the resumption of robust economic growth is highly unlikely. While a return to inflation will be sharply resisted by those who stand to gain so much by preventing it, the forces at play are almost certain to discover this outlet, by accident and design, as a way out of the impasse in which the industrial world now finds itself.

Even if the debt game is not likely to endure, it has left its mark on this phase in the history of capitalism. It seems appropriate that dismal utilitarianism ought to be the ethic of a capitalism whose leading feature is high interest rates.

The capitalism of our time is not strong, resilient and forward looking. It is fearful and defensive, retreating from its former ability to include ever larger numbers of people as its beneficiaries. In generational terms, high-interest-rate capitalism is a vehicle for those in middle age who have already accumulated capital. But these soaring rates are the enemy of the young, and despite all the market rhetoric we hear, they are antipathetic to the entrepreneurial. As capitalism retreats ever further from its capacity to fulfil the needs and aspirations of the majority, it turns ever more to the politics of fear and repression.

But history does not end here. The door is opening to a new generation and a new left.

CHAPTER 10

A NEW CANADIAN LEFT

FEBRUARY 24, 1996, was an historic day in Canada. On that day, one hundred and twenty thousand people demonstrated peacefully in the heart of Hamilton, Ontario, against the right-wing policies of the Harris government. The demonstrators, who arrived in thousands of buses and cars from many parts of the province, were in the city at the same time as the provincial Conservatives were holding a convention there—and they outnumbered the Tories a hundred to one.

Mike Harris tried to dismiss the demonstrators as a "special interest group"—a favourite phrase of his. This time it rang hollow. After the great demonstration had marched past the Tory convention, the marchers convened in an open space in the heart of the city. So huge was the crowd that it stretched to the horizon in all directions. In the whole history of progressive social movements in Canada, there had never been a demonstration on this scale. Activists I know who attended expressed their surprise that they did not encounter a single person they knew, even though they had been involved in progressive causes for many years.

The Hamilton demonstration and the rising tide of protests in many other parts of the country have challenged the media's understanding of public events. In a column in the *Globe and Mail*, Rick Salutin made the point that the "media are having a rough time covering all the protest in the province." Accustomed to reporting on election campaigns, where leaders make the news and the people are little more than a backdrop, the media have suddenly been confronted with protests and strikes where, as Salutin put it, "people who normally 'don't count' become unavoidable."[1]

In the mid-1990s, Canadian politics has taken a crucial shift. Even though the media don't know what to make of it, what they are witnessing is not the populism of the right, which they have grown accustomed to, but the emergence of a popular new politics of the left.

The Hamilton demonstration was a single high point in a crescendo of steadily rising popular mobilization against right-wing policies. In some cases that mobilization has been directed at provincial governments—as in the struggle against the Klein government in Alberta. In other cases, it has been directed at Ottawa—for instance, in the protests of Maritimers against changes in unemployment insurance benefits. But while the Hamilton demonstration was very much the product of immediate concerns about the harsh agenda of the Harris government, it was also the outcome of the many years in which an extraparliamentary opposition has been developing in Canada.

Today the real political opposition to right-wing policies is taking place almost exclusively outside the walls of Parliament. That movement has been building steadily at least since the battle against free trade in the 1988 federal election campaign. It was during that campaign that the inspiration and energy of Canada's progressive politics passed from New Democrats sitting in the House of Commons to the newly forming extraparliamentary opposition. (The Action Canada Network, coordinated by Tony Clarke, played a crucial role in bringing together the labour, nationalist and social activist opponents of free trade.) Since then, those involved in this growing opposition have included trade unionists, students, feminists, gay and lesbian activists, childcare advocates, antipoverty organizers, advocates for the cultural community, those in the Canadian nationalist tradition, aboriginal activists, environmentalists and left-wing intellectuals.

Revitalized trade unions have been indispensable to this emerging political movement. Indeed, the progressive nature of Canada's trade union movement in comparison with its counterpart in the

United States is a crucial factor in explaining why a new left is being born in Canada, where none is evident as yet in the United States.

The rise of the public sector unions over the past two decades and the creation of the Canadian Auto Workers Union (CAW) in 1985, following the separation of the Canadian region of the United Auto Workers (UAW) from the American UAW, have been seminal developments. Bob White, president of the Canadian Labour Congress and former director of the Canadian region of the UAW who was instrumental in forming the CAW, and Buzz Hargrove, his successor as president of the CAW, have combined effective unionism, in an extremely difficult economic environment, with a new brand of social and political unionism. As a result, the public sector unions and the CAW have been involved in an expanding network of social movements. In his recent book, *The Canadian Auto Workers*, Sam Gindin, assistant to the president of the CAW, speaks of "movement unionism" which "includes the shape of bargaining demands, the scope of union activities, the approach to issues of change, and above all, that sense of commitment to a larger movement that might suffer defeats, but can't be destroyed."[2]

In the public sector in many parts of the country, hydro workers, civil servants, teachers and nurses have created a brand of militant, democratic unionism that addresses societal issues along with collective-bargaining concerns. The five-week-long strike of the Ontario Public Service Employees Union (OPSEU), which began in February 1996, showed that if workers held their ground, they could force concessions even from a hard-line, right-wing government. Members of the Harris government expected OPSEU to crumble in its first-ever strike. Instead, the fifty thousand civil servants who took to the picket lines forged a much stronger union than they had had before the strike. OPSEU president Leah Casselman emerged as a sane and tough leader, who easily held her own in the battle for public opinion against Tory Cabinet ministers.

Meanwhile, hit with huge rises in tuition fees, students in universities and community colleges have become politically active on a scale unseen for twenty years. The conventional media wisdom that students are mostly right wingers has always been bogus. While there certainly are right-wing students, and even a few who wear suspenders in an effort to look like David Frum, the political mood on campuses has been shifting to the left in recent years. Even though the media has not yet figured this out, the largest student demonstrations in Canadian history have occurred, not in the 1960s or 1970s, but in the 1990s.

And the women's movement has been undergoing a long-term transformation so that the key focus of the National Action Committee on the Status of Women (NAC) has become the plight of working class and minority women. It is highly significant that women have proven to be a much tougher sell for neo-conservatism than men have been, as evidenced by the emergence of the so-called political gender gap. Throughout North America, support among women for hard-right political parties and politicians is significantly lower than it is among men.[3]

The childcare movement has been instrumental from the very beginning in the battle against the policies of the Harris government in Ontario. In November 1995, the Ontario Coalition for Better Child Care Network organized public meetings and demonstrations attended by thousands of people across the province, and for one day they shut down daycare centres attended by sixty thousand children. These actions helped stave off anticipated deeper cuts to childcare by the Tories.

The Council of Canadians (COC), under the leadership of its volunteer director Maude Barlow, has burgeoned from an organization dedicated to fighting the free trade deals to become a crucial voice in opposition to the right-wing agenda. The council has been successful in attracting a large national membership and in establishing a fund-raising base that allows it to maintain a substantial national office.

Trade unionists, social activists and intellectuals now combine forces each year to present what they call an Alternative Federal Budget. This highly sophisticated exercise has been undertaken by the Ottawa-based Canadian Centre for Policy Alternatives

(CCPA) and Choices, a Winnipeg coalition for social justice with the financial support of the Canadian Labour Congress. The alternative budgets offer detailed proposals for how Ottawa could manage its taxation and expenditures to create jobs and extend social programs. The exercise has turned a spotlight on both the federal Department of Finance and the right-wing think tanks that have played such a key role in designing neoconservative economic policies. The Alternative Budgets have shown that it is possible to reduce the deficit much more effectively through a strategy that creates jobs than through austerity measures, which destroy them. Moreover, the Alternative Budgets have shown that the path back to economic health can be taken much more fairly through a reformed tax system which insists that the affluent and corporations pay their share.[4]

Although environmentalists have had their own particular agenda, their progressive social influence has also been evident. Especially in British Columbia, where the struggle against clearcutting at Clayoquot Sound on Vancouver Island achieved international significance, the environmental movement has transformed the way society understands the relationship between economy and ecology. Although the "cut-and-run" strategy of giant forest product corporations continues, environmentalists have placed it under unblinking scrutiny.

Not all of these movements regard themselves in any explicit way as a part of the left; they have their own points of departure, their own ways of looking at the world. It is clear, though, that they all have been challenging the right-wing agenda of the private sector and of governments and developing a critique of how the politics of the new right are contrary to their own goals.

The case for a coherent left, encompassing a range of social movements, drawing strength from all of them and adding to the force of each of them, has always rested on the way power is held in a capitalist society. Social movements may imagine themselves to be battling for discrete objectives that are meaningful to them alone. Inexorably however, they are in contention against the massed power of capitalism as a system—business, the state and the dispensers of orthodox ideology. In the face of the new global capitalism, the case for a left that understands itself as greater than the sum of its parts is as compelling as at any time in the past two centuries. There is no question that the purpose of the left is to oppose a system of power in which the interests of the majority are subservient to those of a privileged minority, and to organize for a new system of power.

Many of those involved in social movements clearly see themselves as on the left politically. Increasingly, they are combining their activities and that is drawing each of the movements into the wider arena of a general societal struggle. A new Canadian left is forming.

There remain as well the tens of thousands of Canadians who belong to the New Democratic Party. While social democracy has been in crisis, the members of the NDP continue to constitute the largest single component of the Canadian left. NDP members have been influenced by the immense socioeconomic and political changes of recent years, and the large majority of them want their party to return to political relevance. The choices NDP members make about where and how to direct their political energies will be crucial to the future development of the left.

Though it is still in its formative stage of development, the new left is already absorbing the lessons of history as it looks to the political battles to come. A clear set of values infuses its strategic outlook as it copes with the novel, as well as the ancient, features of the capitalism of our age. The new left has learned a great deal from the political battles in which its has been engaged and from the intellectual work it has done. What follows are a number of key elements, essential to the strategic outlook of the new left, which have grown out of that experience. (What this is not is a platform for a political party.)

The return to class politics. At the heart of the new capitalism is a hard-edged division between social classes that has closed the door on the strategy of postwar social democrats. Those at the helm of our social system, and the affluent and wealthy who benefit from it, have hitched their fortunes to the lode star of inequality. The widening division in income and power between the affluent and the rest of society is testimony to that.

Class politics is an inexorable feature of turn-of-the-millennium capitalism. During the golden age of social democracy following the Second World War, social democrats abandoned their former anticapitalist radicalism and embraced the great social compromise. Now the left is unlearning the habits of that era. In the face of the new capitalism and the new right, compromise has become an invitation to be eaten alive. From Margaret Thatcher on, the new right has made an overt point of its contempt for the very notion of compromise, regarding it as a sign of spinelessness and lack of principle.

Social classes are living, breathing entities. If their perimeters were blurred during the postwar decades, they have become distinct once more. While the politics of the great social compromise resulted in gains for those in the working and middle classes, compromise today invariably means concessions, retreats and losses of power to capital. There is plenty of talk in industrialized societies of the need for "reform." But today, the universal assumption is that "reform" must come at the expense of working people. Changes in corporations mean more work, often including virtually mandatory overtime, for a smaller workforce while real wages stagnate or decline. Changes in government programs mean fewer benefits for working people. Starting from the assumption that business holds all the advantages, and can go anywhere in the world it likes, the social dialogue is relentlessly negative for working people.

The left asserts that the changes being made do not flow from abstract necessity, but from the currently superior strategic position occupied by big business. The left works for a change in the strategic balance so that business can no longer impose concessions on the rest of society.

The left seeks a society which affirms the essential equality of human beings and embraces the goal of equality of condition. It does this by defending existing social programs against cutbacks, by advocating new programs such as a universally available national childcare system and by pushing for economic reforms that transfer power to those who work for a salary or a wage.

Resisting the power of capital. The right would not be able to wield such a big stick against labour were it not for the unprecedented global power of capital. Social democrats have been drawn into a self-defeating strategy, where they seek to demonstrate that they can manage the cutbacks and austerity of the new capitalism more humanely than neoconservatives can. Acting as mediators between the social classes is the social democrat's most deeply ingrained political instinct. But where the rush to mediate was once based on the hope of winning gains for working people, today it invariably involves negotiating concessions that favour capital.

History has not ended with the present configuration of capitalism. There is no excuse for social democrats to prostitute themselves to the power of capital as though it were immutable. While there are other powerful tendencies within global capitalism that will provoke challenges to the rule of the bond market, the left has a very particular role to play. Certainly, tensions between different sectors of business will roil the waters of the new capitalism. Retailers and manufacturers and other elements of business who take on the power of the bond market will do so for their own reasons. But only the left will have as its starting point the interests of those who work for a salary or a wage.

The left begins by challenging the idea that some great human purpose is served by the existence of a single global capital pool. The unprecedented separation of capital from the control of the nation-state is a cornerstone of the harsh new capitalism of our era. Politicizing the role of the bond market and the banks is essential. Indeed, this is already happening.

The principle on which the left anchors its position is that capital has a social dimension. Capital is accumulated as the fruit of the labour that goes into the production of goods and services. The reinvestment of capital quite literally determines the priorities of society. This fact has been recognized, in practice, in the host of regulations on the investment of capital that have been deployed in advanced capitalist societies. At one time or another, most countries have imposed capital controls of various kinds to limit the investment of domestic capital abroad. For instance, in Canada it remains the case that registered pension funds may contain no more than 20 percent of foreign investments.

Banks and other financial institutions, backed by right-wing think tanks, strive to reduce the remaining state regulations on the financial sector and to eliminate all forms of capital controls. The left opposes the idea that the deployment of capital is a private matter. Gaining social control over the investment of large sums of capital is crucial to the redemocratization of society. Popular sovereignty has to include democratic control over setting priorities for capital investment.

The left asserts the right of Canadians to set priorities for the investment of capital. Allowing banks, other financial institutions and fund managers to decide how capital is invested forces federal and provincial governments to govern according to the dictates of the bond market. It robs Canadians of economic sovereignty, just as, historically, the control of large parts of the economy by American manufacturing and resource companies robbed them of sovereignty.

In contrast to the right-wing globalization agenda, which prevents whole nations from setting their own economic course, the left affirms the importance of community-based economic development. To that end, the left supports policies aimed at strengthening cooperatives and credit unions, whose goal is to reinvest capital in local communities.

Pension funds have become an enormous source of capital, which is the direct product of the efforts of labour. At a time when capital is being invested with little thought for the communities whose labour created the capital, pension funds can be a powerful tool for an alternative investment strategy. The left favours policies that place pension funds in the hands of the representatives of workers so that these funds can be invested to increase the decision-making power of labour in the workplace and to enhance domestic economic development. (Quebec's pension plan, the Caisse de dépôt et placement, unlike Ottawa's Canada Pension Plan, has accumulated a huge pool of capital, which has been invested at the discretion of the province and has succeeded in supporting indigenous enterprise in Quebec.)

The left affirms the principle that the federal government should set priorities for the investment of capital so as to serve the interests of the Canadian people. Chief among those interests is the creation of a sufficient number of jobs that pay a living wage to return Canada to full employment.

Chronic unemployment and underemployment are outcomes of the current economic system. They are not immutable facts of nature or the necessary consequence of contemporary technology. The left believes that it is the responsibility of government to play a direct role in the creation of productive jobs, as well as an indirect role through the establishment of a regulatory framework that motivates the private sector to create jobs instead of shedding them. (Corporate tax policies that reward job creation and inhibit job shedding, as well as environmental regulations that promote proper resource management, are examples of this type of regulation.)

Embracing diversity. Encompassing the social movements that are at the heart of progressive political struggles, the newly forming left is diverse, democratic and nonsectarian. No single vision of the way forward characterizes it.

Canadian society has become heterogeneous in ways that would have been virtually incomprehensible at the time the first social democratic government was elected in Saskatchewan in 1944. In recent decades, immigration from the Caribbean and Asia has transformed the nation's major cities, making Canada much more than a union of anglophones and francophones.

There have also been dramatic changes in the lifestyles of Canadians. The two-parent family, with the husband in the workplace and the wife in the home, was seen as the norm in the postwar decades. Today, most women participate in the paid labour force, divorce is immensely more common and the number of children raised in single-parented and blended families has sky-rocketed. Gays and lesbians, once unacknowledged, have fought for and achieved visibility and increasing social legitimacy. Feminism and environmentalism have transformed the culture to such a degree that the definition of what is mainstream has itself been significantly altered.

Although the advance of our society toward heterogeneity is unstoppable, it continues to provoke significant waves of back-lash, which have benefitted the right politically. In recent years, conservatives have made much of their commitment to traditional values, rededicating themselves fervently to the defence of social norms they claim to have inherited from the past. By making itself the defender of the family, religion and small business, con-servatives have played on the stresses in a multiracial, multi-lifestyle society. Newt Gingrich, the U.S. Republican speaker of the House of Representatives, has become the exemplar of this kind of politics. Meanwhile, in Canada, the Reform Party and the right-wing Tories have reinforced the misconception that there is a link between violent crime and the presence of immigrants, plac-ing a strong emphasis on deportation of immigrants found guilty of crimes. The right ignores data that shows that violent crime has not been increasing and it never points out that the rate of violent crime is higher in cities like Victoria, British Columbia, than it is in multiracial Toronto.[5]

The right has fanned resentment against employment equity policies, seeking to hone the anxieties of white males. In a period when there has been little job creation, the right has attacked measures to overcome long-term, systemic discrimination in the job market against women and minorities. Against what it claims is reverse discrimination, the right calls for an abstracted "equali-ty" among all people, which takes no account of the different cir-cumstances people face as a consequence of race and gender. Front-line victims of these policies have been the disabled, who have been hit with cutbacks to education, transportation and social assistance and whose hopes for greater access to the job market have been crushed by the right's insistence on "equality."

During the election campaign that won them power in Ontario, the Harris Tories focused on employment equity in their television advertising, pledging that they would eliminate what they called the "quota" law when they formed a government. In these ads, the Tories caricatured the employment equity legislation of the Ontario NDP government, which required employers to establish targets and timetables for the hiring of women and members of minority groups. The Tories simply swept the history of systemic discrimination under the carpet.

Similarly, the right has positioned itself to benefit from any backlash against advances toward equality for gays and lesbians. In the last days of the Rae government in Ontario, the Harris Conservatives opposed the extension of benefits to same-sex couples. When he was running for the Republican Party's presidential nomination in the winter of 1996, Pat Buchanan said he would not allow gays or lesbians to work for the federal government if he was elected. Everywhere, the right has added gays and lesbians to its list of so-called "special interests" in its populist quest to win the votes of "regular people."

Whatever the short-term political costs paid for this, what most fundamentally distinguishes the left from the right is that the left is open to everyone. Its humanity is not restricted to elites, the propertied or those of particular races, religious affiliations or sexual orientations. The right, by contrast, has always defined itself through its exclusions. Today's right-wing menu consists of a main course of greed, garnished with bigotry and sweetened with "family values." Particularly among the young, racism and homophobia are increasingly falling on deaf ears. In the long term, the left's greatest political advantage is that it embraces everyone and not the exclusive few.

The deepening of democracy. Traditional social democracy has talked a good game when it comes to democracy. But its practice has been less lustrous. Democratic theory has coexisted with the entrenched habit of crucial decisions being taken by a few. In my experience in the NDP, the rule—not the exception—has been that decisions have been taken in the back rooms. Election strategy has been set by the party leader, provincial or federal, and his or her close advisers. Party conventions and election strategy committees have had little real impact on strategic decisions. Indeed, by the time the average delegate gets to an NDP convention—if he or she is not a member of a key committee—the important decisions concerning policy have already been made. Today, NDP leaders pay a lot more attention to polling data than to the resolutions adopted at conventions.

The new left insists on real intraparty democracy. The top-down model of political organization, now so prevalent, has to go. This hope for a renewal of democracy within the left is more than pious, precisely because the grassroots social movements just described have grown so much stronger than electoral social democracy. Movement politics is breaking the pattern of bureaucratic politics, so long a feature of the NDP.

The achievement of a synthesis between movement and party. In recent years, the relationship of the NDP to social movements has been ambivalent. As the NDP's electoral fortunes have waned, some party spokespersons have pointed a critical finger at the social movements, arguing that if their leaders had only devoted themselves to the NDP, the party would have fared much better in the 1993 federal election.

Such criticism misses the mark. Over the past two decades the NDP has become a political organization run by professionals, for whom politics is a career. It is firmly in the hands of those in office, those who seek office and those who dream of seeking office. The gap between this cohort of professional social democrats and social movement activists has never been wider. And this has weakened the party's power. Over the course of its life, the CCF-NDP has moved from a genuinely radical analysis and political prescription, to the hollow rhetoric that suffuses today's offerings. Electoral success at the provincial level over the past two decades has speeded the party's headlong rush toward the political centre and away from the more challenging aspects of the analysis that was offered in the past. The federal NDP has become the beached whale of Canadian politics, gasping for survival.

It cannot be assumed that social movements will be included in the constituency of a political party, just because it claims to espouse progressive politics. The new left will have to be built through an evolving consensus and a developing sense of mutual trust among movements that have a very strong sense of their own individual identities.

If the NDP is to renew itself as the political voice of the left, it will have to become fully involved in the battles for social justice that have been joined by social movement activists on so many fronts. The new Canadian left will remain incomplete until a political party expresses its views and participates in the electoral fray at the provincial and federal levels. The NDP may yet remake itself as that political party, or it may not. That remains an open question.

If New Democrats are certain to make a huge contribution to the new left, so too can people who are rooted in other political traditions. There have always been progressive Liberals and Conservatives in Canada. Today, many of these people are in despair as their political parties embrace right-wing policies. The door is open to them to become a part of and to shape the new progressive politics of our era.

An environmentally sustainable economic policy. In an age when too many industrial practices and patterns of resource use threaten the well-being and even the survival of the human race, the left is committed to the idea that economy and ecology can no longer be viewed as separate realms. Economic policies must pass the test of being sustainable so as not to rob future generations of essential resources.

Necessarily, the pursuit of environmentally sound policies— higher water-quality and auto-emission standards, stringent limiting of the production of greenhouse-enhancing agents, policing the disposal of toxic chemicals, and requiring product recycling— imposes higher costs on business. The left rejects the current drive on the part of business to reduce environmental standards on the ground that this is necessary if we are to be competitive in the new global economy. Short-term pursuit of profit at the expense of the environment means the potential sacrifice of health and well-being, long-term generational inequity and possible eventual environmental catastrophe.

A Canadian strategy. Despite their nationalist tendencies in the past, Canadian liberalism and conservatism have adopted globalization as a fundamental aspect of their worldview. Notwithstanding the sentiments of many individual liberals and conservatives, these ideologies are no longer compatible with the ideal of a Canadian society that is economically, socially and politically distinct from that of the United States. Indeed, neoconservatism is deeply hostile to those features of Canadian society that have most distinguished it from the U.S.

The new capitalism and the new right have placed Canada on the road to dissolution. The medicine the new right applies to Canada is the kind of quackery from which the patient is lucky to escape alive.

The automatic reflex of Canadian neoconservatism is to believe the state should always do less. Neoconservatives reject the proposition that the survival of Canada requires a continuous strategy of government intervention in the economy, communications and culture. Canadian survival once was linked to the toryism of John A. Macdonald. Neoconservatism is an entirely different matter. In less than a generation, market-first policies have pushed the country into incoherence, indeed to the brink of disintegration. Only social democracy is capable of providing a consistent rationale for the existence of a Canada that amounts to more than a geographical expression.

The left can make an indispensable contribution to keeping alive the values on which Canadians can sustain the effort to keep building their own nation on this continent. The American empire has passed its zenith and has entered its era of decline. There is every reason to preserve Canada, with its traditions and values, for a future in the global age that is to come after the decline of American hegemony.

First Nations. The left affirms that justice cannot be achieved in Canada without justice for First Nations. Canada has been built on the territory of aboriginal peoples, whose societies have experienced deep suffering as the victims of European colonization. Over the past quarter-century, aboriginals have struggled to achieve recognition for their place in Canada as distinct peoples who have the right to self-government. Aboriginals have transformed their self-definition, emerging from the long shadow of colonialism, to assert their right to live and to thrive according to their own lights.

The new right seeks to extinguish aboriginal land claims by insisting that they be subordinate to private property rights. For its part, the left supports struggles to achieve constitutional recognition for aboriginals as peoples within Canada, self-government for their communities and the just settlement of their land claims.

Partnership with Quebec. Since the founding of the NDP in 1961, social democrats have sought a new partnership between English Canada and Quebec. The new left rejects the idea that Quebec is simply one of ten provinces and affirms Quebec's position as a national community with the right to decide whether or not to remain within Canada. English Canada and Quebec need a renewed economic and political partnership if both are to survive next door to the United States. The left values the historical association of Quebecers with other Canadians, and seeks a broader understanding of the nature of Quebec and Canada which is the necessary precondition for a new partnership.

Internationalism. The great political battles of our era will not be fought in watertight national compartments. The new capitalism is a regime based on a highly complex series of arrangements among the world's governments. These arrangements make it possible for a global financial market to operate and for multinational corporations to function effectively in almost every part of the world.

To an overwhelming extent, the opponents of the new capitalism fight their battles from isolated national bastions. While trade unions, social movements and left-wing political parties certainly talk to each other across borders much more than they have in the past, they have hardly begun to counter the ability of capital to use its global position to apply leverage against them.

In North America and Europe, progressive political movements are meeting much more regularly to work out strategies for dealing with NAFTA and the European Union. The goal must be for such movements to coordinate their plans so that they can present a united front against the game of "lowest common denominator" being played by business. Corporations are now in a position, as never before, to threaten to go where labour and environmental standards and social programs are the weakest. To counter this strategy, social movements need to do internationally what trade unions have done nationally over the past century—present a common front, which stops business from playing people off against each other.

Essential to the new internationalism of the left is the rejection of comprehensive trade agreements that enshrine the rights of capital and disenfranchise working people. In that spirit, it is clear that NAFTA cannot be remade to serve the interests of the working people of North America. Similarly, the newly established World Trade Organization (WTO) is a rule maker on behalf of capital and against the interests of labour.

The left remains what it has always been—the party of equality. And the right continues to be what it has always been—the party of inequality. All the specific questions in our politics—globalization, competitiveness, the deficit, unemployment, taxation and the welfare state—are really debates about equality versus inequality.

The right believes that society must be led by an entrepreneurial elite, that this elite opens the way for new technologies, products and services, that it creates jobs, and above all, that it rewards only those who are ambitious and hard working. For the right, inequality is essential.

Contemporary conservatives, bent on restoring the social inequality of earlier historical periods, revel in the language of revolution and love nothing more than to castigate their opponents on the left as reactionaries. When Brian Mulroney was crusading for free trade in the 1980s, he described his critics as "neoreactionaries," "prophets of doom," "timorous, insecure and fretful" and, above all else, "apostles of the status quo." This is far from being the first time in history that the forces of political reaction have gone on the offensive and masqueraded as revolutionaries. In 1787, the French nobility, determined to resist the monarchy's plan to increase their taxes, dressed themselves in the cloak of opponents of the status quo. It was this so-called "révolte nobiliaire" that fatally undermined the French state and opened the door to the real revolution of 1789, which promptly consigned the nobility to the dustbin of history.

Those on the right who play-act at revolution by attacking the status quo run the risk of opening the door to real change from the left. That is because as they tear up an existing social contract between capital and labour, they force labour to rethink its position as well. And that involves the possibility of potent radicalism from below, exactly the antithesis of what is sought by the "revolutionaries" of the right.

Indeed, the right's assault on the welfare state is already converting defenders of the status quo into people who have little to lose by attacking it. During the postwar epoch, the majority of Canadians gained a stake in the existing order of things to an extent never before attained. Since then, however, capitalism has turned its back on the majority. While that has always been true in the developing world, it is now true again after a relatively brief hiatus, in the developed world.

This is a moment for bold initiatives. We have no more reason and no more right to be immobilized by despair than had the progressives who met in Calgary in 1932 and in Regina the following year to create the CCF.

Their watchword was clear: "We aim to replace the present capitalist system, with its inherent injustice and inhumanity, by a social order from which the domination and exploitation of one class by another will be eliminated, in which economic planning will supersede unregulated private enterprise and competition, and in which genuine democratic self-government, based upon economic equality will be possible."[6]

On the eve of the millennium, the human future is poised in uncertainty between the potential for a broadening of freedom and the spectre of a dark age in which a technological elite controls the mass of humanity. The present course of capitalism is clear enough. Despite its populist tendencies, it is headed away from democracy and in the direction of a global corporate order, underpinned by revolutionary technology. As it has become ever more global in character, capitalism has become ever less democratic in its practice, if not its theory. Corporations have become ever more remote from those they employ and those to whom they sell their products. Despite the ludicrous notion, regularly advanced by apologists for the system, that it is consumers who steer the global behemoths, the reality has never been more different. And while corporations, particularly financial corporations, have become more powerful and more footloose, the state has retreated from the egalitarian, social democratic impulses that were so pronounced in the postwar decades. Just as the postwar state contributed to and reflected the capitalism of that time, the present state contributes to and reflects the capitalism of our time.

For its part, the left believes in the essential equality of human beings. It looks forward to an end to the extremes of wealth and poverty, and to the disappearance of vast disparities in power among people. The left rejects the notion that the business elite is the source of progress. It believes that releasing the energy and creativity of the vast majority of the population is the real way to raise living standards, and more important, to open the door to a society in which the economy will be seen as a means to an end and not an end in itself.

The left can be, and often is, badly led. It can be divided, morose and underfunded. It can suffer famous defeats.

What causes the party of equality to spring back from the very edge of extinction, however, is the reality of the human condition. It is wealth, privilege and the power of a few to decide the fate of the many that gives rise to a new left when an old one falls by the wayside.

ENDNOTES

CHAPTER 1   THE BEST OF TIMES, THE WORST OF TIMES

1. *Toronto Star*, 14 December 1994.
2. Thomas Walkom, *Rae Days: The Rise and Follies of the NDP* (Toronto: Key Porter Books, 1994), p. 142.
3. *Globe and Mail*, 10 May 1995.
4. Author interview with Gerald Caplan, Toronto, April 1995.
5. Author interview with Joseph Levitt, Ottawa, April 1995.

CHAPTER 2   DEMOCRACY IN PERIL

1. Alan Bullock, *Hitler and Stalin: Parallel Lives* (Toronto: McClelland & Stewart, 1991), p. 974.
2. Armine Yalnizyan, T. Ran Ide and Arthur J. Cordell, *Shifting Time: Social Policy and the Future of Work* (Toronto: Between the Lines), p. 25.
3. Michael Harrington, *Socialism: Past and Future* (New York: Arcade Publishing, 1989), pp. 248–78.
4. For this perspective on welfare, see Charles Murray, *Losing Ground: American Social Policy 1950–1980* (New York: Basic Books, 1986).
5. Ontario, Ministry of Community and Social Services, "Managing Social Assistance in Ontario: Finding the Problems and Fixing Them," October 1994, p. 7.
6. "The Common Sense Revolution," pamphlet issued by the Progressive Conservative Party of Ontario, 1995, p. 10.
7. *Toronto Star*, 7 June 1995.

CHAPTER 3   THE GLOBAL CRISIS OF SOCIAL DEMOCRACY

1. Alexis de Tocqueville, *Democracy in America* (New York: Schocken Books, 1970), vol. 1, p. 202.
2. Cited in Samuel Eliot Morison and Henry Steele Commager, *The Growth of the American Republic* (New York: Oxford University Press, 1962), vol. 2, p. 221.
3. Eduard Bernstein, *Evolutionary Socialism* (New York: Schocken Books, 1961), p. xxii.
4. U.S. Bureau of the Census, *Statistical Abstract of the United States*, 1994, 114th ed. (Washington, DC, 1994), p. 867.
5. Leo Panitch, "The Role and Nature of the Canadian State," *The Canadian State: Political Economy and Political Power*, ed. Leo Panitch (Toronto: University of Toronto Press, 1977), p. 7.
6. Conrad Black, *A Life in Progress* (Toronto: Key Porter Books, 1993), pp. 415, 416.
7. Author television interview with T.C. Douglas, April 1979.
8. *Globe and Mail*, 22 July 1995.

9. Leo Panitch, "The Role and Nature of the Canadian State," p. 13.

10. For a summary of the Mitterrand program, see Howard Machin and Vincent Wright, eds., *Economic Policy and Policy-Making under the Mitterrand Presidency 1981–1984* (London: Frances Pinter, 1985), pp. 1–35.

11. Janice McCormick, "Apprenticeship for Governing: An Assessment of French Socialism in Power," in Machin and Wright (eds), *op. cit.*, pp. 44-62.

12. Christian Stoffaes, "The Nationalizations: An Initial Assessment, 1981–1984," in Machin and Wright, eds., *Economic Policy and Policy Making*, p. 144.

CHAPTER 4   THE NEW CAPITALISM AND THE NEW RIGHT

1. *New York Times*, 25 February 1996.

2. Ottawa, Department of Finance, *Agenda: Jobs and Growth* (Ottawa: Queen's Printer, 1994), p. 32.

3. Author television interview with Michael Foot in London, England, June 1979.

4. James Laxer, *Canada's Energy Crisis* (Toronto: James, Lewis and Samuel, 1974), p. 32.

5. *Wall Street Journal*, 14 March 1974.

6. *Toronto Star*, 12 December 1977.

7. Ibid., 12 December 1977.

8. Ibid., 5 December 1993.

9. Lester Thurow, *Head to Head: The Coming Economic Battle among Japan, Europe and America* (New York: Morrow, 1992), p. 30.

10. U.S. Bureau of the Census, *Statistical Abstract of the United States, 1995*, 115th ed. (Washington, DC, 1995), p. 805.

11. As cited in Eric Hobsbawm, *Age of Extremes: The Short Twentieth Century 1914–1991* (London: Michael Joseph, 1994), pp. 573–74. Quotation from Bairoch is from Paul Bairoch, *Economics and World History: Myths and Paradoxes* (London: Hemel Hempstead, 1993), p. 164.

12. *New York Times*, 26 February 1996.

13. World Commission on Environment and Development, *Our Common Future* (New York: Oxford University Press, 1987), p. 31.

14. *New York Times*, 19 June 1994.

15. Bob Woodward, *The Agenda: Inside the Clinton White House* (New York: Simon and Schuster, 1994), p. 270.

16. Linda McQuaig, *Shooting the Hippo: Death by Deficit and Other Canadian Myths* (Toronto: Viking, 1995), p. 85.

17. Statistics Canada, *Canada Year Book*, 1994 (Ottawa, 1993), p. 194.

18. Statistics Canada, *Earnings of Men and Women*, cat. no. 13217, 1992.

19. Susan D. Phillips ed., *How Ottawa Spends 1993–1994* (Ottawa: Carleton University Press, 1993), p. 500.

20. David Frum, *Dead Right* (New York: HarperCollins, 1994).

21. *Harper's Magazine*, April 1995.

CHAPTER 5 TOMMY, DAVID AND THE BIRTH OF THE CCF

1. *Globe and Mail,* 5 July 1962.
2. *Winnipeg Tribune,* 23 April 1964, as cited in Doris French Shackleton, *Tommy Douglas* (Toronto: McClelland & Stewart, 1975), p. 245.
3. *Saskatoon Star-Phoenix,* as cited in Shackleton, *Tommy Douglas,* p. 245.
4. Ibid., p. 17.
5. U.S. Bureau of the Census, *Statistical Abstract of the United States,* 1993, 113th ed. (Washington, DC, 1993), p. 849.
6. CCF Convention Proceedings (1956), p. 8, as cited in Gad Horowitz, *Canadian Labour in Politics* (Toronto: University of Toronto Press, 1968), p. 4.
7. Norman Penner, ed., *Winnipeg 1919* (Toronto: James Lewis and Samuel, 1973), pp. 56, 57.
8. Ibid., p. 208.
9. Ibid., pp. xxvi, xxvii.
10. Hugh Thorburn, ed., *Party Politics in Canada,* 6th ed. (Toronto: Prentice Hall, 1991), p. 533.
11. Walter Young, *The Anatomy of a Party: The National C.C.F., 1932–61* (Toronto: University of Toronto Press, 1969). The full text of the Regina Manifesto is reproduced in the appendix of this excellent book.
12. David Lewis, *The Good Fight: Political Memoirs 1909–1958* (Toronto: Macmillan of Canada, 1981), p. 13.
13. See Horowitz, *Canadian Labour in Politics,* pp. 93–94.
14. Lewis, *The Good Fight,* p. 441.
15. Thorburn, ed., *Party Politics in Canada,* 6th ed., p. 533.
16. Ibid., p. 533.

CHAPTER 6 THE NDP'S UNCERTAIN JOURNEY

1. Thorburn, ed., *Party Politics in Canada,* 6th ed., p. 533.
2. Ibid.
3. Ibid.
4. *Harper's Magazine,* December 1994.
5. As cited in Sam Gindin, *The Canadian Auto Workers: The Birth and Transformation of a Union* (Toronto: Lorimer, 1995), p. 226.
6. *Toronto Star,* 4 June 1993.
7. Ibid., 4 June 1993.
8. *Globe and Mail,* 4 August 1993.
9. Bob Rae, letter to NDP supporters, undated, February 1996.
10. Alan C. Cairns and Daniel Wong, "Socialism, Federalism and the B.C. Party Systems, 1933–1983," in *Party Politics in Canada,* ed. Thorburn, p. 469.
11. Ibid., p. 480.
12. *Globe and Mail,* 11 November 1995.
13. *Globe and Mail,* 25 April 1996.

14. Ibid.

CHAPTER 7 THE WAFFLE: A CHILDREN'S CRUSADE
Closing quotation: CAW, Discussion Papers, 4th Constitutional Convention, Quebec City, August 1994.

CHAPTER 8 SOCIAL DEMOCRACY AND CANADIAN SURVIVAL
1. George F.G. Stanley, "The 1870s," from *The Canadians 1867–1967*, ed. J.M.S. Careless and R. Craig Brown (Toronto: Macmillan, 1967), p. 60.
2. Donald Creighton, *The Empire of the St. Lawrence* (Toronto: Macmillan, 1956), pp. 6, 7.
3. Linda McQuaig, *The Quick and the Dead: Brian Mulroney, Big Business and the Seduction of Canada* (Toronto: Viking, 1991), p. 121.
4. See James Laxer, *False God: How the Globalization Myth Has Impoverished Canada* (Toronto: Lester, 1993), pp. 39–88.
5. *International Herald Tribune*, 24–25 June 1995.
6. Ibid.

CHAPTER 9 TWO SOCIETIES
1. *Financial Times*, 3 February 1995.
2. Monitor, April 1996 (Ottawa: Canadian Centre for Policy Alternatives,1996).
3. E.P. Thompson, *The Making of the English Working Class* (London: Pelican, 1968).
4. McQuaig, *Shooting the Hippo*.
5. Ibid., pp. 283, 284.
6. McQuaig, *Shooting the Hippo*, pp. 283, 284.
7. *Globe and Mail*, 6 March 1996.
8. Dr. James Stanford, "Growth, Interest and Debt: Canada's Fall from the Fiscal Knife-Edge" (Ottawa: Canadian Centre for Policy Alternatives, 1996).
9. Elmar Altvater, *The Future of the Market* (London: Verso, 1993).
10. Ibid., p. 176.
11. *Globe and Mail*, 20 December 1995.

CHAPTER 10 A NEW CANADIAN LEFT
1. *Globe and Mail*, 30 March 1996.
2. Sam Gindin, *The Canadian Auto Workers: The Birth and Transformation of a Union* (Toronto: Lorimer, 1995), p. 268.
3. *Toronto Star*, 27 April 1996.
4. See "Alternative Federal Budget 1996" (Ottawa and Winnipeg: Canadian Centre for Policy Alternatives, and Choices).
5. *Toronto Star*, 28 November 1993.
6. Walter Young, *The Anatomy of a Party: The National CCF, 1932–61* (Toronto: University of Toronto Press, 1969), appendix.

INDEX